Books should be returned on or before the
last date stamped below.

ABERDEENSHIRE
LIBRARY &
INFORMATION SERVICES

WITHDRAWN
FROM LIBRARY

NORTH EAST of SCOTLAND LIBRARY SERVICE
MELDRUM MEG WAY, OLDMELDRUM

MCWILLIAM, Colin

Scottish townscape

1.   AE

D1615268

N E S L
889542

SCOTTISH TOWNSCAPE

SCOTTISH TOWNSCAPE

Colin McWilliam

COLLINS
St James's Place, London, 1975

William Collins Sons & Co Ltd
London · Glasgow · Sydney · Auckland
Toronto · Johannesburg

AE
1.
889542

First published 1975
© Colin McWilliam 1975
ISBN 0 00 216743-3
Maps by John Flower
Set in Monotype Scotch Roman
Made and Printed in Great Britain by
William Collins Sons & Co Ltd Glasgow

TO CHRISTINE

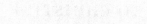

CONTENTS

		page	*plates*
	Foreword	9	
I	THE TOWN SCENE	11	1–3
II	THE MEDIEVAL BURGH	26	4–7
III	JAMES VI AND THE SEVENTEENTH CENTURY	45	8–11
IV	THE EIGHTEENTH CENTURY	65	12–15
V	NEW TOWNS OF THE EIGHTEENTH AND NINETEENTH CENTURIES	86	18–20
VI	THE EARLY NINETEENTH CENTURY	109	21–25
VII	THE VICTORIAN TOWN	137	26–28
VIII	THE TWENTIETH CENTURY	171	29–30
IX	CONSERVATION	191	31–32
X	TEN TOWNSCAPES	216	33–40

Walks in: Aberdeen · Ayr · Banff
Cupar · Dumfries · Edinburgh · Glasgow
Haddington · Inverness · Montrose

	Map of Royal Burghs		16
	Map of Regions		17
	Further Reading and Reference Books	245	
	Index	250	

PLATES between pages 80–81, 160–61, 240–41

FOREWORD

This is an attempt to describe the appearance of Scottish towns and how they came by it.

Apart from Edinburgh and perhaps a dozen other towns whose quality is recognized, are they worth looking at? Hurrying through towns whose main streets have now become trunk roads, there may well be some doubt about this. But what if the traveller stops and looks at them or if, lured in the first place by the better-known beauties of the Scottish landscape, he finds himself in places more remote and unexpected?

What he will discover is first of all a kind of town that quietly, and always with good functional reason, exploits its natural setting. He will see a modest range of building types, variously adapted to many circumstances of which this setting is one of the most important. He will then see how these types were gradually modified by Georgian progress, with more attention to rational planning than to fancy building. He will find how crisp and satisfying is the urban stonework of the late Georgian period, which in Scotland as in England (but more substantially) saw the highest achievements of deliberately planned townscape. He may be surprised to see that the Victorians continued and adorned this achievement; and that they not only managed to develop a real urban style from old Scottish sources, but looked abroad for other themes which they adapted with great scholarship and ingenuity to their own town scene. And finally in looking at the better work of the twentieth century he will notice that Scotland's twin architectural virtues (a plain functional tradition and an ability to digest new ideas) have not quite disappeared.

But that is only the architectural face of the subject. Although this book must to some extent be an account of town buildings in Scotland, its main object is to reveal and explain the town

9

scene as a whole. Based chiefly on visits and research in 1973, it cannot be timeless; some places have changed – not always for the worse. Of particular omissions I am very much aware. My inadequate excuse for leaving out a number of good towns (Bowmore, for example, and the other planned towns of the Island of Islay) is also an unhappy confession; I have not seen them. Only in historical terms does it attempt to be comprehensive, but even here I must admit to a serious gap. I have not discussed the new towns of the twentieth century because to do them justice would have been to upset the balance of the whole story. A critical survey of their architecture and townscape is still needed. For one thing it would help to defeat the prejudice against things new, which has done almost as much harm in this century as that against things old.

To bridge this gap between old and new was my main object in writing this book. I hope it will give some useful guidance not only to anyone who wants to study and enjoy Scottish towns, but also to those who will have to make decisions about their future.

*

The dedication is to my wife Christine. There are many others whom I have to thank for their help; notably the staff of the National Monuments Record at the Royal Commission on the Ancient and Historical Monuments of Scotland, Professor Christopher Smout who read and commented on the first typescript, and innumerable librarians, town clerks, policemen and passers-by. For my opinions and my errors I am responsible.

Colin McWilliam

Plates. Birch of Cupar 35c. Country Life Ltd and Jonathan M. Gibson 40. John Dewar 38a. East Lothian County Planning Office 9b. Gillespie, Kidd & Coia 30b. Glasgow Museums and Art Galleries 13b. Michael Laird 29e and f. Sir Robert Matthew, Johnson-Marshall & Partners 29c. The National Library of Scotland 4. Perth Museum and Art Gallery 21a. The Royal Commission on the Ancient and Historical Monuments of Scotland 10e, 12e, 35b and 38c. The Scottish Tourist Board 18a. Wheeler and Sproson 32c. Reece Winstone 18c. The remainder by the author.

I. THE TOWN SCENE

1880 Lord R. Gower *Figure Painters in Holland* 66:
It is a landscape, or rather a townscape.

1889 Hissey *Tour in Phaeton* 263:
Some of the quaint townscapes (to invent another word) of our romantic, unspoilt English towns

Townscape . . . a picture or view of a town.
New English Dictionary, Oxford 1926.

Townscape, a portion of a town which the eye can view at once; a picture of it; the design or building of part of a town.
Chambers's Twentieth Century Dictionary 1972.

It was Gordon Cullen, in his contribution to the important series of articles that began in the *Architectural Review* in 1948, who really established the word. He also gave it an extra meaning. Gower used it about the picture of a town, Hissey applied it to the town itself. Cullen, though the recent dictionary definition excludes this meaning, pointed out that townscape is seen by the moving spectator. He also noted its close connection with the function of towns. Had he done so more emphatically we might have been spared the outbreak of 'applied townscape' which followed from his still further use of the word in the sense of a creative skill. In the introduction to the 1971 edition of his *Townscape* he rightly condemns the meaningless outbreaks of cobbles, the pedestrian precincts with nothing for pedestrians to do, which had been the immediate result of his missionary enthusiasm.

THE IDEA OF TOWNSCAPE

Every town is useful and, as soon as anything in the least memorable has happened there, historic. Use and history

11

collaborate with geography to give each place its characteristic townscape, a visual bonus which does not necessarily owe anything to aesthetic decisions. Like the creation of townscape, its enjoyment is primarily a matter of use, and need not involve conscious aesthetic appreciation. The older Dutch word *stadsgezicht* or townview, meaning whatever you may happen to see of a town without the implication that you are deliberately studying it, comes nearer to admitting this more casual but perfectly reasonable attitude to the town scene.

Nevertheless the visual idea of townscape, as distinct from the experience of it in other ways, has long been recognized. A 'picture or view' is often the town's trademark; Delft across the water, Princes Street disappearing in a long perspective past the Scott Monument [pl. 24a]. These are views sanctioned by paintings and postcards, bait for visitors and souvenirs for exiles. They can recall the reality of a town and even add to it, or extend it into the past, but they cannot bring the experience of it to someone who has never been there.

Pictures can give clues. Verbal descriptions, even if they are not visually specific, can do more. Dorothy Wordsworth could sum up the experience of a town in a single matter-of-fact sentence. Scott, going to the opposite extreme of length and imprecision, evoked vague images of places and built his own vaguely baronial seat at Abbotsford. Yet he posthumously inspired an immensely successful revival of traditional Scots architecture in country and town alike. Trollope made Barchester a real if generally unseen presence, and could bring it into sharp focus when he wanted. In his own way Barrie did the same for the actual town of Kirriemuir. Hardy, an architect by training, used architecture, landscape and townscape not merely as scenery but as symbols sympathetic to his story. Victor Hugo had done the same before him. All of them describe people and places together, and both become more real in the process.

THE ANALYSIS OF TOWNSCAPE

There are four ways of examining townscape. Geography is a matter of where a town is, and its importance does not need to be stressed. No town can be described without reference to the shape of the ground, the colour of its local materials. There are always good geographical reasons not only for the siting of towns but for their ability or inability to adapt themselves to new needs later on. Edinburgh, a defensively sited town that expanded against heavy geographical odds (a fact responsible both for its difficulties and its character) is one of the exceptional towns which have argued with nature and won.

Then comes use, and the question of how a town works. Between the form and the function of a town there is a two-way relationship. Function plays a primary part in forming a town for particular purposes at particular times. But as soon as it has taken shape, the town imposes its own functional pattern on everything that goes on in it; positively generating some kinds of activity but discouraging those to which its form is not congenial.

History can give the answer to forgotten but none the less important questions which come up under the other headings. Why and by whom was a town founded just where it is, and for what purpose? How, if that purpose has ceased, has it survived and even grown? It also sheds light on the visual content of townscape, and on the aesthetic decisions that may have helped to form it.

Finally there is visual analysis, which has recently become as essential a part of the study of towns as it was in the early nineteenth century, though rather less effectively. It cannot of course be considered without reference to the other three factors with which it has such a close connection. But as the product of these factors, the visible presence of a town is what townscape is about. Its analysis in visual terms can sometimes assist in its enjoyment, but can never be a substitute for the visual experience of the townscape itself. Nor can it begin to include the other, though closely related, experiences that towns provide. Its real justification is creative; to identify the visual qualities of a town which may have been obscured by change of custom and use, or by neglect (itself a symptom of change) and then, in the words of the *Civic Amenities Act* of 1967, effectively preserve and enhance them.

TOWNSCAPE IN ABSTRACT

In its strictest sense, visual analysis ignores everything but abstract form. It sees a town as a total sculptural space, every solid inflection complemented by that of the enclosing air. Robert Adam, in the preface to his *Works in Architecture* (1773), defined a similar concept in relation to buildings, based on the idea of movement which is fundamental to townscape as well as landscape:

> Movement is meant to express, the rise and fall, the advance and recess, with other diversity of form, in the different parts of a building, so as to add greatly to the picturesque of the composition. For the rising and falling, advancing and receding, with the convexity and concavity, and other forms of the great parts, have the same effect in architecture, that hill and dale, fore-ground and distance, swelling and sinking have in landscape: That is, they serve to produce an agreeable and diversified contour, that groups and contrasts like a picture, and creates a variety of light and shade, which gives great spirit, beauty and effect to the composition.

Bearing in mind Adam's own work as an architect uncommonly sensitive to townscape and landscape, his careful definition of the 'great parts' is significant. In the arrangement of the smaller parts he was always at pains to achieve a more static effect in which movement is resolved, if not eliminated.

Of Adam's contribution to Scottish townscape more will be said in chapter IV. But the terms he used in his definition of movement have an application far beyond his own individual buildings or anyone else's. 'Rise and fall, advance and recess' suggest a three-dimensional grid in which any building, or for that matter any townscape, can be plotted as if by radar. In less general terms, there are words to describe the relationships between the parts of a building, or between one building and another; diversity, group, contrast. Some words have a particular suggestion of space, like concavity and distance. In townscape the crucial relationships are not only between building and

14

building, space and space, but equally between buildings and spaces.

Diversity and contrast are vital parts of townscape, but it is important to realize that they must always depend (as they obviously did in the eighteenth century) on a degree of sameness; certain conventions against which diversity is valid. As to what kind of diversity can be effective in each particular case, it is far easier to judge in retrospect than in advance. The most blatant contrast in the whole of Scottish townscape is the colourful, finicking, half Anglicized and half timbered conglomeration of Ramsay Garden, seen from Princes Street at the head of the great grey prospect of Edinburgh's old town [pl. 32a]. It was designed in 1892, at a time of wild disregard for townscape conventions everywhere. But Sir Patrick Geddes, who commissioned it, was an academic planner with a rare grasp of how towns grow and function, and knew what he was at. In this nearly north-facing scene Ramsay Garden is like a permanent burst of sun and colour. Only on summer evenings is the whole incredible scene brilliantly lit and the contrast between this group and its sombre neighbours is forgotten in view of the greater contrast between hillside and buildings, which earlier in the day were merged in shadow.

Some diversity of scale, closely linked to that of status, is taken for granted as an ingredient in townscape. Most towns have a hierarchy of buildings and spaces that are more or less large or important in relation to each other and form a sequence in place or time. One of the few executed products of Adam's own ambition to design public buildings on the very grandest scale is the entrance front of the Old College of Edinburgh University (1789). But alas, it is only a front; the internal sequence of small and large court which was to have followed on behind it was never carried out.

Scale, of course, is an entirely relative term of comparison not only between buildings or spaces but between their parts, right down to doors and windows and small units like bricks and stones, glazing and paving, until it becomes virtually a matter of texture. If a Georgian terrace were revisited by its designer, what would most startle him would be the break in scale through

15

the introduction of the larger units of more recent technology; the plate glass windows, flush doors and continuous asphalt road surfaces, things which in varying degrees we can now accept even if we do not approve of them. In fact the only absolute sense in which scale can be discussed is that of 'human scale'. This will be done in another context.

Abstract values, the geometrical play of solid and void, are created just as often by accident as design. But the 'accident' is far more likely to be brought about by function than by chance, being the result of functional constraints that eliminate the need for design decisions. Towns cannot be called abstract creations, but since they are nothing without function they abound in the abstract quality to which function gives birth.

CONSCIOUSNESS OF TOWNS

If towns are not abstract, still less are the ways in which people look at them and talk about what they see. In his book *The Image of the City* Kevin Lynch coined the ugly but useful word 'imageability', which means the property of certain objects in the townscape that enables people to remember and describe them in visual terms. A stranger asks the way to a distant part of the town. The resident, even if he knows the route through constant use, may have difficulty in describing it in the visual terms from which the stranger will be able to recognize it. 'You can't miss it,' says the resident, meaning that he is conscious of his inability to describe something he knows so well.

Visual qualities are thus taken for granted, but a visit to a strange town – and indeed the subsequent return to one's own – can be an eye-opener, stimulating a conscious reaction. So can a view of a known town in unfamiliar conditions, like Words-worth's view from Westminster Bridge. Change in a home town also brings visual images and concepts to the surface, quite apart from any practical considerations like that of whether a new building adequately serves a purpose of which one approves. The familiar scene gives reassurance while change, at least until one gets used to it, does not. The awkward, or convenient, fact that people will eventually become visually accustomed to anything that does its job moderately well, is a good reason for guarding rather than relaxing the accepted usages of townscape.

THE FARAWAY TOWN

The first event in townscape is often the town-mark, the signature with which a town announces itself at a distance. It may be a natural landmark like the citadels of Stirling or Edinburgh, Dumbarton Rock or North Berwick Law [pl. 2b], all of which are volcanic hills; so are Edinburgh's eastern hills, including the Calton [pl. 10a]. Most often it is the silhouette of one or more tall buildings first glimpsed on a first approach, and thereafter not forgotten. Few of the great medieval churches still perform this role except as ruins, like the cathedrals of Elgin or St Andrews, or in restored form like the tower of Dunfermline parish church which used to be the Abbey. The majority of towns owe their characteristic profile to towers and spires of the last 250 years, sometimes those of parish churches but more often of tolbooths or town-houses, designed no less to impress the stranger than to welcome the home-comer. *Proud when our tower comes in sight,* an unknown nineteenth century Renfrewshire poet wrote; he might well have been thinking of the town-house spire of the weaving village of Kilbarchan.

Such also are the spire of Montrose parish church (p. 140) seen across the basin that makes the town almost an island, and of Haddington town-house (p. 68) over the trees or, tallest of them all, the distant needle of the town-house of Ayr (p. 134). Sometimes it is a compound signature with more than one town-marking feature. Irvine, a dozen miles further up the Ayrshire coast, has three; a parish church demurely Georgian, a skinny Grecian town hall and a powerful, big-skirted gothic free church. They have lately been joined by a cluster of tower block housing of less distinctive profile.

In Holland, where churches and town halls hoist their bulbous outlines like weather signals over the polders, they have a flamboyant variety which the need for identification made desirable and imported timber and metal made possible. The Dutchman John Slezer, honorary captain in the British Army, obviously enjoyed the variety of spires that similarly if more modestly marked the towns of seventeenth-century Scotland. They are an important and indeed exaggerated feature of the twenty-eight Prospects of Scottish towns in his *Theatrum Scotiae* (1693).

THE PROSPECT AND THE PANORAMA

What Slezer calls a Prospect is a view of a town in its setting from a selected vantage point. Comparison of his Prospects with their subjects as they are today [pls 1a, 1b] shows that the majority are still recognizable at least by the lie of the land or their former town-marks, though the latter are usually so engulfed by subsequent town growth that they have ceased to perform this function. Culross is one of the minority which have not grown far outside their seventeenth century margins, but it has gained a tolbooth tower from the eighteenth century, and lost its shore line (as well as the distinctive twin towers of the Abbey House) in the twentieth. Falkland, with its town-marking royal palace, is one of the least changed of all.

Change of itself need not be deplored, but of all townscape views the prospect is most vulnerable to it. The merits of a prospect lie in limitation, whether of boundaries, patterns, colours or textures. From this view any backyard developments, from garden sheds to factories, occupy the front of the stage. In a prospect the townscape must be its own apologist. We do not yet have the vital evidence, justification even, that is provided at a closer view by the sight of the people who made, or who now use, what appears to be some glaringly inconsistent development.

It is hard to draw a firm line between a prospect and a panorama. The latter implies a wider view and a greater variety, and thus applies to distant views of cities and large towns. Except on the skyline it is less vulnerable than a prospect, for it is intrinsically diverse, a counterpane pieced together from successive growths and developments. The panorama of Dundee, a city whose development verges on the chaotic, still provides

one of the most impressive of all urban views. A vast hillside
sprawl of docks, town hall, steeples, mills and mansions, tenements and tower blocks, it rushes towards you from the other
end of the Tay road bridge; the bare summit of the Law emerging,
with a diminutive town-mark at the very top.

THE ENTRY

Fortunate indeed, where townscape is concerned, is the town
whose edge is clearly defined by nature or, which is much less
common, by man. A still greater advantage from the point of
view of the approaching spectator is the barrier which, while
effectively preventing sprawl, still offers points of entry; a wall
with openings or a river with bridges. Dundee and the Tay
provide an extreme and dramatic example. Drive up river
towards Perth, and you find a gentler but still perfectly distinct
sequence; first the great landed mansions of the Carse of Gowrie,
then the well-treed Victorian villas of Kinnoull and finally the
Georgian toll-house village of Bridgend, from which it is only a
short jump across the same (but now narrower) river by
Smeaton's bridge into Perth's centre [pl. 21b]. Stirling's eastern
entry [pl. 3a] is the most sophisticated in Scotland.

Most towns have a fringe, a rough edge like thinly-distributed
iron filings at a distance from the town-magnet. On a small
scale it can be a filling-station or a couple of bungalows. But it
can also be a ribbon suburb trailing out for miles along the
roads which are the urban lines of force, half obliterating any
real places in its path as the Glasgow road has done to Edinburgh's neighbouring village of Corstorphine. There are also
the neutral zones, belts of specialized use which, though they
often happen to be bounded by large roads, do not acknowledge
them as lines of force at all. Indeed the roads themselves, with
their increasingly specialized job of carrying traffic, tend now to
divide the urban areas which they once drew together. The
approaches to many a Scottish town have suffered in this way,
and to explore the townscape quality of most suburbs it is
necessary to get off the main roads that sever them. More
acceptably from the town's own point of view, and often more

19

excitingly from your own, you can still arrive at or near certain privileged town centres by train (p. 169).

PEOPLE AS TOWN MAKERS

Once inside a town, the meaning of townscape stems from the people concerned (of whom you are now one) and the things they do there. A dead or sleeping town may have an interesting form, but it immediately poses questions to the memory and imagination. How and by whom has it been made and used? What will happen here tomorrow?

People are involved with towns in three degrees; the individual, the corporate and the public. A town could be represented by a large number of individual boxes nesting into bigger corporate ones, these in turn fitting into the biggest which is the town itself. But of course it is impossible to cast people in such rigid roles. In practice their concerns and activities overlap in an infinite number of ways, many of which are quite unpredictable. No one in a town, except the occupants of graveyards and other places of permanent confinement, does the same thing in the same place all the time.

The same complexity is expressed in the actual fabric of the town. It is easy to mark a town plan so as to show to what category of owner each piece of ground belongs; John Wood did it in many of his Town Maps (p. 123), actually marking each plot with the name of its private, corporate or public owner. But as soon as he puts up a building, the owner is plainly not acting just for himself; even the private or corporate owner is now doing something of public concern. He is not only placing a building of a certain appearance and use in a certain place, but in some measure he is physically defining the public space between his and all the other buildings. It may be any sort of space; open suburb, street or square, down to the narrow alley or the left-over, man-size space that might be useful for sitting down and selling newspapers. But what all these spaces have in common, unless they are fenced off and accessible to the eye only, is that they are public, and by mutual consent you can do anything in them that is not obviously illegal.

Georgian new towns like Craig's Edinburgh layout [pl. 14a] with their formal pattern of buildings, spaces and uses, achieved a fine balance between all the interests involved. The individuality of the single house in Charlotte Square [pl. 15a] is merged into the corporate character of the terrace. This in turn defines and adorns a public space which has a definite relationship with the other spaces in the town. Medieval towns, less formal in every way, are no less intelligible.

THE HUMAN SCALE

Scale means relative size, and can only be said to have any absolute meaning in relation to the one universal measure, the human figure. Yet in practice even this standard is extremely flexible. No building is literally of human size except the sentry box or the telephone kiosk which are designed to enclose an individual man-space with minimum room to spare. Human scale in fact implies domestic scale, and most people naturally acquire their idea of this from the places where they live, which means (in Scottish towns) a ceiling height of anything between two and four metres, with doors and windows to match. In corporate or public buildings we are quite accustomed to seeing larger versions of these same units in a hierarchy of scale that corresponds with a hierarchy of status, that is with the number or importance of the people concerned. Traditional construction with pierced load-bearing walls has hitherto made it easy for buildings to supply this evidence of status and thus identify themselves in the townscape. Current building practice however offers a choice between two extremes [pls 29e, f]; the pre-cast wall and window sections which establish human scale and then repeat it indefinitely, at best making a satisfactory pattern out of it, and the curtain wall which may lose it altogether. Neither sort of building gives a clue to its real importance except in crude terms of size.

SCALE AND STYLE

Along with the adaptability and explicitness of the load-bearing wall we have inherited the huge vocabulary of architectural style which still enlivens our townscapes although it is beyond our means and ability to use much of it today. A Victorian church spire of moderate quality, a minor orgy of terra-cotta ornament which somebody ordered out of a catalogue a century ago; even these humble exercises in the use of style can give life to what would otherwise be a dreary place. But it is the classical style in all its variations that does most for our towns. Brought to perfect fluency by the Georgians, and in Scotland further developed with particular tenacity by the Victorians, it unites the town scene in a way that can too easily be taken for granted. All over a Georgian town, columns and piers and pilasters provided a system, sometimes structural and sometimes ornamental, that brought together all sorts and sizes of buildings and their parts under common rules of proportion, so that in a sense these elements are stand-ins for people; the only comparable system, as we have seen, is based on the human figure. The columns of a doorpiece are of human scale, but if these same elements are applied two storeys tall to a terrace of private houses they give it a larger, corporate scale; once again Charlotte Square [pl. 15a] is a familiar example. Or large and small columns, pilasters or whatever, can stand side by side doing both jobs together. On a public scale they may come into their own as supporting members holding up a portico which could be the open, outdoor ante-room of an important interior. With equal propriety a column can stand by itself thirty metres high in masonry, in the middle of a public square; or be one of many in painted wood, a mere two metres high, between a row of little shop windows [pls. 33a, 14b, 19e].

PERMANENT PEOPLE

If the classical system is effectively an extension of human scale, a more literal one is provided by the town's statues. To put up one of these, unless one is simply adding to a perfunctory line-up of notabilities like that of the Pincio gardens in Rome, is to undertake a major commitment in townscape. Its subject may well have been a living character in the town and as such he will have been related to it like anyone else, but the relationship is now to be permanent and formal. Whatever can be conveyed of his personality or attributes (Sir Walter Scott's dog, William Pitt's nose) must be subsidiary and if possible relevant to the statue's main job, which is to inhabit and demonstrate a town space [pl. 3b]. In Edinburgh three very diverse figures perform this role at the three successive junctions of George Street with its cross-streets [pl. 15c]; the histrionic King George IV, the suavely rhetorical prime minister Pitt, the convinced, expository cleric Thomas Chalmers; the two benign politicians of Montrose do the same job (p. 243). Always concerned with space, when statues stand before a building they look away from it; thus the Duke of Wellington, conscious of form as always, leads the charge from the door of the Register House on his prancing war-horse, right across the already powerful axis of Waterloo Place and over the bridge to Edinburgh's old town. In Glasgow, leaving heroics to the mighty portico of Stirling's Library, he sits more ceremonially and on a quieter mount to look down Ingram Street (p. 235). Not all Glasgow's statues are so well sited, some of them having been displaced by traffic. The magnificent early-eighteenth-century equestrian bronze of William III which used to dignify the line of Trongate [pl. 13b] has been unhappily penned in a small fenced-in plot near the Cathedral. As real as people (in some respects more so) and substantial as buildings, statues form a link between the two; a link also in time, for they are witnesses not only of times past but of times passing, as sundials through bright days, bird-perches always, sadly dripping in the rain, snow-hatted in winter.

THE EXPERIENCE OF A TOWN

What do people demand of towns, apart from the predictable necessities? In total it seems to be a balance of opposites; public and private life, industry and idleness, the natural and the man-made, the material and the transcendant. The travelogue cliché which sums it up, 'city of contrasts', can be applied to any town worthy of the name, regardless of size. The larger the town, the wider the extremes it can embrace and the greater their variety. A small town or village offers less diversity, but the essential quality is the same. It is an area of co-existence, a meeting place for people and things.

In terms of function, a town is a place of activities known and unknown, separate or shared, of business or pleasure or a combination of both. Its most characteristic function, the selling of goods and services, is an intensely sociable one; that of moving about and buying them is even more so. Despite (or rather because of) the good functional reasons that may be behind them, the social encounters of town life become important in themselves, encouraged and confirmed by their setting in the townscape.

The same sort of requirements can be stated in terms of place. Here the town's first job is to define space, starting with the ground and finally coming to terms with the sky after accommodating people and their activities on the way. In this definition it must first be intelligible, but it must also be partly mysterious, even if only a short interval of time separates you from the answer to the mystery. Both needs are satisfied by the spacious medieval market street with its half-hidden exits and narrow pends; or even by the mysteries of private lives glimpsed through the windows of a square. People can, if they want, be passive in a town, but spaces cannot and buildings should not. A building, for example, must have a very good excuse for confronting a public space with a blank wall; a seventeenth-century town house has a good historical reason for this (p. 60), but for a twentieth-century office which has an empty wall on street level there is no excuse at all.

Finally a town is seen in the medium of time; of regular functions, chiming clocks. It is a place where one looks for the oldest things and the newest. Time also provides the sequence in which a town is seen; not only by sitting in one place and watching it as a theatre of half-planned activity, or observing its own performance as a sundial, but by moving on from one

24

part to the next. The entry from large spaces into small and back again, the reassurance of a half-unseen but manifestly symmetrical layout, the gradual working out of the question posed by a curved street, encounters with buildings and their quick-change act into space-defining screens, the pursuit of distant signals; these are familiar parts of the experience of walking, with whatever purpose in mind, through the town.

II. THE MEDIEVAL BURGH

At first sight there is so little left of the town scene of medieval Scotland that it would seem reasonable to begin the story with the reign of James VI, 1567–1625, from which the earliest coherent townscapes, like that of Culross, survive.

But there are three good reasons for starting earlier. First is the existence of some of the more durable medieval buildings such as bridges [pl. 5a] and burgh kirks, and the castles and religious houses with which many towns were associated. Taken with the geographical evidence, these often shed light on the siting and the subsequent success of a town. Then, even more durable, there is the layout of streets and lanes; the former sometimes known as gaits and the latter always as wynds, for there is a Scots vocabulary of town topography, as of building. Street plans are often as old as the towns themselves and many medieval layouts, lined with a succession of newer buildings, still exist today, the majority still working as town centres. Third and perhaps most important, the constitution of Scottish burghs, the machinery by which town communities made decisions about their whole way of life and their physical environment, spring from acts of government which go back to the beginning of the twelfth century. The reorganization of Scottish local government under Lord Wheatley's proposals in 1975 was not merely the first radical change in a system eight centuries old; it virtually brought the system to an end. To understand Scottish towns it will now more than ever be necessary to be something of a historian.

The emergence of Scotland as a nation is closely linked with the rise of the colonizing Scots who came over from Ireland and to whom she owes her name. Duncan I, descended through seven generations from Kenneth MacAlpin King of the Scots, succeeded in 1034 and became in effect the first king of Scotland. It was less a nation than a multi-racial group assembled by conquest, dynastic management and treaty. Even in territorial terms it differed from the country we know, for Norway still held the outer isles and some of the mainland, and the southern frontier was still to be fixed. Duncan was killed as all the world knows (but in battle, not in bed) by the rival claimant Macbeth, likewise descended from MacAlpin. His son Malcolm Canmore, or Big-head, avenged him in 1057 at the battle of Lumphanan in Aberdeenshire. This was Malcolm III, who is remembered less for his efforts to organize Scotland on English (that is on Saxon) lines than for his English second wife Margaret, a refugee from the Norman invasion. Among her achievements were a considerable programme of reform in the Scottish Church and the foundation of Scotland's first Benedictine abbey at Dunfermline.

Despite Malcolm's opposition to the Normans, by whom he was killed in battle near Alnwick, the eldest of his three sons succeeded him with Norman support. But it was the youngest, David I, 1124–53, who had the vision and ability to undertake the constructive government of Scotland as a single nation. This he did by imposing upon it, as far as was then practicable, a version of the feudal system which the Normans had already established in England. The key to it was the perpetual and heritable possession of land by the grant of a feu from the feudal superior to the feuar, subject to any conditions or obligations which the superior might lay down. As feudal superior of all Scottish land, David disposed of it to whom he wished, in exchange for payment in kind or for services or (in the case of the Burghs) for money. His feuars might sub-feu in turn, and theirs might do the same, but all such arrangements were part of the same feudal pyramid, at whose apex was the king. Today not much is heard of this ultimate feudal obligation to the monarch, while the principle of feudal control, with its immense disciplinary influence on the Scottish landscape and townscape, is itself disappearing and may soon be abolished. Many superiors of town land have sold their right to collect feu-duty, and their successors, who may have purchased the superiority only as an investment, are no longer interested in the prerogative of control that goes with it.

THE KING'S BURGHS

David I disposed of his land in various ways. Some he retained for his own domestic purposes or gave it to his officers in return for their court duties. To bishops and abbots he made generous grants not only for their immediate use but often well outside their precincts, as an endowment. Sheriffs were appointed and given sheriffdoms which they governed from royal castles. Usually attached to burghs, or to settlements which in time were erected into burghs, the early castles were of the motte and bailey (mound and rampart) type with wooden palisades. It is clear that the whole machinery of order and defence was the result of formal provision; so was that of trade, in which the burghs played a vital part. An early use of the term *burgus* is found in the famous charter of 1159 to Kelso Abbey, now in the National Library of Scotland. Here King Malcolm IV, whose portrait is coupled with that of his grandfather David I in the two halves of his illuminated initial M, confirms a number of previous grants. Berwick and Roxburgh (the former lost to England in the fifteenth century, the latter now totally sub-merged under green fields) are both given the title of *burgus*, but Kelso itself is still only a *villa*, or village. The earliest surviving burgh charter is that of Ayr, granted by Malcolm's brother William the Lion in the first decade of the following century. Settlements had of course existed at communication points, or ancillary to places of defence or worship, long before their erection as burghs, or the planting of new ones. An unclassified town of this kind appears in the charters as a *villa*. What then was special about a burgh?

A *burgus* is literally a fortified enclosure. But fortification is not the main point. In the feudal context a burgh can be described as a protected and privileged commercial centre whose administration is in the hands of its burgesses. The formal erection of burghs indicates Scotland's change from an agglo-meration of self-supporting rural areas to an organized mercantile system, with arrangements for selling its surplus products and buying those of others by means of the silver coinage that David I introduced.

The Royal Burghs (though they were simply called 'my burgh' in the relevant charters, the royal title being first applied to Whithorn in its charter of 1511) were initially the commercial centres of sheriffdoms, the sheriff or captain affording the protection of his castle and acting as the administrative link with the king and his chamberlain; within the burgh however he had no jurisdiction. The burghs had the exclusive right to trade within their sheriffdoms and to hold weekly markets and annual fairs, and from these they levied petty customs which they paid to the king. Similar rights in the export trade were granted to coastal burghs and paid for in 'great customs'. Their burgesses, the English, Norman, Flemish and Scots merchants who were given land in the burghs, paid feu-duty to the king; Edinburgh (1319) and Aberdeen (1329) being the first burghs to purchase the charters of feu-ferme which exempted them from this burden. The burghs were thus unique among the king's vassals or feuars in that they could and did pay him in hard cash.

None of the original charters of erection survive for any of David's burghs, but fourteen of them are mentioned in other charters and documents: Berwick, Roxburgh, Dunfermline, Edinburgh, Perth, Stirling, Aberdeen (not Old Aberdeen), Forres, Haddington, Peebles, Renfrew, Rutherglen, Elgin and Linlithgow. Inverness and Montrose are possible additions to the list. Of these the 'Four Burghs' of the south, Edinburgh and Berwick, Roxburgh and Stirling, seem to have adopted during his reign a code of Burgh Laws adapted from those of Newcastle and subsequently taken over without much variation for the charters of many other Scottish burghs. These '*Leges Burgorum*' start with an affirmation of the rights of the king:

In primis videndum est quid sit redditus domini regis in burgagiis.

– or in Thomson's vernacular form:

> In the first what is the rent of our lord the kyng in borowagis [burgess holdings].

Most of the laws are devised to protect the mercantile rights of the burgesses, but those concerning the sale of bread, meat and ale imply fairness to the customer as well. They also shed some light on the town scene:

> And wha that takis brede to sell aw nocht for to hyde it bot sett it in thair wyndow or in the mercat that it may be opynly sauld.

> Wha that wyl sell flesche . . . he sal sett his flesche opynly in his wyndow that it be sene communly till al men that will tharof.

> And ilke broustare sal put hir alewande ututh hir wyndow or abune hir dur that it may be seabill communly till al men.

Brewing was for many centuries a kitchen industry supervised by ale-wives like Bessie Bar, a sixteenth-century maltstress in Culross. Bulk sales at the market are mentioned in a more general context in one of the laws added by William the Lion:

> And it is commandit be the King that the merchandises for said and all other merchandises salbe presentit at the mercat and mercat croce of burghis and thar at the lest salbe profferait to the merchandis of the burgh effectuouslie wythout fraude or gyle. And the custom tharof salbe payit to the King.

The *Laws of the* [merchant] *Gilde* of Berwick include an early and typical attempt to deal with the problem of refuse in public places:

> We ordain that no one presume or dare to place filth or any dust or ashes on the common way or in the market place, or on the banks of the Tweed, to the hurt and skaith of the passers by.

A related hazard, that of fuel or combustible rubbish left in the open, was dealt with by a law *Anent fyre in townis* in 1425.

The Court of the Four Burghs was formally convened in 1292 and four years later they joined the burghs of Perth and Aber-

deen in sending representatives to the parliament held in Dun-
fermline, where they affixed their seals to John Baliol's treaty
with France. Thenceforth the burghs became, with the nobility
and the church, one of the Three Estates of Parliament in
Scotland. From 1369 the Court consisted of Edinburgh and
Stirling, Lanark and Linlithgow (the two latter in place of
Berwick and Roxburgh) and their meeting place was fixed in
Edinburgh by an Act of 1454. Finally, a general Convention of
Royal Burghs, including the southern with their Court and the
northern with their Hanse, was constituted by an Act of 1487

> for dealing with the welfare of merchandise, the gude rule
> and statues for the common profit of burrows, and to provide
> for remied upon the skaith and injuries sustained within the
> burrows.

The powerful position of the burghs, reinforced by the Act of
1469 which gave each town council to nominate its successors
year by year instead of submitting to burgess elections, was
gradually eroded by the success of the mercantile system that
had brought them into being, and by the introduction of more
equitable forms of government. But the Royal Burghs still have
their formal (if less influential) Convention based in Edinburgh,
and although the individual burgh has virtually ceased to be a
force in local government, its eight centuries of supremacy have
left an indelible mark on the Scottish townscape.

Royal Burghs still hold this courtesy title although many have
recently lost some of their former civic importance. Of the
thirty-one administrative counties existing in Scotland till 1975
(taking Morayshire and Nairnshire as single counties and likewise
Perthshire and Kinross-shire), sixteen had county towns which
attained Royal Burgh status before the death of William the
Lion in 1214, and eleven more of them were to gain it by 1700.
Lerwick, the county town of Shetland, was a second generation
burgh (of barony), while the remaining three were all replace-
ments for old county towns in their eponymous counties: Duns
for Berwick, Newton St Boswells for Roxburgh and Stonehaven
for Kincardine. Dundee, which like Edinburgh, Glasgow and
Aberdeen had county status, is also like them a Royal Burgh;

as are ten out of the twenty-one towns which had until 1975 the administrative title of Large Burghs. Certainly not all Royal Burghs have been equally successful in terms of growth. Glasgow now has a population of 896,000, Culross of 520 (p. 143). But it was as Royal Burghs that most of today's important town centres took on their present shape. The main exceptions are the new industrial centres of the nineteenth century and six of the seven post-war towns of the twentieth. The other, Irvine, is based on a Royal Burgh.

BURGHS OF BARONY

As well as erecting its own independent burghs which subsequently became known as 'royal', the crown had the prerogative of allowing barons and prelates to establish burghs on the lands it had granted to them, and to take the duty payable on burgess holdings, markets and fairs. Until the middle of the fifteenth century, when the growth of internal trade began to justify the founding of many more of these baronial burghs, their existence is a sign either of exceptional royal favour or that the influence of the baron, in his own lands at least, was greater than that of the king; even if only temporarily, for most of the early burghs of barony (including all those mentioned here) later came or reverted to the crown. But a Royal Burgh could become baronial. Nairn, a burgh newly planted by the king about 1190, complete with its sheriff's castle, was given by King Robert the Bruce to the Earl of Moray along with his two other burghs of Elgin and Forres. The king's burgh of Kirkcudbright was alienated about 1369 to the Lords of Galloway as a burgh of regality, this title indicating a jurisdiction almost equivalent to that of the crown itself.

There were also ecclesiastical burghs of barony whose prime purpose was to endow the religious foundations from which they held their privileges. St Andrews and Glasgow started as cathedral burghs, with charters from David I and William the Lion. Arbroath, Canongate and Kelso were abbey burghs, Whithorn a priory burgh. But not all the great churches were funded by their neighbouring burghs, even where these existed.

32

The rich and powerful abbey of Dunfermline, for example, was adjacent to a king's burgh but drew its money from huge properties in Fife and Lothian, including its own baronial burghs of Kirkcaldy, Queensferry and Musselburgh. Among the later erections were that of Paisley in 1488 for the benefit of the abbey, and in the following year that of 'Old' Aberdeen for the cathedral [pl. 4]. The charter of 1488 that made the village of Paisley into a burgh of barony is typical of its kind, specifying not only the usual qualifications for carrying on local trade but the particular commodities that were likely to be bought and sold. Here the burgesses were to enjoy

> the full and free liberty of buying and selling in the said burgh, wire, wax, woollen and linen cloths, wholesale or retail, and all other goods and wares coming into it; with power and liberty of having and holding in the same place, bakers, brewers, butchers, and sellers both of flesh and fish, and workmen in the several crafts . . .

> . . . likewise to possess a cross and market for ever, every week, on Monday, and two public fairs yearly, for ever; namely one on the day of St Mirren, and the other on the day of St Marnoch.

BURGH LAYOUT

The dominant factor in burgh layout was of course geography, which often indicated the site for a castle, provided the natural amenity of a harbour, or allowed through traffic routes which in turn might demand river crossings. The most important of these routes (often the one across the river) became the *hie gait* or high street and thus normally took on a second job as a market place. Others were linked directly to it without any of the formality characteristic of Georgian planning or any of today's inhibitions about congestion and functional separation.

In order to serve its purpose as a market the main street or *hie gait* was wider than the others for at least part of its length. Its commonest shape is a long triangle or wedge, but it may also be tapered at both ends or square at both, much depending on the pattern of the connecting streets. A square end may be formed by a T junction or it may be the sudden constriction just before a town gate or port, as at the former Netherbow Port in Edinburgh and the North Port in Montrose; both gateways have now gone, but the distinctive street form remains (pp. 232, 244). The tolbooth (p. 61) occupies a position of vantage at the blunt end of the street or in the middle of one of the long sides, or sometimes on an island site in the middle like Edinburgh's old tolbooth, the 'Heart of Midlothian'. The mercat cross stood in the open nearby. In busy towns its modern fate is to be surrounded almost permanently by motor traffic like that at Cupar [pl. 35b], or moved to an unhistorical but safer position up against the tolbooth wall; this is what has happened to the cross at Banff, a much weathered but still beautiful crucifix which serves to remind us that the great majority of surviving mercat crosses and virtually all tolbooths are of post-reformation date. Although the tolbooth had to contain a meeting room for the council and provide security for money and the confinement of criminals and debtors, it was seldom distinguished by any special architectural status from the ordinary houses of the burgh until the reign of James VI.

These burghs were 'planned' insofar as their layouts were the result of deliberate decisions by the first burgesses and their successors. The layouts were 'organic' not because of any lack of planning, but because natural constraints were accepted and functional needs fulfilled with the basic minimum of expense and formality, the latter being embodied in the mercat cross. They are thus both planned and organic towns, in which the two principles are very seldom opposed. Dualities and contradictions did nevertheless arise where this system could not produce an answer that would obey all the constraints and satisfy all the needs. Settlements established for one purpose may or may not be able to satisfy another, or there may simply be natural difficulties. Ayr, for example (p. 218) offered a good harbour near its river mouth and the early settlement was as close to it as possible, about 200 m. upstream where the river could be forded. It had one wide street in line with the ford, later called Sandgate, or more properly Sandgait. The 'new' medieval town

adopted what was in some ways a better site, with its *hie gait*
planned along the route south to Alloway (both Ayr and Alloway
still have their medieval bridges). The new site was more
sheltered, and the burgesses with plots between *hie gait* and
river were able to build their private wharves. The result was a
real conflict of importance between the new and old streets,
and by the late eighteenth century it seemed to have been
settled in favour of the latter. Not only had the tolbooth been
resited in the middle of Sandgate, but in 1785 this street was
extended over the river by way of the New Brig. Meantime the
High Street had suffered the indignity of houses encroaching on
its triangular market space. The conflict was to a great extent
resolved in 1828 when the Sandgate tolbooth was demolished
and Thomas Hamilton's magnificent town steeple [pl. 34] was
erected at the corner where the two streets come together.

Where anything like a rectangular pattern appears in the
essentially linear layout of a medieval Scottish burgh, it is the
result of the rather unusual arrangement of two or more important streets running approximately parallel as they do at
Crail and St Andrews, and at Perth which was laid out with
exceptional formality within its town wall. A river or coast line
at right angles to the main route also helps to set up a pattern
of this kind.

There is very little evidence on the actual operation of laying
out the gaits and wynds, the burgess plots which lined them and
the vennels or passages between them, though 'lynaris of land'
(presumably surveyors) were employed at Elgin in 1540. The
burgh's specialist supervisor of building comes on the medieval
scene in the person of the Dean of Guild. He was the head (and
is still the titular head) of the merchant guild, an organization
which existed in Aberdeen by 1222, in Cupar by 1369 and in
Ayr by 1430. His earliest duties seem to have included the
supervision of the burgh's standard weights and measures
(Culross still has a fine set of these, now at the 'Study') and the
repair of the burgh's own buildings including the kirk. In
Edinburgh in 1403 Simon de Schele was 'Dene of Gilde, and
Keeper of the Kirk Work', but the minutes of the Dean of
Guild Court, which go back to 1529, are concerned with such

matters as dykes (walls), rights of access, measures and nuisances. A new constitution of 1584 gave the Court the right to adjudicate between neighbouring proprietors, and in 1674 another Act of the Council gave them something like their present absolute authority over building works within the city; the enforcement of building regulations and the upholding of public and private rights and safety. They also have to authorize demolition works, but the safety of existing buildings is the direct responsibility of the city engineer. Other burghs have a similar system but it is not always operated by a Dean of Guild. Aberdeen, for example, terminated this office in 1876 and new building came under the surveillance of a Plans Committee. The 1947 Planning Act relieved all such authorities of their duty to adjudicate in matters of amenity and architectural design, and with the reorganization of 1975 still more of this pattern has now gone into the past tense.

TOWN WALLS

Defence had a limited importance in burgh layout. National strategy depended more on strong points (the royal and other castles) than on fortified towns, and only Edinburgh, Stirling and Perth were surrounded by stone town walls in medieval times. King William the Lion made a compact with the burgesses of Inverness that he would have a ditch made round the burgh and they would erect and maintain a good palisade above it. Medieval Aberdeen had an earth wall and most Scottish burghs seem to have been similarly protected. In 1503 it was

> statute and ordanit that all tounis and portis on the sey side, sik as Leth, Inverkethin, Kingorne, Disert, Crail and otheris, war spend their commone gudis one the wallis of thair toune to the sey side with portis of lyme and stane. [The Common Good was the burgh revenue from its own lands.]

This burgh law, although it was enacted in the year of James IV's marriage to Henry VII's daughter Margaret, was a national precaution against the growing power of the English navy. Its slightly ambiguous terms suggest stone walls with gun ports on the coastal flanks of the towns alongside their harbours, and Dunbar has an early seaward wall which may date from this time.

The splendid half mile of towered wall on the south-east side of St Andrews, rebuilt in the early sixteenth century, is in fact the precinct wall of the Priory, entered by the earlier gateway known as the Pends. At the west end of the burgh is the double towered Southgait Port of 1589 [pl. 7a]. This is supposed to have been modelled on Edinburgh's Netherbow Port, but is much more like James V's gateway at Linlithgow Palace; apart from the 'Wishart Arch' across the Cowgait in Dundee, saved by its alleged connection with the famous preacher, it is the only Scottish burgh port still in existence. The wall that formerly linked up to it, much of which can still be seen on the walk along the Lade Braes, is not a burgh wall proper but was formed, as was the usual practice, by the continuous walls at the outer ends of burgess plots. Of burgh walls in the proper sense, the two latest examples are those of Edinburgh, still building the 'Flodden' wall at the end of the sixteenth century and extending it with the Telfer wall to take in the grounds of Heriot's Hospital in the second quarter of the seventeenth; and Peebles, which walled its 'new town' (that is the present town) in 1570. Whether publicly or privately financed, the main function of the wall was to be a customs barrier. Entry and exit for the ordinary traveller was restricted to the ports, which could also be closed in times of plague.

BURGH AND CASTLE

Today it is not always easy to appreciate the importance of the castle as an element in burgh planning, for it has usually disappeared. It is still pre-eminent in Edinburgh, where the main street (not a through traffic route) grew down from it (p. 230). Likewise at Stirling; but there a similar ridge site gives just enough room for Castle Wynd to fork into two, the long wedge shape of Broad Street accommodating the market while St John Street provides the main road downhill. This unusual division of mercantile and traffic functions was in this case dictated by the site. Linlithgow, before the building of the palace [pl. 1], had a sheriff's castle in nearly the same position on the promontory overlooking the loch. The round castle of Rothesay with its moated wall is surely the most impressive in itself, and none the less so for being stranded in the uncommonly festive townscape of a Victorian resort. Tarbert's castle, ruined and inaccessible, is the most forlorn.

Castles, albeit late ones, play an important part in two Shetland towns. In 1600 Patrick Stewart, Earl of Orkney, built the 'castellated mansion' whose ruin still looms above and behind the strung-out houses of Scalloway, a name that literally means 'the huts on the bay'. The castle at the north end of Lerwick was built even later, then burned by the Dutch against whom it had been built, and finally reconstructed in 1781 as Fort Charlotte. Lerwick's main street is the most beautiful of the narrow main streets of the islands (Stromness runs it a close second) which have never allowed for heavy through traffic. Pedestrian precincts by right of history, they combine the importance of a main street with the intimacy of a close; people immediately become more important.

Dumbarton, Inverness [pl. 39a] and Jedburgh are all overlooked, from natural hill sites, by the appropriate successors of their sheriff's castles; and each is approached by a *castle gait* or wynd bearing the more recent name of Castle Street. More often however, as at Aberdeen's Castlehill, the street name is the only clue to a castle's position. Forres still has the hillock where its castle once stood on the axis of the *hie gait*, and a similar mound just off Castle Street in Forfar also marks the castle site. The most spectacular of these now empty defensive positions, though a little way outside the town, is the Bass of Inverurie. Elgin's Castle Hill retains the vestiges of its royal fortress, and is called Lady Hill from the dedication of its chapel.

Many baronial burghs had castles too, like the one in the High Street of Maybole which still houses the office of Cassillis Estates. Dornoch [pl. 5b], an ecclesiastical burgh of barony, has its bishop's castle across the street from the cathedral, though considerably altered and now used quite suitably as a hotel. The episcopal castle at St Andrews is a ruin, and the remains of that of Glasgow were cleared altogether at the end of the eighteenth century to make way for the Adam infirmary, whose Edwardian successor will soon be replaced itself. Burntisland is rather deceptive, for Rossend Castle which overlooks the harbour was neither a royal castle (the place only became a Royal Burgh in 1540) nor in the proprietary sense a baronial one.

THE GREAT CHURCH

The tower of the abbey church of Dunfermline, boldly restored by William Burn in 1822 in such a way as to advertise it as the burial place of KING ROBERT THE BRUCE in skyline lettering, still dominates the faraway view of the much enlarged burgh. Many others, if the towers had survived or been replaced, would do the same. But on closer inspection it is clear that there was no very intimate relation between the parent abbeys and the mercantile burghs that were often their late offspring. Even a cathedral may stand apart from the burgh created nearby. The extreme example is that of Brechin; the high street turns its back on the old ecclesiastical site, and it would be quite possible to spend a day in the town without being aware of the Cathedral or the tall round tower that was probably built about the year 1000. An opposite case is that of Kirkwall, a Norse town until 1469 when James III accepted Orkney in lieu of a dowry on his marriage to Margaret of Denmark. Here the old town centre, and the mercat cross of the king's burgh formally erected in 1486, were at the west front of the cathedral of St Magnus.

The little towns of Dornoch and Fortrose cluster round their cathedrals, but although they both became king's burghs and the former in time a county town, they scarcely grew beyond their old ancillary settlements. Dunblane [pl. 6a] has the nearest mainland equivalent to an English cathedral close, and at Dunkeld [pl. 32d] the market street of the bishop's burgh (now called the Cross) is an isosceles triangle aside from the main route, one of its long sides continuing along the line of the former chanonry (now Cathedral Street) until it meets the cathedral's east end. The canonry of Old Aberdeen has a more spacious layout but lacks any visual link with the burgh [pl. 4]. In both these cases the canons' manses have been replaced. Glasgow however still boasts its Provand's Lordship at the foot of Castle Street. Built in the late fifteenth century, it is the earliest surviving town house in Scotland, even pre-dating the bishop's burgh whose *hie gait* was to run (though not quite directly) between cathedral and river crossing. The burgh laid out with most regard to its great church is St Andrews [pl. 7b], which had an enormous medieval diocese. Its two main streets, almost parallel, are processional ways converging on the coastally sited cathedral; the market street, not a main route, is relegated to a subordinate position between them.

THE BURGH KIRK, AND OTHERS

Scotland began to be divided into parishes in the middle of the twelfth century, and these roughly correspond with the territories awarded by the crown to the barons, who might of course be bishops or abbots. It was up to them to build the parish churches, and among the first of these was the splendid Romanesque church at Dalmeny in West Lothian, whose masons had come on in about 1150 from Dunfermline Abbey; a later set of marks at Dalmeny correspond with some of those at Leuchars in Fife. Some of the early kirks adjoined a hamlet or a burgh, but very few of them form part of the town scene today. The church of Dunning in Perthshire still boasts a Romanesque tower, but the village that grew up around it did not even become a burgh of barony till 1511. With certain apparent exceptions which will be explained, the later medieval parish church is not an important type in Scotland. The main reason is that the large religious foundations, who increasingly took over the parish churches from the barons, saw them rather as a source of income than as offering opportunities for fine building. This, where it occurs, is much more often found in the burgh kirks, built by the burgesses who were proud of what they had achieved in this world and apprehensive about what might happen to them in the next. The title 'burgh kirk' is rarely used today, but would correctly be applied to the principal parish churches of most Scottish towns.

Of the exceptions, the most obvious are (or rather were) the establishments which the various religious houses built for themselves in some of the towns, like the Abbey of which a fragment still stands in the High Street of Kilwinning, the mid-fifteenth-century Carmelite priory church at South Queens-ferry, and the Priory whose guesthouse survives at Pittenweem. There were also, in most of the larger towns, the friaries. Elgin has the finest surviving example of a friary church, that of the Franciscans or Greyfriars, beautifully restored by John Kinross in 1896. The ruined north transept of the early-fifteenth-century church of the Dominicans or Blackfriars can be seen in South Street, St Andrews. More often there is nothing left of them except the name still applied to a town district or parish. The Greyfriars' establishment in Edinburgh was demolished about the time of the Reformation, but gave its name to the burial ground and soon afterwards to the new church which forms part of the present one. The *Maison Dieu* or hospital connected with the cathedral at Brechin was not the only one of its kind, but a Victorian parish church still bears its title.

The other kind of medieval church which was not strictly a parish kirk was the collegiate foundation, a church built by a baron in which the mass would be said or sung for himself and his descendants in perpetuity. Some of these were sited in towns, like the collegiate church of St Nicholas, Dalkeith, whose choir (always the most important and sometimes the only completed part) still stands as a curious ruined annexe to the restored nave that became the burgh kirk after the Reformation [pl. 10d]. Many other town churches were originally collegiate foundations, and St Monance church, built as a votive chapel by David II in 1362, may count as one of them. Its nave was never constructed, but the simple geometry of tower and spire, choir and transepts rising above the sea walls, make it the most conspicuous of all the town-marking churches of the Fife coast as seen from the seaward side; like many other uncompleted collegiate churches it anticipates the T-plan post-Reformation kirk, and this indeed is what most of them, including St Monance, were to become.

Of a second type of collegiate church, that which was connected with a university, the finest are those of King's College in Old Aberdeen (1500, pl. 4) and St Salvator's College in St Andrews (1450). Both are marvellously complete in their fabric, their town setting, their continuing function and even their plenishings, and in their very different ways they are the truest of all survivals from late medieval Scotland; the first lying back from the long, narrow high street whose scale is that of a village, and sporting a stone crown of the holy Roman empire on its stumpy tower, the other (though sadly deprived of its window tracery) with its tall plain tower and buttresses lined up along North Street, from which it has a direct entrance.

The great age of the burgh kirk, as of the collegiate church, began about the middle of the fifteenth century, and to a large degree the two were complementary; the Church establishment having concentrated on its bigger buildings, the other two of the Three Estates were providing for their own religious needs. Of combined burgh and collegiate churches there were very few; family chapels added to parish churches were more frequent in country parishes than in town, and Bothwell church, where Archibald, Earl of Douglas, built a new collegiate choir on to the nave of the existing parish kirk in 1397, is exceptional. Sometimes however a burgh church became collegiate, as did St Giles' in Edinburgh [pl. 36b] and St Mary's in Crail. The latter, its nave arcade built in the early thirteenth century, has the distinction of being the earliest of all burgh kirks in the true sense of the term.

Continuing use has brought continuous alteration, and even the quality of historical development has been lost when a burgh kirk has been piously but lifelessly restored. Of the three crowned churches of the Lothians, only St Giles' in Edinburgh still has this feature in its original form, but its great width occasioned by rows of side chapels has been clad in geometric ashlar that does not conform to our present idea of a medieval church. St Michael's, lying close below the palace of Linlithgow, has fared better as far as outside appearances are concerned, and has even won a shiny new spire [pls 1, 30a]. St Mary's across the river from Haddington has had a curious fate, for only the nave was used by the reformed church and the remainder, having survived as a lovely ruin, has recently been brought to life again in a brilliant and valid partial restoration by Ian G. Lindsay and Partners. A fourth tower for which a crown was probably intended still forms a conspicuous feature of the characteristic skyline of Dundee.

The most dramatically sited of all medieval burgh kirks is that of the Holy Rude in Stirling with its bluff apse (1507), crow-stepped at the head and deeply buttressed, standing at the head of St John Street. Those of Perth (mid-fifteenth-century, pl. 6b) and St Andrews (1410) are fitted more prosaically into regular burgh plans, the latter built on six half-length burgess strips with a west front formed later on a seventh. The largest was the formerly collegiate church of St Nicholas in Aberdeen [pl. 4], but of the original work only the late-twelfth-century transepts and the fifteenth-century crypt under the eastern apse survive. The post-Reformation history of the remainder has been regretted in the past, for it was divided into two parish churches; on the Aberdonian James Gibbs's rebuilding of the nave (the West Kirk) in 1741 Hill Burton produced the following dolorous judgement:

> . . . as if emphatically to show that the fruits of his genius were to be entirely withdrawn from his own countrymen, the only building in Scotland known to have been planned by him, this church in his native city, combines whatever could be derived of gloomy and cumbrous from the character of the Gothic architecture, with whatever could be found of cold and rigid in the details of the classic.

So much for pedantic criticism, for to us, looking through the Union Street screen across the burial ground at this immensely dignified presbyterian monument, it is evident that Gibbs, the gayest designer when occasion demanded, was displaying in his last work the sense of time and place which is the hallmark of the Scots architect. The crossing and tower were rebuilt in 1878 after a fire by William Smith, and by then the choir had been replaced (1835) in lightweight gothic by Archibald Simpson of all the altered burgh kirks this is the truest to its history and its situation. Elgin, where Simpson's Grecian kirk took the place of its medieval predecessor on a proud site in the middle of the High Street (1826, pl. 6c) provides an example of total renewal – the sort of case that modern developers are fond of quoting in support of still further change. The architects and planners of every age are responsible for weighing up the advantages of old *versus* new. Renewal in Elgin gave the town something very good (it would be even better in townscape terms if the paved island site were not isolated by modern traffic). The last two chapters will unhappily record more losses than gains through redevelopment; losses which are even more severe in townscape than in architecture.

III. JAMES VI AND THE SEVENTEENTH CENTURY

Of town buildings which were standing at the time of Mary, Queen of Scots (1542–67) precious few survive today; most notably the royal works with which her father James V claimed a place in the architectural history of the European renaissance, so that it is not absurd to compare Stirling Castle with Amboise which Mary herself knew, or Falkland Palace [pl. 11a] with the double-towered entrance of Langeais. Moreover each of them is related to its town in much the same way as its French counterpart. We still have the old tower at Holyroodhouse to which she came in 1561, built by her grandfather but now scarcely distinguishable from its late-seventeenth-century twin at the other end of the palace frontage.

With lesser buildings, legend has generally outlasted fact. Lamb's House near the shore in Leith is popularly named after the merchant who entertained the Queen after she had set foot in Scotland. Like 'Queen Mary's Bath' (probably a gate lodge of Holyroodhouse) it actually dates from the early part of the next century. Queen Mary's House in St Andrews, with its stone oriel overlooking the garden, is the town building most genuinely associated with her.

JAMES VI

The long reign of James VI effectively began in the 1580s, and it is about this time that Scottish townscape ceases to be a mere matter of speculation based on street patterns, documents and deduction, and moves into the realm of demonstrable fact.

45

James was born in Edinburgh Castle in 1566 and became king on Mary's abdication the following year. The last of four regents was the Earl of Morton, a fragment of whose house survives in Blackfriars Street, Edinburgh. His execution in 1581, the promotion for the time being of James Stewart of Bothwellmuir after the foiling of the Ruthven kidnap attempt, the Black Acts of 1584 which subjected the reformed church to the crown; these are among the tactical devices of the first part of James's reign. His strategy lay in the control of two of the estates of his realm, the nobles and the church, and the encouragement of the third, the burghs. His objectives were the raising of money (albeit at first by the crudest of methods which devalued the efforts and the revenue of the already expanding burghs) and the achievement of the crown of England.

In all this he succeeded. The outcome of many desperate moves was a balance which Scotland had not known before and which made the seventeenth century a modest but distinctive plateau in the fortunes of Scotland in general and the Scottish burgh in particular. This reached its full height when the English and Scottish crowns were united in 1603.

The creation of a string of Royal Burghs along the coast of Fife (he called them the fringe of gold on a grey cloth mantle) is the most celebrated application of a policy designed to bring in the hard assets of foreign trade. In *Rob Roy* Sir Walter Scott puts the following speech into the mouth of Andrew Fairservice, the anecdotal gardener of Osbaldistone Hall:

> The pedlar, your honour means? But ca' him what ye wull, they're a great convenience in a country-side that's scant o' borough-towns, like this Northumberland – That's no the case, now, in Scotland – There's the kingdom o' Fife, frae Culross to the East Nuik, its just like a great combined city – Sae mony royal boroughs yoked on end to end, like ropes of ingans, with their hie-streets, and their booths, nae doubt, and their kraemes [stalls], and houses of stane and lime and forestairs – Kirkcaldy, the sell o't, is langer than ony town in England.

This picture of a Jacobean megalopolis, if one can forget its modern equivalent, is not altogether misleading. Kirkcaldy (still known as the *lang toun*) merges into Dysart [pl. 32c], while in the east neuk St Monance, Pittenweem, the Anstruthers and Cellardyke are as nearly continuous as the coastal terrain permits. Some of these places were ecclesiastical burghs of barony which James VI seized in 1587 along with all other church properties and made into Royal Burghs from which he would be the chief beneficiary; Anstruther in the same year, Culross and Earlsferry in the two years following, and St Andrews in 1620. Crail [pl. 9a] had been a Royal Burgh since the reign of David I. The similar erection of Arbroath into a Royal Burgh in 1599 shows that this policy was not limited to Fife, and it should be remembered that James was equally attentive to the established trading burghs such as Leith and Kirkcaldy, Dundee and Aberdeen.

Exports consisted mainly of wool and coarse cloth, hides and sheep-skins, fish and grain – and occasionally coal; this, like the salt from the pans which it fired, was of poor quality and chiefly used at home. Salt good enough for pickling came back, and so did timber from the Baltic, iron from Sweden, hemp and flax and the finer works of art and craft. From the Netherlands, among many varieties of skilled manufacture (the craftsmen themselves sometimes following suit) came bells for the towers of tolbooths and kirks; those at Crail have inscriptions in Dutch which read, respectively

> I was cast in the year of Our Lord 1520,
> Peter Van den Ghein cast me in the year 1614,

the former a reminder that the North Sea trade, for all that James did to encourage it, was already established before his time.

After the union of the crowns the export of livestock to the newly accessible markets of England enriched the border counties. Here the rich ecclesiastical burghs of Galashiels and Kelso were given ordinary baronial status under new superiors. But the lack of exclusive territorial trading rights (a well-guarded prerogative of the Royal Burghs) inhibited their growth and encouraged the foundation of other commercial centres round about.

THE STREETS; MERCHANTS AND CRAFTSMEN

The burghs had always had their descriptive street names; the *hie gait*, the *kirkgait*, the *cowgait* along which cattle were driven to the common pasture, and so on. Gladgate in Auchtermuchty is a rarity; it was the way to the royal falconry with its hawks, or *gleds*. In the sixteenth century such functional names became more numerous; in Glasgow for example *St Thenew's Gait* was renamed Trongate after the common weighing-place which had been set up there, and *Walcargait* became the Saltmarket. In many burghs these specialized markets had their own crosses and even their trons; there was a butter cross in Forfar and a butter tron in Edinburgh, and Elgin still has a Muckle Cross and a Little Cross. The same century also saw a gradual increase in the status of the crafts, which sometimes gave their names to the streets where the craftsmen lived and worked and sometimes sold their manufactures. Bishop Leslie of Perth enjoyed the appropriateness of this arrangement in 1578:

> Is nocht honest, that everie craft (of quilkes thair is no smal number) occupie his awne gaite asyde?

It was a fair enough system, for many crafts, like that of tallow-boiling in Edinburgh's Candlemaker Row, were distinctly offensive and were therefore segregated.

It had always been possible for a craftsman to be a burgess if he had sufficient means, but that was precisely the difficulty. A Burgh Law of 1466 decreed that *na man of craft use merchandise*, and it was nearly a century later that the craftsmen in Royal Burghs, against the opposition of the merchants, began to win the right to sell their own products. Craft guilds became fairly widespread in the sixteenth century, but one of the first guild halls of any architectural significance was that which was established in 1614 in the former Magdalen Chapel (Cowgate) by the wealthy Hammermen's or smiths' guild of Edinburgh, and was subsequently used by other trades as well. Only in 1583, by decree arbitral of James VI, did the craft guilds obtain formal representation on the town councils, most of whom had long been dominated by the merchants. Sixty years later the trading monopolies of the Royal Burghs (both at home and abroad) were confirmed by parliament. But they were already under pressure from an expanding economy that neither wanted nor needed its trade to be channelled through privileged markets, and in 1672 their monopoly was removed from all staple commodities and confined to luxury goods only.

By this time however the enterprising merchants and their guilds were hardly in need of protection. The merchants of Glasgow, for example, were beginning to claim a share of the Virginia tobacco trade in defiance of the Navigation Laws of Charles II. They had already built their own guild hall which was finished in 1659. Its tower still stands, a status symbol old fashioned even in its time, ascending in gothic-windowed stages to a Dutch style balustrade and a spire which puffs out into a small balloon near the tip. This is curious in that it is the only obvious Scottish quotation from the flamboyant skyscape of contemporary Holland with whom Glasgow had a considerable trade, using the little port of Bo'ness on the Firth of Forth (now completely closed) as a convenient back door.

CLOSES

Most burghs managed to expand with little or no increase in their boundaries, on the basis of the original street network. The key to this was the old burgess holding system, and St Andrews, as so often, provides a range of examples. To start with there are the untouched strips or *lang rigs* [gardens], like those behind South Street which still have their burgess houses (or their successors) fronting the street, and long gardens to the rear. Some of the walls between the rigs have little recesses on one or both sides to indicate single or shared ownership. No. 46 even has a doocot, which is of eighteenth-century date like the house. The *lang rigs* being the units of land ownership in the burgh, the present Greyfriars' Garden shows how one of them could be made into a new public thoroughfare. Louden's Close, at the west end of South Street, illustrates a far more common arrangement which is universal in old Scottish burghs, and continued until twentieth-century regulations made the generous provision of daylighting a condition of survival for a house in a close; Mitchell's Close in Haddington has survived thanks to the planned introduction of other uses (p. 238, pl. 9b). Here as elsewhere, the original burgess house is redeveloped with a new street-front building which incorporates a tunnel or 'pend' giving access from the street into the close. On each side of the close more houses are built at right angles to the street line, and the whole close (as in this instance) shares the name of its developer and the protection of a lockable door or *yett* at the opening of the pend. The best site naturally comes at the tail of the strip on which the close is developed; the lucky owner can build a house whose front blocks off the close and from whose back he can enjoy what is left of the garden, with uninterrupted views of the country beyond. Such is the town *ludging* of the laird of Leckie at the end of the close behind No. 24 Bow Street, Stirling, and later examples can be seen to the north of Montrose High Street. A still further development of this theme can be seen at the rear of No. 23 in the High Street, Dunbar. Here a two-storey house of about 1600 faces you as you walk down the close, but allows you to penetrate into still further back lands by way of its own pend, picturesquely placed under the platt of an outside stair.

BUILDING REGULATIONS

A Scottish equivalent of the 'great rebuild' in England was under way by the middle of the sixteenth century, and pressure was put on the owners of sub-standard property by an act of 1594 *Anent the uphalding of decayed landis within burgh.* This is particularly interesting in its assertion of the rights of the feudal heritors to deal with problems arising from joint ownership or tenancy. A *land* means a building, but the term was later applied to tenements, that is to multiple buildings in general and blocks of flats in particular; it is now only used in proper names, like 'Shoemakers' Land' and so on.

> Oure Soverane Lord, with avise of his estatis in this present parliament, ratifies and apprevis the actis and statutis maid by his Hienes maist noble progenitouris, of worthie memorie, concerning the uphalding of landis gevin in conjunct infeftment, als weill to burgh as land,
>
> and for the better execution thairof and reparation of the decayed policie within burgh, statutis and ordanis that the provest and bailies of ilk burgh sall, at the instance of the heritouris of the landis within the same, tak summar cognitioun of the estait of the landis within the same, upon citatioun of pairtie, tak summar cognitioun of the estait of the landis, housis or tenementis within the burgh, be ain condigne inquest of the nichtbouris thairof,
>
> and gif the samyn be found auld, decayed and ruinous in ruif, sklattis, durris, windois, fluringis, loftis, tymer wark and wallis, or ony of them, and ane land biggit built of auld and throw lang tyme decayed in sic sort that it be alreddie inhabitable [sc. uninhabitable] or that within schort time may become inhabitable . . .,
>
> in that cace to decern that the conjunct feuar or lyferenter sall repair the saidis landis in the partis thairof decayed, as salbe found be the said inquest, within the space of yeir and day nixt efter thai be requirit thairto be the heritouris, and falzeing thairof declairis that it salbe free to the saidies heritouris to enter to the possession of the same . . .

TOWNSCAPE; THE SCOTS STYLE

Within its tight medieval pattern and the even tighter form in which it developed, the late-sixteenth-century burgh now begins to devise a townscape style that will persist for the next hundred years, and in many essentials for the next two hundred. Thrift, in space, labour and materials, is essential to it. But so (for those who can afford them) are identification and status, which

51

reach their final expression in the prestigious and frequently macabre townscape of the kirk-yard:

> Life is a city full of streets,
> Death is the mercat where al men meets,

and when there it is well to be recognized.

Houses hug their allotted length of street front, to which the richer houses present their long sides, the less privileged (with narrower plots) their chimneyed gable ends. The contrasting motifs of level eaves and pitched gable become the standard profile of the Scottish street, indefinitely repeated and varied. Gables are crowstepped; the eaves may depart from the straight line and sprout into gabled dormers of one and sometimes two storeys, or even pretend to be gables themselves so as to provide more chimneys at the wall head. Slates cover the better houses, and the majority, as Slezer shows (p. 17), are thatched until pantiles become more easily available in the early eighteenth century. Thatch is still seen at Glamis [pl. 10c] and Auchtermuchty.

On street level the angular jostle of houses is mitigated by bold curves and chamfers to minimize damage by animals and carts or avoid too tight a squeeze between the packed buildings of a close; above it, rounded corners return to the square as quickly as possible, or the squared angle bulges into a round turret. Many a turnpike stair has a little room at its head [pl. 8a], and so that you can get into that, another stair turret with snuffer top is pushed out (as are the walls themselves) into the shrinking air space overhead.

This is a style so intimately connected with function that it can hardly be called a style at all. If you took it away, you would take away the useful parts of the building. It has the abstract quality of all useful things, and this is almost everywhere enhanced by the use of harl, a rough rendering thrown on to rubble walls. Functionally this is a continuous weatherproofing coat over walls that are mostly built of rough or field stones and soft lime mortar, the available freestone being saved up for the margins and openings, or more exceptionally for sculptured trimmings like skewputts, or initialled and dated lintels.

Abstractly, harling is an enveloping, neutral blanket which has the effect of making a building into sculpture [pls 8a, b and c].

STONE

Field stones were available almost everywhere for the cheaper sort of walling but from the beginning of the seventeenth century they are increasingly supplemented by random or roughly squared stones from the quarry. There are a few places in Scotland where geology helps the quarryman by providing stones that are easily split and thus practically ready to use. In Orkney and Caithness you can pick up tough, heavy slabs and stand them on edge to make a fence, or pile the narrow ones neatly into a good dry wall. Some of the sandstones are fairly easy to split and thus make a naturally coursed wall such as you often see in Angus [pl. 10c] the greenish ones weathering badly but the pink being tough enough to use for slates. On unharled rubble walls the most spectacular colouring can be seen in the variegated sandstones of East Lothian which are heavily stained with iron, the most austere in the grey granites of Aberdeenshire. Whin, an immensely hard basaltic rock which requires great skill to split, is not much used for walling until the eighteenth century.

Both for rubble walls and dressed stonework and in all the numerous varieties of each, yellow-grey sandstone is sufficiently common to make other local types and colours conspicuous. Of these sandstones some of the whitest are found near Edinburgh and in Stirlingshire. A warmer yellow is much more common, sometimes shading into pink so that both colours occur in the same town, as at Lanark or Dornoch; in Girvan yellow and red come together. Deep red sandstone is the characteristic material of Annan and Dumfries, and of a whole region extending further into the south-west until it mingles with the granites of Kirkcudbrightshire. Similar strong reds can also be seen in the east at Dunbar in East Lothian, Edzell in Angus and Turriff in Banffshire, but the brightest of red stone towns is Mauchline in Ayrshire. One of the pinkest is Kirriemuir in Angus; this county, with Perthshire and Kincardinshire, provides a great variety of pink stone grading into purple, buff and green; they can all be seen together in Arbroath. Only in the late nineteenth century was the discipline of local materials broken, most noticeably by the import of Locharbriggs and other red sandstones from Dumfries-shire to nearly every part of Scotland.

One of the most characteristic stonework details is the crow-stepped gable. This could perhaps be explained as being the easiest way to finish off a wall as it rises, course by course, above a pitched roof. But most gables at this time are built in rubble, and it seems more likely that crowsteps were made partly for functional reasons; they could be climbed in order to repair roofs or sweep chimneys. If both gables of a house were stepped it was possible to lay a narrow plank from one to the other, bringing any part of the roof within reach for thatching, slating or tiling. Continuous skew stones forming a plan triangular gable did not have this advantage, and were harder to make than the small blocks which form crowsteps. On both types of gable the lowest stone or skewputt was often treated decoratively, the straight skew turned up into a scroll, or the last crowstep projecting from the wall as a concave bracket that might have a human mask carved on it. Rarer types of skewputt include sundials (as at Ormiston) or date stones, one of which may be seen on the gable of the house by the cross in Culross, bearing the very early date of 1577 [pl. 8c]. The church at Alness in Easter Ross, though not strictly a town building, has a gable which is a further refinement of the dated skewputt – in fact there are three of them, the latest (1775) being in the usual place at eaves level and the two earlier ones (1737, 1625) forming steps in the skew, at the head of which is the little early-seventeenth-century bell-house of dressed stone, preserved by piety and thrift through two rebuildings.

WOOD

It would be difficult to discuss the stonework of this period any further without mentioning the wooden construction from which many of its features developed. Stone houses were so rare in the sixteenth-century burgh that in some places they are given as special points of reference in title deeds. The *ludgings* of the church establishment or landed gentry were often stone built, but not always, for it happens that the only known house with a full timber structure is the Earl of Kinnoull's *ludging* (*c.* 1600) in Watergate, Perth. Or rather it was, for it was demolished in 1965. The possibility of finding another example concealed behind the cement and plate glass of a more recent frontage is still very real, especially in the unusually little-disturbed centre of Perth.

There was however an intermediate type, the stone building with a timber frontage. Burgess houses fronting a public space continued to follow what seems to have been the medieval pattern, with storage and shop on street level, and an outside stair leading to the house above. The shop or booth stood forward from the house frontage, its roof supported by posts. In burghs where space was short these single-storey extensions were developed upwards so that each house or tenement might be fronted by a range of galleries, either left open to the air or boarded up to provide more habitable space. The result is noted by John Ray in his *Itineraries*; the same entry, which is for 16 August 1661, also mentions the half shuttered windows that were usual at the time.

> They [the Scots] have a custom to make up the fronts of their houses, even in their principal towns, with fir boards nailed one over another, in which are often made many round holes or windows to put out their heads. In the best Scottish houses, even the King's house, the windows are not glazed throughout, but in the upper part only; the lower have two wooden shuts or folds to open at pleasure and admit the fresh air.

MacGibbon and Ross were able to give a very detailed account of two of these timber fronted buildings in Edinburgh's Lawn-market, for they had witnessed their demolition [pl. 11c]. The more famous of them, whose image survived well into the present century as the trademark of Nelson the publisher, was the tenement at the head of the West (now Upper) Bow. The timber and plaster-faced upper rooms projected seven feet from the wall behind, each successive storey being bracketed a little further out. Its destruction in 1878 was followed five years later by that of Mary of Guise's House, built in 1580. This had a wood-framed front which did not rest on posts but was cantilevered out from the masonry wall behind.

In 1674 the construction of such a building became illegal in Edinburgh, an Act of Council declaring that

> when a house or tenement is or shall be ruinous or burnt, or when a new one is built, the same shall be built in such a way as shall be most fit and suitable to the honour of the Kingdom, and for the ornament and security of the City, and of the inhabitants thereof, and all others concerned.

> That is to say, that the front and fore-parts, and all other parts of the same, shall be built altogether with stone and lime, and no part thereof, nor any forestairs of the same, shall be built with timber.

Nevertheless Edinburgh still has two houses which, though not fully timber fronted, are both good examples of a transition from wood to stone and may equally owe their survival to apocryphal owners. 'John Knox's House' as we see it from the outside [pl. 10a] is largely from the time of Knox's contemporary, the goldsmith James Mossman, from 1556 to 1573. The stonework, extraordinarily advanced in design for its time in Scotland, bears his own and his wife's initials, a sundial, and pious allusions to the commandments. 'Huntly House', in what was the separate burgh of Canongate, has its timber framed gables in a continuous rank of three and bears the date 1570, when it was built by the landed family of Acheson. Long known as the 'speaking house', its Latin inscriptions are a little defensive in tone; *Today it is my turn, tomorrow yours, so why are you anxious?* and perhaps in case tomorrow did not bring the promised good fortune *There is another hope of life*.

Despite frequent fires and the regulations designed to avert them, there was perhaps a special reason for the late survival of timber buildings in the capital in that Edinburgh's Georgian extensions had taken away much of the pressure for change and redevelopment from the old town. But anywhere in Scotland, whenever old frontages are stripped of their rendering there is a chance that the sawn off stumps of cantilever beams may come to light, as they did in 1962 during the restoration of the Gyles tenement near the harbour at Pittenweem.

Both the post-supported and the cantilevered types of wooden front were developed in stone. Another building in the Lawnmarket, Gladstone's Land, has a stone front (possibly in place of timber galleries) built forward from an earlier masonry wall. Its two arches on street level show the evolution of a timber colonnade into a stone arcade. A fragment of a similar arcade can be seen on the south side of the High Street near Hyndford's Close. Elgin was famous for its arcades or 'piazzas' (a name also applied to wooden stalls or booths), and they survive in restored form at Nos. 7 and 50 in the High Street, both originally built in 1694 [pl. 10b]. Until the middle of the nineteenth century the finest series of arcades used to be in Glasgow's Drygate, where they formed a sort of cloister below the frontage of the Duke of Montrose's *ludging* and the prebendaries' manses, presumably for social rather than mercantile use; the same applies to the arcade (formerly open) of the Glencairn *ludging* (1623) in Dumbarton High Street. An idea of the prestige of the stone-arched front was given by the astonishing early-seventeenth-century block in Dundee's Greenmarket which is now no more. On its peninsular site this set out to be a sort of Holyrood, complete with corner turrets. Miniature arcades were corbelled out right round its bulging perimeter, but this uncommon expense at low level may have curtailed the appropriate display higher up; a double pitched roof, truncating the turrets, came surprisingly down over the whole affair.

The stone equivalent of a cantilevered timber front is seen on the lower storeys of 'Huntly House' and a little later at Sailors' Walk, facing Kirkcaldy harbour. In both cases stone corbels take the place of wooden brackets. Even the gallery treatment similar to that of Mary of Guise's house went on being interpreted in stone. The house built about 1705 in the West Bow, Edinburgh, by Thomas Crocket of Johnstounburn [pl. 31b], repeats precisely the old pattern of timber rails and uprights –

but in dressed stone with harled rubble panels between. This lovely frontage also shows the fullest development of one of Scotland's most characteristic townscape features, the wall-head gable. Its late-seventeenth-century neighbour up the hill, whose lower floors are architecturally organized by making the sills on each level into a continuous string course, is crowned with the traditional crowstep gable; this is unusual in having a *doocot* [dovecot] with two flight holes at the head, Northfield House at Prestonpans being its country counterpart. But the main point is that it is not a true gable at all, but a sort of over-grown dormer, with a narrow strip of the main roof running down on each side. Crocket's Land goes further, its gable covering the full width of the house and thus concealing the fact that it is not one of the gables of the main roof. In this it differs from the continental practice which obviously influenced its graceful curly outline. The real 'Dutch gable' of a seventeenth- or eighteenth-century frontage in the Netherlands belongs to a roof whose ridge and eaves run back from the street, and it seldom has a chimney as its crowning feature. Often, if it belongs to a merchant's house, it has a door and winch serving the storage space in the garret. This arrangement is not found in the equivalent Scots house, but may not have been quite un-known for it was conjecturally restored, on circumstantial evidence, by Robert Hurd in one of the crowstepped gables of 'Lamb's House' in Leith (1959). As to the curved profile of the Crocket's Land gable, although it found its way into this chapter for other reasons, its type does not belong to the seven-teenth century any more than its date. This shape was widely adopted in early-eighteenth-century Scotland for reasons which will be suggested in due time (p. 72). Apart from the splendid curved gable of the Canongate Kirk, the only example which may have been earlier is illustrated by William Simpson in his *Glasgow in the Forties*, where he quotes the bookseller and antiquarian Robert Stuart as having dated this house on the corner of Clyde and Stockwell Streets at 1668. The most in-teresting feature of the curly end gable that faced the river was its combination of the truly Dutch crowning pediment with the usual Scots chimney.

Yet another difference between Scottish and continental practice was in the treatment of the ground floor. In the Dutch merchant's house it consisted of a lofty principal room with a mezzanine often sandwiched into its height along the front, and an internal stair. Its Scots counterpart continued the medieval tradition of a ground floor used for cellarage, with the principal rooms on the first floor reached by an outside stair. On the grander merchants' houses and town *ludgings* this stair was enclosed in a tower. The 'Tower' at 103 High Street, Elgin, bears the initials of Andrew Leslie of Glen Rothes and his wife and the date 1634, while the 'Study' in Culross [pl. 8a] and the Kellie *ludging* in Pittenweem High Street were possibly built a little earlier. These have stair towers projecting into the street, while that at Abertarff House in Inverness is built out into a close, the rest of which has disappeared (p. 241). In all these cases there is a little room on top of the tower and bulging out from it. Little angle turrets appear on corner houses like No. 1 High Shore, Banff [pl. 9c] and the Fordell *ludging* at Inverkeithing, both for show and for the advantageous views they afford. So in appearance and very largely in function these are quite literally country laird's houses come to town, and are part of the Scottish baronial tradition. Very few would look out of place if they were suddenly transplanted to an open site, as indeed happened to the 'Wallace Tower' in Aberdeen (1963). Another quite freely baronial house is 'Maclellan's Castle', or more properly *ludging*, in Kirkcudbright. Concessions to the town environment are rare, as when the flattened stair tower of 'Lamb's House' betrays the fact that it used to stand in the very narrow Willie Waters' Close.

In 1618 John Taylor the Water Poet set out on his *Pennilesse Pilgrimage* in search of wonders to make good copy, and duly reported on Edinburgh and the Canongate:

I observed the fairest and goodliest street that ever mine eyes beheld, for I did never see or hear of a street of that length . . . and from that Port the Nether Bow, the street which they call the Kenny-hate . . . the buildings on each side of the way being all of squared stone, five, six, and seven stories high, and many by-lanes and closes on each side of the way, wherein are gentlemen's houses, much fairer than the buildings in the high street.

He does not note the wooden galleries and gables, and it is doubtful whether, in the Canongate at least, the aristocratic exodus from the main street was as complete as he implies. It was more important to move the door off the public way than the house itself, which even if it fronted the street was often entered from a close, like 'Huntly House', or through a gate leading into a private courtyard. Taylor was to go on to Culross, and before his exciting visit to the underwater coal workings he saw the house of their owner Sir George Bruce, enlarged after his knighthood so that the triangular dormers of the west range are inscribed *GB 1597* and those of the north range (a separate building apparently designed as a sort of royal guest house) *SGB 1611*. The walled forecourt is entered by a gate from the Sandhaven. Tankerness House in Kirkwall is another assembly of buildings round a gated court, but there are plenty of examples of a more formal arrangement, all from the latter part of the sixteenth century; the Earl of Eglinton's 'Seagate Castle' in Irvine, with its round arched pend and weird revivalist ornament; then Mar's Wark, which presents to Castle Wynd in Stirling a great deal of reading matter and of grotesque sculpture inspired by that of the neighbouring royal castle, and finally on the opposite side of the street the slightly later Argyll *ludging* [*c.* 1630, pl. 11b], Scots in the position of a staircase tower in one angle of the courtyard, European in its ornament and internal organization. A high but isolated achievement in the street architecture of the Scottish renaissance is Moray House in the Canongate (*c.* 1628) whose polyglot renaissance decoration suggests that it may be the work of the architect of Winton Castle, William Wallace. At the time of its building, Wallace was starting work on George Heriot's Hospital, whose fantastic towers and highly wrought detail perpetuate the good name of the banker and royal goldsmith.

THE TOLBOOTH

Originally a tax-office as its name implies, the medieval tolbooth was also a council chamber, court house and prison. During the reign of James VI it began to be an embodiment of burghal prestige, very often by means of a tower. This was secure, it could be built on an ordinary burgess site, and it could be seen from afar, or heard by the sound of its bell which had probably been imported from Holland or Denmark.

By 1600 many burghs had their tolbooth towers like those of Crail and Pittenweem, both of which stand at the junction where you turn off the high street to go down to the harbour. There were also the more ambitious towers; the fiercely turreted Canongate tolbooth of 1591 (with a pend underneath and a close to the rear) and its masonry twin at Tain, both symbolizing civic power in the baronial manner. According to tradition the tower of Musselburgh tolbooth, with its curious belfry like a slated windmill, was already standing in 1590 when the burgesses added a more horizontally planned building adjacent to it. Using stone from the convent of St Mary of Loretto, they achieved a much more solid and splendid tolbooth than that of Edinburgh, and so did the Canongate whose tolbooth was started – complete with tower – about the same time; both have a veritable castle air.

The crowned spire of Glasgow's old tolbooth (1626, pl. 13b) out-tops all the rest, and the stone spire added to the existing tower (now belonging to the parish church) at Pittenweem is more typical. It is indistinguishable from those of many of the burgh kirks of the time, and this remained a popular pattern in both roles for another hundred years and more. Culross tolbooth was built in the early seventeenth century, the ceiling of its council chamber decoratively painted on the boards and joists in the fashion of the time. Its tower with ogee slated roof is much later, but took its cue from those of the corner towers of the Abbey House up the hill. The similar tower of Clackmannan tolbooth likewise follows that of Alloa kirk. Of wooden belfries one of the earliest is that which was added to the tolbooth

tower at Crail in 1602. It is hard to find a continental model for
it, but the spire and belfry of the old tolbooth of Aberdeen
(1627, now hemmed in by its Victorian successor) may have
been derived from those at Flushing. A closer parallel can be
found between the early-seventeenth-century tolbooth of
Dunbar (in the big, un-Scottish crowsteps of its end gable and
the skirted profile of its slated and leaded spire) and an old
building, now destroyed, in Middelburg. Unfortunately no such
continental source can be found for the apparently Dutch belfry
first seen at Holyrood chapel (1633, since demolished), and then
at the tolbooths of Linlithgow (now replaced), Stirling and
Dumfries [pl. 36a], as well as on numerous churches.

THE BURGH KIRK AFTER THE REFORMATION

The period from the Reformation to the end of the seventeenth
century was not a great one for church building, for the existing
churches could usually be made over for reformed worship by
internal rearrangement, and the larger by subdivision. Even the
new kirks could be conservative in layout like Edinburgh's
Greyfriars Church begun in 1612; and the spire of Glasgow's
Tron Kirk, still a salient feature of Trongate [pl. 13b], has an un-
mistakable likeness to that of the Cathedral.

Yet the first great post-Reformation burgh kirk, that of
Burntisland, (1592), is an astonishingly logical answer, if also an
elaborate and expensive one, to reformed church requirements;
a large square, with galleries and pews whose woodwork bears
witness to the way the town's prosperity had caused it to out-
grow the old building. It has no formal place in the plan of the
burgh, but must have presented a distinctive appearance seaward even before 1750 when it received a stocky central tower of
timeless Scots-classical aspect; this had probably been intended
from the first, for it is supported on the massive diagonal arches
that span the interior – as if the crown of St Giles had been taken
indoors. Church spires of seventeenth-century date, mounted in
more orthodox fashion on towers, are a feature of eastern Scotland; essentially they are of the traditional type with a short
octagonal spire rising from behind a parapet, but now more in

the Dutch fashion, the spire belted and windowed (as indeed were Glasgow's Cathedral spire and its small descendant of 1620 at the Tron), and the parapet transformed into a balustrade. Cupar in Fife was one of the first (1633), followed by a simpler version at Anstruther Easter (1644).

The most serviceable type of reformed church, and one which retained its popularity well into the nineteenth century, was planned in a T shape. Typically it had galleries or lofts in all three limbs (often betrayed on the outside by two-storey fenestration) and the pulpit stood against the long wall at the top of the T, flanked by tall, uninterrupted windows. Not surprisingly it made an early and widespread appearance in the ardent presbyterian country of the south-west, and one such kirk was built in 1653 in Ayr (on the site of the old Greyfriars Church) when Cromwell took over the pre-Reformation parish church of St John in order to build his citadel around it; the army duly made a contribution to the cost of the new work. The three lofts that face the (still original) pulpit belong respectively to the merchants directly in front, the trades to the left and the sailors to the right, the last with a model ship hanging above. The earlier T-plan church at Kirkintilloch (1644) has survived as a museum.

The location of a tower on such a church presented something of a problem, and from the beginning of the eighteenth century (as at Gifford, pl. 18a) this was most neatly solved by placing it against the cross-bar or long side of the T. However at the Tron Kirk in Edinburgh, a T-plan building which has unfortunately suffered the partial loss of two of its limbs and the complete amputation of the third, the tower intrudes into the church and originally incorporated the pulpit. Designed by the king's master mason John Mylne who was also master of works to the city, its architectural treatment is an unorthodox but perfectly assured mixture of classic and gothic. Christ's Kirk at the Tron, to give it its full title, was begun in 1637, the very year of the riot in St Giles against the ill-fated episcopacy imposed by Charles I, and his name appears on the tablet over the door at the base of the tower. Not many years afterwards, the parish church at Berwick-on-Tweed was rebuilt in a more solemn version of the same transitional style, a Commonwealth equivalent to this joyous late display of renaissance court architecture.

Other seventeenth-century churches give hints of what lies ahead. The Greek cross plan church at Lauder (1673, pl. 10f), probably designed by Sir William Bruce who worked for the Lauderdales at the nearby Thirlestane Castle, looks forward to the church of similar form by William Adam in the burgh of Hamilton (1732), though the latter did not follow the simple logic of its tower directly over the intersection. In the Canongate James Smith built the loveliest of all seventeenth-century churches in Scotland (1688). Its boldly curving gable which honours the street is innocently prophetic of those hundreds of churches that were to hide themselves behind more or less relevant architectural screens during the next century and a half. But for the formal placing of a church in the town scene, most conspicuously in the work of the improving landowner, we have to wait until the following century.

IV. THE EIGHTEENTH CENTURY

The eighteenth century began with a national disaster and ended with a stock-taking. The year 1700 saw the final collapse of the scheme for a Scottish colony at Darien, for which no English help had been forthcoming. Two years later Anne (daughter of James VII and II and the last of the Stewart monarchs) became Queen of the United Kingdom. Terms for a political union were negotiated over the following years with a special view to preserving the freedom of the kirk and the law of Scotland and her overseas trade. The matter of internal duties was more complicated and in the event more troublesome, but all this bargaining took place on the assumption, confirmed by both parliaments, that fuller union was desirable. So in 1707 Scotland sent forty-five commoners and sixteen representative peers (the latter number being still the same today) to the united parliament in Westminster.

At the close of the century the member for Petersfield had just finished his *Statistical Account* of Scotland, a perfect planning tool (as indeed he intended it) but shaped for a national situation which was soon to change the neat urban structure of county-towns and villages. He was Sir John Sinclair of Ulbster, whose vocation to national management was such that in the alternate periods when his own constituency of Caithness was not (by the system of that time) represented in parliament, he was obliged to look further afield for a seat; a search that took him not merely to Hampshire but for a time to Lostwithiel in Cornwall.

The Scottish townscape of the century's early years reflects the peculiar status of the country following the Act of Union. Native traditions continue and develop as if nothing had happened, merely adding a solid and thrifty classicism to the ordinary way of doing things. New ways are introduced either along the lines of political influence from England (sometimes indeed through military control) or increasingly by the spontaneous endeavour of certain Scots who see the creation of towns and villages as desirable for their own part of Scotland and thus for the whole. But here too, native tradition intervenes, usually hand in hand with economy. Street plans of great consequence are filled up with houses which in themselves are seldom remarkable, for architecture and layout have not yet found common cause. It was Robert Adam who perfected towards the end of the century the sort of lucid architectural argument that matches the rational plan (p. 83), and to him also belongs much of the credit for devising the picturesque all-purpose classicism that became the common language of Scottish and English townscape in the early 1800s.

SCOTTISH TOWNS AFTER THE UNION

Professor Youngson in his *Making of Classical Edinburgh* has given the lie to that simplified view of the Union which pictures it as a confidence trick and Scotland as its victim, rebellious and depressed in the first half of the eighteenth century and then, having lost all pride of identity at Culloden in 1746, a sort of stuffed dummy toeing the Georgian line in the second. The Jacobite dream was based on much more than romance, for it recalled a period in which Scotland had flourished under her own royal dynasty. But the Union, which promised a further increase in this material prosperity, found its own enthusiastic following. Towns and villages are the index of its spectacular success in the lowlands, its relative failure over most of the highlands.

The growth that had begun in the seventeenth century was certainly not stopped in its tracks. Frequent laws in favour of the linen industry, for example, had culminated in the Act of 1681 which forbade the import of linen, cotton and woollen fabrics and the export of thread. From the earliest years of the eighteenth century there was a spectacular rise in the linen trade to satisfy not only home demand but that of the foreign markets which had (officially at least) been closed to Scotland by Charles II's Navigation Laws. Paisley and Dunfermline became the two most celebrated linen towns (the former in course of time was to turn over to cotton) but the prosperity of dozens of smaller places was similarly based. In 1727 the Board of Trustees for Fisheries and Manufactures was convened in Edinburgh and spent almost half its annual grant of £6000 on the widespread promotion of the linen industry. Beith, which had begun to trade in woollen cloth in the year of the Union, started selling linen yarn as well in 1730. The ghost of a mid-century cottage-industrial town, once substantial but now ever less so, can still be seen there.

The agricultural market towns also benefited. Crieff, on the edge of the highlands, became the gathering place for cattle on the long drive south to England; the return, as in many another place, was in the shape of money and the new skills required for its application. Here George Drummond, a Lord Provost of Edinburgh whose namesake appears later in this story (p. 78), had feued a number of sites for the development of the expanding town before 1716, when it was burnt by a band of supporters of the would-be James VIII. Fifteen years afterwards it was recreated on a new plan by its superior James Drummond, after whom the Square is named. He also built a linen factory (presumably to service a cottage-based industry) but this was itself burnt at the '45 rising. For his complicity in this, Drummond's lands were sequestered and between 1752 and 1784 the town was under the control of the Commissioners of Forfeited Estates, who introduced the new industries of bleaching, tanning and papermaking and also gave their name to the new Commissioners' Street; a spacious thoroughfare but not a very useful one until, that is, the elongated hexagon of Burrell Square was laid out at one end of it in 1809. Except for the Commissioners' interregnum Crieff was a baronial burgh right up to the Reform Act of 1832; the handing back of forfeited lands to their former holders was proof that the Westminster government recognized the importance of the improving feudal owner; he was in fact the hero, playing his part with enlightened self-interest, of Georgian Scotland.

Of the newly prosperous market towns, Haddington (p. 237) is the most complete and lively survivor. The Nungate woollen factory ambitiously founded in 1681 (with the help of skilled labour from England) was not successful. But there is plenty of evidence of the wealth brought in by more efficient farming; not only in the good-quality tenements which are the surest indication that an eighteenth-century burgh was doing well, but in the palace-fronted merchants' houses built alongside them in the narrower streets – a distinctive Haddington type of which 'Carlyle House' [pl. 38c] is the oldest and most famous. In everything except its miniature scale it resembles the work of William Adam senior, master mason to the Board of Ordnance and, it might be said, architect by appointment to the Union and its supporters. He did design the town-house on its almost axial site nearby, though it was later overlaid by a westward extension and Gillespie Graham's tall new spire (1830).

TOWN GROWTH AND HOUSING

The first official census, carried out in 1801, shows that Scotland's population was 1,608,000, an increase of about fifty per cent since the beginning of the century. Edinburgh (from about 40,000) and Glasgow (more spectacularly from about 12,500) were both past the 80,000 mark. The textile centre of Paisley had recently risen to third place with 31,200, just ahead of Dundee and Aberdeen which had begun the century as much larger towns with something like 6000 each; Perth had started with the same total but was now left behind. In 1700 perhaps a score of the more important market and harbour towns had a population of two or three thousand, but that of the others could be numbered in hundreds. By the close of the century nearly every burgh created under the old system had risen well above subsistence level, and the twin inducements of prestige and leisure had begun to change the face of their streets.

This growth of urban population, though modest compared with that of the nineteenth century, involved the extensive expansion and redevelopment of those burghs which were taking advantage of new opportunities in marketing and industry.

The builders of new towns, about which there is much more to be said in chapter V, were to develop specialized forms of workers' housing, but certain patterns can be seen everywhere; for example families engaged in cottage industries lived in one- or two-storey houses, each with its ground-floor weaving room or workshop. On the edge of a town there was room for such houses to front the street, but the typical unit of central redevelopment was still the burgess plot; a house or often a tall tenement towards the street, penetrated by a pend giving access to the houses, or more tenements, behind.

In these buildings the discipline of the Georgian manner always takes precedence over its trappings. Materials remain the same – generally harled walls with stone dressings – but everything is done to achieve symmetry and regularity. Staircase turrets for example are banished to the back, and any sort of tower on a street front is a rarity; the late-eighteenth-century Morgan Tower tenement in Dundee's Nethergate is a charming exception, but it is hard to say whether it looks forwards in time with its generous Venetian-window bow, or backwards as its old-fashioned, ogee-slated roof would suggest. Far more typical of what was being built in all the more prosperous Scottish towns right through the eighteenth century is the plain tenement, sometimes built speculatively, sometimes by an investing agency like the Shoemakers' Incorporation who built (or at least reconstructed) in 1787 the fine example in Banff High Street (p. 222). This is three storeys high on each level and three apartments wide, the centre ones served by a traditional gabled chimney at the wall head, the central axis being further emphasized by the little round-headed window at the top and the pend at the bottom. Sometimes the latter is enriched with pilasters or a channelled masonry surround of the kind that can still be seen at one or two of the tenements in Dunbar High Street. On a smaller scale, the most celebrated example of this last and most austere generation of the Scots vernacular style is the 'Arched House' in the High Street of Ecclefechan; with a Venetian window as its one token of fashion and status, it has an arched pend and a now somewhat-altered close to the rear. This was the birthplace of Thomas Carlyle, whose mason father and uncle built it in the last decade of the eighteenth century.

Where special show was required, classical features were at first used as mere adornments to town houses that were basically in the old Scots style. In 1705 the Laird of Strathmartine was by no means ashamed of putting a stair tower in the middle of the frontage of his Dundee lodging, and loaded it with the pomp and circumstance of international classicism. A more disciplined alternative was the Dutch Palladian manner that was to culminate in Edinburgh's new Exchange (1754, pl. 13a). Its domestic use in Scottish towns goes back to Queensberry House in the Canongate which had an ogee roof when built as the Hatton lodging in 1680, but it lent itself especially well to public buildings. Gordon's College in Aberdeen has the same double-pavilion plan, plus a spired belfry and a central Venetian feature whose middle compartment accommodates a statue of the founder; William Adam's original design of 1731 had curly gables on each pavilion. The H plan of King James VI Hospital in Perth gives it a semi-courtyard on each side of its main block; it is dated 1750 but the crowning lantern which confirms its William-and-Mary look is a happy afterthought, given in 1764 by the Duke of Atholl from the demolition of the House of Nairne.

There was also the English Palladian town mansion, heralded by the Campbell of Shawfield house (p. 75) of which the finest provincial version is a house (*c*. 1760, pl. 12c) in Nith Place, Dumfries. This is finely situated athwart a downhill vista, bending the tail of the High Street towards the riverside. The elaborate palace-fronts of eighteenth-century Haddington (an unusual type north of the border) have already been mentioned. The more orthodox classically-trimmed town mansion found some of its finest interpretations in Aberdeen granite; notably at 53–7 Gallowgate which may have been built as early as 1721 with its splendid pilastered pend, and at many such houses as 61 Schoolhill which probably dates from fifty years later.

From these and other sources, including in time the graceful pattern-book neo-classicism that permeated Britain in the course of the eighteenth century, something very like a Scottish Georgian style emerged, Scottish because it shows so clearly what was considered important in the closely related fields of building and design. A tradition very much concerned with the edges of buildings, the corners and the openings where rubble walls have to be strengthened and defined with dressed stone, was able to accept architectural fashions which showed new, formalized ways of doing these jobs; channel-jointed or alternately long and short quoins, bracketed window-sills and deep, water-shedding cornices. The same preoccupation with edges and profiles prompted an interest in shaped gables and rounded openings. The picturesque irregularity of the former (not a quality the Scots mason had much interest in retaining) put them out of favour by mid-century. There was still however a long future for the wall-head chimney gable, and it was often used as a crowning feature on frontages of lesser rank or even formalized into a chimneyed pediment. This was indeed to be a feature of much low-rise late-Georgian housing in west central Scotland. Hundreds of houses in the weavers' terraces of Paisley have now been demolished, but there is still a good number in the High Street of Kirkintilloch [pl. 23f].

Another roof form was now available which enabled the builder, if he wanted, to dispense with gables altogether and achieve a level wall-head. It was a notable event when the builder of the 'Ark' house at the centre of the many-gabled burgh of Culross decided, probably about 1700, to give it a level, corniced wall-head and a piend (that is hipped) roof. As to the arched or circular openings that were the test of a mason's skill and his client's purse, these would be given pride of place at the very centre of a new frontage, round-headed windows often being amplified into Venetian form by the addition of a flat-topped one on each side. Front doorways, although it was some time before they increased in actual size and acquired generous fanlights, retained their traditional job as announcers of status. A good specimen at 16 Canongate in Jedburgh is dated 1729 on the keystone and has rusticated quoins. Another type (square blocks and moulded frame in alternate courses) is associated with the great Aberdeen-born architect James Gibbs, who used it at St Nicholas' Church (p. 43). All these architectural motifs, once adopted, were absorbed into the continuing native style,

71

with the result that similar buildings are often found to differ widely in date; one of the most impressive of many Gibbs-detailed houses for example, despite its small scale, is at 61 High Street, Huntly (p. 98); it is most unlikely that it was built before 1770. Outside Edinburgh, Kirkcudbright is one of the best places to see the maturity of the late-eighteenth-century town house [pl. 20c]. Inveresk is a curiosity; a grand suburb on the basis of an older village [pl. 12b].

THE 'DUTCH' SURVIVAL

In what might be described as the delayed renaissance that followed the Union, the formal classic manner had a popular rival. One of the principal themes of Scots practice was the gable, and this could easily be classicized; one way was to insert a Venetian window in it, and the use of a false window in the round-topped centre light (as commonly in Edinburgh, and in one of the blocks which face the harbour at Arbroath) would allow a central flue to the crowning chimney. Another possibility was to give the gable a curly 'Dutch' profile, a bland but very effective supplement to the traditional domestic style. The Forbes lodging at Boyndie House in Banff is dated 1740 (p. 223), and other curved gables appear about this time in Clackmannan, Eyemouth, Fraserburgh, Haddington, Irvine, Portsoy and St Monance. All these (unlike the end gables of Parleyhill House near Culross Abbey) are wall-head chimney gables in the Scots manner, some of them showing the eaves of the main roof on each side. Common in their time, not one of them is now expendable. The lovely example in Edinburgh's West Bow, already mentioned (p. 57, pl. 31b) narrowly escaped demolition as a dangerous structure in 1969. Another in the High Street of Dalkeith was knocked down a few weeks after I had photographed it [pl. 10d].

The continued use of the Netherlands style may have an additional explanation. The burghs, and especially the royal burghs, had lost many of the privileges that went with their original role as incubators of trade. But they still had their share of opportunity, and laid claim to it by means of civic buildings and even churches which were calculated to advertise their past and continuing commercial status. Dutch-inspired buildings had already been seen in seventeenth-century Scotland (p. 49), most notably at Glasgow's merchant hall steeple. But why did Allan Dreghorn, who finished St Andrew's Church in the Gibbs manner nearly a century later in 1765, giving it a steeple resembling that of St Magnus Martyr, impale a ball in similar fashion on its topmost spike – an outdated quotation from Dutch practice at a time when trade with the Netherlands was relatively unimportant? Both here and in other like cases the answer may be that the architecture of the Netherlands was the architecture of trade. Its use is like a burghal affirmation of commercial prestige.

Thus many civic buildings and even churches of the early eighteenth century look back, almost patriotically, to the age of Scotland's closest relationship with the Netherlands. Auchtermuchty, Strathmiglo and Coupar Angus (1767) were quite happy to adopt the Fife-Dutch steeple type for their tolbooths although – or perhaps because – it had now been established in the east of Scotland for more than a century. So were the 'Steeple Committee' of Kinross [pl. 12d], though the public meeting which convened them in 1742, with the minister as convener and the schoolmaster as clerk, had not actually had a tolbooth in mind. It had been minuted that

> considering it was in contemplation to build a new church, a steeple might with great propriety be added thereto.

In the event the church found another site, but the steeple was finished in 1751 complete with a clock presented by Sir John Bruce of Kinross, son of Sir William Bruce (p. 91), as superior of the burgh. A town-house was subsequently added to it. Twenty years later another public building at the town centre was proudly inscribed:

> This County House was repaired by the Crown.
> Robert Adam Knight of this Shire decorated this front at his own expense.

This is one of the first generation of county court houses erected

73

after 1748, when all feudal landowners like Sir John had surrendered their inherited judicial functions in exchange for financial compensation. In 1826 a new court house by Thomas Brown was built on the northern edge of the burgh.

The tolbooth steeple at Stirling was designed by Sir William Bruce himself in 1702, and its pavilion belfry is evidently a loyalist reminder of the original at Holyrood (p. 62); but not an isolated one, for Tobias Bachup repeated it on the tower of the charming tolbooth he built a year or two later in the middle of the High Street of Dumfries [pl. 36a]. There is nothing in the coincidence of names, for *fries* in Gaelic means wood – Dumfries the wooded hill; in Dutch it means an edge or indeed a frieze, so that Friesland is simply coast-land. But it is appropriate that this little building, dominant in position but domestic in scale, should be the meeting-place of the old and the new style in the public architecture of Scotland.

CIVIC CLASSICISM

The first full-fledged Palladian town hall was designed (possibly by William Adam) in 1731 for Sanquhar, a royal burgh whose progress was greatly assisted by the enterprise of its neighbouring landlord the third Duke of Queensberry in opening good roads to east and west and joining with the Board of Trustees (p. 67) to help the town's stocking industry. Sanquhar's dumpy classical town hall has a northern counterpart in Kintore three years later, imitating its five-bay frontage, twin forestair and belfry, but sacrificing further refinements to the hardness of granite. The same basic design, without the forestair, was used by George Jaffrey in 1788 for the town-house that closes the vista of Old Aberdeen's High Street, but it was one storey higher and two bays narrower. This tall classicism, crisply interpreted in granite which by now is rather more smoothly dressed, brings yet another Dutch nuance to eighteenth-century Scotland. But for the grandest example of this first Palladian type we must go back to the splendid town-house which William Adam designed for Dundee in 1734 (p. 198) based on an arcaded loggia that became affectionately known as the Pillars (there is still a pub of that name near the site) and crowned with a Gibbsian steeple. This agreeably stodgy brand of municipal classicism is still seen at Inverkeithing in 1770 [pl. 12a].

Two other Palladian types were represented in the town-houses of Edinburgh and Glasgow. The former [pl. 21a] was built in 1754 as the Exchange, and as such it had been first on the list of specific ideas put forward in the *Proposals* of 1752; a commercial centre in the capital to which other Scottish burghs were successfully invited to contribute. Based on a design by William Adam's eldest son John, it repeats the general form of the Cloth Hall at Leiden in Holland (1639) and applies it with the most sumptuous effect to the close-packed, high-rise townscape of mid-eighteenth-century Edinburgh. In this context the great forecourt is an ultimate expression of status; its scale is emphasized by giant pilasters and a pediment, while it is at once cut off from and united to the High Street by the arched loggia running across the front. It had rooms for the use of the Council from the start, but only became known as the City Chambers in 1811. Glasgow's town-house [pl. 13b], begun in 1737 and developed under Allan Dreghorn's direction, was of greater significance in the history of civic design because in the Trongate, where it stood next to the old tolbooth, it was more than just a magnificent interlude. It showed the way towards the idea of continuous grandeur above, utility below, which is our highest conception of the formal city street. Indeed by 1760 it had been enlarged from five to ten bays, its grand rhythm repeating in formal fashion the Trongate motif of tenement over 'piazza' which Daniel Defoe had noted in his *Journey* of 1827.

THE GROWTH OF GLASGOW

Andor Gomme and David Walker have detailed the architectural ancestry of this town-house, in which Inigo Jones' Covent Garden has pride of place. They have also shown that the Shawfield Mansion in Argyle Street (1712, demolished 1795) was the first executed design of Colen Campbell and a pioneer work of the Palladian movement in eighteenth-century Britain. As its owner Daniel Campbell of Shawfield represented Glasgow in parliament it was the target of public demonstration against Walpole's malt tax of 1725, a measure which also caused a brewers' strike in Edinburgh. But it none the less established a vogue for this type of detached town mansion as Glasgow spread westwards, gridiron fashion, from the old High Street. Miller Street was laid out in 1762 and one such house may still be seen there, built by John Craig in 1771 and now stranded amid the piecemeal commercial developments of the next two centuries. The little English Chapel of St Andrew by the Green is a free-standing version of the same type. The 'nineties saw the building of Charlotte Street away to the east, with six such mansions formally arranged down each side, one of them built by the mill-owner David Dale.

The Adam brothers may have designed not only Charlotte Street but the very different single block scheme of tenements and shops in Wilson Street in 1790. The first, apart from a few callously mauled fragments, survives in name only, its vista pathetically marked by the triumphal arch made up by Provost McLennan from the demolition of the Adam Assembly Rooms of 1792 [pl. 30b]. On the second, a rather less severe change of use and status have merely inflicted grievous harm. Essentially this building differs little from the plain frontages of Candleriggs which represent the bread-and-butter street architecture of eighteenth-century Glasgow. But upon it has been laid by way of punctuation, to emphasize the ends and maintain the interest in between, the effective but quite unostentatious classical system of which Robert Adam was the master. 'Warehouses laced up the seams' was Horace Walpole's scathing description of the Adelphi. Was this the view of the architectural purist who wanted a uniform building to be uniformly treated, or rather of the social purist or snob, who felt that a row of houses should not give itself airs above its station? Warehouses are indeed what this block has become. The elegant detail has been obscured, a mansard added to the top, and the open arcades on street level filled in with shop windows, but enough remains to plead its own case for restoration. An equally deserving subject would have been the twin blocks of University staff residences which James Adam designed in the High Street (1793, pl. 15b).

These were different again, a curious mixture of the old charm with a new monumentality that looked forward to the more pompous elements in the street architecture of the next century. The Old College that looked between them down College Street disappeared in the mid nineteenth century, the railway yard that displaced it became defunct in the twentieth. By 1973 the pigeons which occupied the south block were waiting for the north one to be vacated by a plastic bag factory, but they were to be disappointed; both buildings were declared unsafe, and the demolition men went in first.

EDINBURGH'S PLAN

The eighteenth century growth of the capital was very different. Glasgow's steady expansion westward from Virginia Street (1753) to Jamaica Street (1771) tells in these two names the story of the enterprising tobacco town that diversified into West Indian sugar and cotton in the decade when the war with the former American colony would otherwise have brought commercial disaster. In 1777, when John Gibson wrote in a letter that 'every stranger is charmed with the appearance of Glasgow', the plan of Edinburgh's First New Town was still largely on paper.

But it was a plan. Professor Youngson has lucidly assembled the contemporary evidence of its long genesis; Fletcher of Saltoun's observations on the backwardness of the city in 1698, the visionary pamphlet written five years later by the exiled Jacobite Earl of Mar who, as an architect, was able to specify real works of improvement, and finally in 1752 the *Proposals for carrying on certain Public Works in the City of Edinburgh*. In each of these the way ahead is seen with increasing clarity. It was the most hazardous and vulnerable type of plan because its purpose was not just to accommodate growth, but to anticipate and generate it. In this it differs not only from what was going on at the time in Glasgow, but from Edinburgh's own piecemeal expansion to the south, where Brown Square and Argyle Square inside the city boundary (both in the area of what is now Chambers Street), and George Square outside it from 1763, had already creamed off a great many of the well-to-do families on whose interest the new residential development would depend. Its siting to the north of the old city, in spite of the obvious geographical difficulties, was in fact the most practical feature of a project that was in all other respects a simple act of faith in the future importance of the capital, for two miles to northward lay the port of Leith.

The first obstacle in the way of a road to Leith was the valley of the North Loch. Acquisition of land for a bridge was made possible by the Act of 1723, but a contract for this was only signed in 1765. The following year saw both the competition for the layout of the New Town on the ridge to the north, and the death of George Drummond who was chief begetter of the *Proposals*. Six times Lord Provost of the city, and founder of the Royal Infirmary (1738, demolished 1879) whose gate piers still stand in Drummond Street, it was he who had galvanized a static situation and made possible that rarest thing in national and civic government (indeed he saw it as the concern of both) the plan which anticipates events. He was not to see its fulfilment, but his vision was clear enough. The words recorded by Thomas Somerville from a meeting with Drummond which probably took place in 1763, and quoted by Professor Youngson, must be quoted again;

> Look at these fields, said Provost Drummond; you, Mr Somerville, are a young man, and will probably live, though I will not, to see all these fields covered with houses, forming a splendid and magnificent city. To the accomplishment of this, nothing more is necessary than draining the North Loch, and providing a proper access from the old town. I have never lost sight of this object since the year 1725, when I was first elected Provost.

In 1767 the *Scots Magazine* reported as follows:

> The project of enlarging of the City of Edinburgh begins now to take effect. An Act of Parliament was passed May 20 for extending the royalty of the City; on the 3rd of June the magistrates complimented Mr James Craig, architect, with a gold medal and with the freedom of the City in a silver box.

and later in the year:

> On the 26th of October the foundation stone of the first house in the new town was laid, by Mr James Craig, architect, the gentleman to whom the premium was given for designing the best plan of the town; and the building of that in Thistle Court and other houses is now going on.

Craig's plan is that of an ideal city [pl. 14a], though laid out by consent and not by autocratic decision. Specifically it is an ideogram of the United Kingdom of England and Scotland, and the names leave one in no doubt of this; a square bearing the name of St Andrew, linked to another for which Craig intended that of St George (but to avoid the obvious confusion it was actually called after Queen Charlotte) by an avenue named after King George himself; the ancient princedom of Wales had a relatively junior place in St David Street, and the subsequent union with Ireland was to receive qualified recognition in the Second New Town's Dublin Street. The north and south facing terraces parallel to George Street are loyally called Princes Street and Queen Street, and the names of Thistle and Rose (the two flowers appear together in many a cornice and chimneypiece in Georgian Edinburgh) maintain the idea of the Union in the lesser streets 'for tradesmen and others' which run between them. The disposition of the central avenue between two squares is strikingly similar to that of Richelieu; even more so on the ground than in the plan published by Tassin. So is the hierarchy of parallel streets. The difference is that Richelieu (1633) is a walled town whose vista leads inescapably to the gates of the Cardinal's chateau (now utterly destroyed). The mid-eighteenth-century vista at Nancy leads up with much greater architectural ceremony to the Palais du Gouvernement. There is virtually no similar display of power in the planning of any Scottish town. Dunbar's broad High Street existed long before an eighteenth-century provost built his house at the north end. In 1790 the Earl of Lauderdale engaged Robert Adam to enlarge it so that it filled the entire seaward view. In 1859 it became (suitably enough) a barrack, but is now used as a social centre.

Craig's plan significantly looks outwards – southward to the old town and northward to the Forth. It also looks inwards, for both ends of its central vista are closed, not by a seat of authority but by a church; at least they would have been, had not the parvenu grocer Sir Laurence Dundas, who had made a fortune as Commissary General to the Army, managed to snap up from the absent-minded city the site intended for the eastward Church of St Andrew [pl. 14b]. Architecturally the house he employed Sir William Chambers to build there for him in 1772 is a great success, standing back quite modestly from a forecourt which is like an easterly extension of George Street. Symbolically it is rather a pity, the more so since 1794 when it acquired the handsome but none the less authoritarian coat of arms of HM Customs. In 1825 it changed its use again, and St George's to the west has become an extension of the Scottish Record Office, so that the house and church confronting each other down the vista are in fact a bank and a filing-cabinet. Neither could have had a better fate, and indeed these uses are suitable enough in the new circumstances which in the following century made this into the city's business quarter. Craig's plan has stood up well to the change, its geometry punctuated and reinforced by the statues at the intersections of George Street and its cross-streets; the first of these commemorates the visit in 1822 of George IV, the eldest of the Princes after whom one of the world's most famous streets was named.

With an absence of architectural formality which may have surprised – as it still surprises today – the visitor who has seen the contemporary work of the younger John Wood in Bath, Edinburgh's first new town started in earnest on the north side of St Andrew Square and grew slowly westward through the remainder of the century. Building plots were feued to private developers (some building speculatively, but most for themselves) by the city, who saw that the houses and the occasional tenements were built along the lines of the plan; the forty-eight foot regulation height from area to eaves was only insisted upon from 1781, but of earlier buildings only the tenements, with their archaic chimney-gables at the wall head (minimally politer versions of the cliff-like frontages of Nicholson Street) actually

I. THE TOWN SCENE

1 Linlithgow: **(a)** the 17th century Prospect from the north in *Theatrum Scotiae*; **(b)** the same from the motorway, with the Palace (pp.37-8), Burgh Kirk (pp.42-3) and modern housing (p.181).

a

b

c

d

e

2 **(a)** Edinburgh from the south-east across Queen's Park. To left of Holyrood Palace and Abbey Church are the spires of the old town; to right Regent Terrace (p.116) along the slope of Calton Hill. **(b)** North Berwick from the harbour, with the town-marking Berwick Law (p.17). **(c)** Killearn: the entry, with Kirk and toll-house. **(d)** Doune: the town centre and Mercat Cross; **(e)** the town end.

a

b

3 (a) Stirling: the entry from the east; the main road sunk between Melville Place and Melville Terrace, forming a triple carriageway (p.19). **(b)** Leith: the Robert Burns statue surrounded by the 19th century tenements and commercial buildings of Bernard Street (p.110).

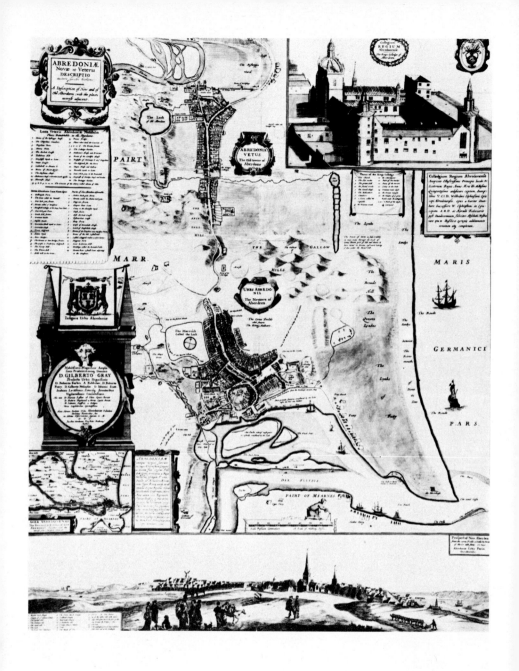

II. THE MEDIEVAL BURGH

4 Aberdeen: James Gordon's Map of 1661, with New Aberdeen on the Dee to the south, and a Prospect of it at the foot; Old Aberdeen (p.33) on the Don to the north with a vignette of King's College and its crown-spired Chapel.

5 (a) Dumfries: the 15th century bridge crossing the Nith onto White Sands, and the spire of Greyfriars Church on the mediaeval friary site (p.228). (b) Dornoch: the Cathedral and the Bishop's Castle (p.38).

a

b

c

6 (a) Dunblane: the approach to the Cathedral from the Cross (p.39). (b) Perth: the Burgh Kirk of St John (p.43). (c) Elgin: the High Street, with the Georgian Burgh Kirk of St Giles on the site of its mediaeval predecessor (p.44).

a

b

7 St Andrews: (a) the West or Southgait Port (p.37) at the entry to South Street (b) which is now lined with Georgian buildings: the ruined Cathedral in the distance (p.40).

III. JAMES VI AND THE 17TH CENTURY

8 Culross (p.199): **(a)** the Black Causeway climbs up-hill past new housing to the 'Study' and Mercat Cross **(b)**; **(c)** the same looking back past the house gable dated 1577 (p.54) and down to the Town-house.

a

b

c

9 (a) Crail: the harbour, dominated by the customs house to left. (b) Haddington: Mitchell's Close (p.238) and (c) Banff: the High Shore (p.59).

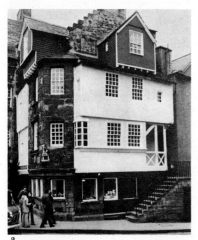

10 *Traditional house types.* **(a)** Edinburgh: 'John Knox's House' (p.56); **(b)** Elgin: No. 7 High Street (p.57), with the Museum to right. *Continuing vernacular.* **(c)** Glamis: 18th century thatched cottages. **(d)** Dalkeith: chimney gabled tenement (p.72) by the Burgh Kirk (p.41). **(e)** Cupar: Preston Lodge in Bonnygate (p.225). **(f)** Lauder: the Burgh Kirk to left (p.64) and the island-sited Tolbooth.

a

b

c

11 *The long Renaissance.* (a) Falkland: James V's Palace gatehouse of 1537 (p.45) with 19th century cross and fountain. (b) Stirling: the Argyll Lodging, 1674 (p.60). (c) Edinburgh: the Lawnmarket in the late 19th century; from left, Mary of Guise's House (p.56), Mylne's Court (1689) and Bowhead (p.55).

IV. THE 18TH CENTURY

12 **(a)** Inverkeithing: Tolbooth tower (p.75) and Mercat Cross. **(b)** Inveresk: the village nucleus, with the Manor House to left (p.72). **(c)** Kirkcudbright: 18th century houses, looking towards the Tolbooth (p.72). **(d)** Kinross: Steeple to left, old County Buildings to right (p.73). **(e)** Dumfries: looking down Nith Place to No. 24 (p.70).

a

b

13 (a) Edinburgh: the Royal Exchange, now City Chambers (p.75) from *Modern Athens* (p.118). (b) Glasgow: Trongate, painted by John Knox in 1826. From left, the Tron Kirk Steeple (p.62), the Town-house (p.75), William III statue (p.23) and the Tolbooth steeple of 1626.

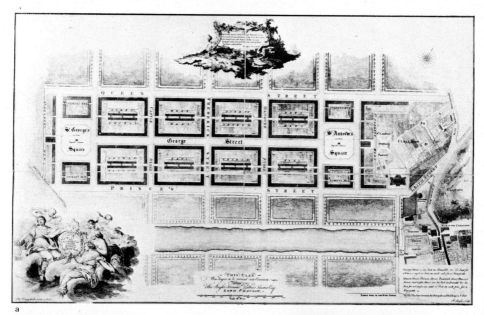

a

b

14 Edinburgh: **(a)** James Craig's plan for the first New Town (p.79). **(b)** George Street (p.79). St Andrew's Church to left, the Assembly Rooms portico of 1818 to right; the George IV statue, Melville Column and Dundas Mansion (p.80) on the main axis. In the background the St James's Centre (p.182).

a

b

c

15 *Adam in Edinburgh*, **(a)** the north side of Charlotte Square (p.82). *Adam in Glasgow*, **(b)** in the High Street (p.76). **(c)** Edinburgh: bowed fronts in north Castle Street (p.81), with the Chalmers statue to left.

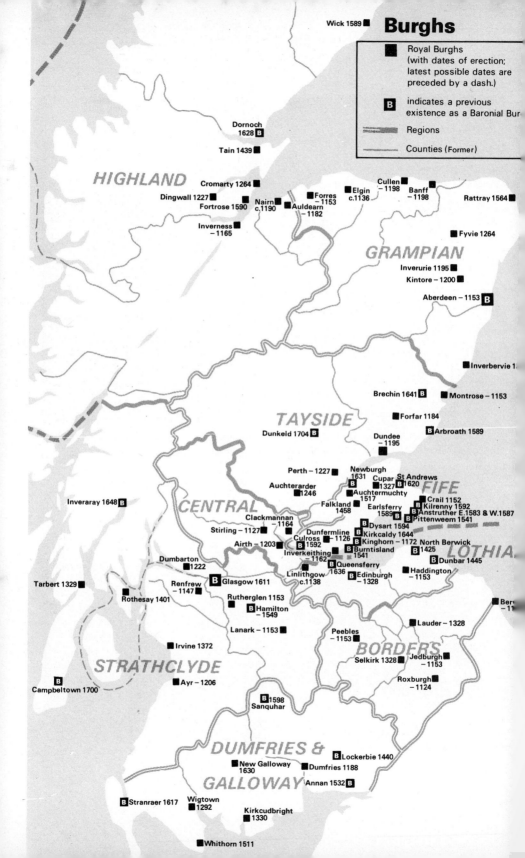

Burghs

■ Royal Burghs (with dates of erection; latest possible dates are preceded by a dash.)

B indicates a previous existence as a Baronial Burgh

▨ Regions

— Counties (Former)

Wick 1589 ■

HIGHLAND

Dornoch 1628 B
Tain 1439 ■
Cromarty 1264 ■
Dingwall 1227 ■
Fortrose 1590 ■
Nairn c.1190 ■
Auldearn – 1182 ■
Forres – 1153 ■
Elgin c.1136 ■
Cullen – 1198 ■
Banff – 1198 ■
Rattray 1564 ■
Inverness – 1165 ■

GRAMPIAN

Fyvie 1264 ■
Inverurie 1195 ■
Kintore – 1200 ■
Aberdeen – 1153 B
Inverbervie 1
Brechin 1641 B
Montrose – 1153 ■
Forfar 1184 ■
Arbroath 1589
Dunkeld 1704 B
Dundee – 1195

TAYSIDE

Perth – 1227 ■
Newburgh 1631 ■
Cupar 1327 B
St Andrews 1620 ■
Auchterarder 1246 ■
Auchtermuchty 1517
Falkland 1458
Earlsferry 1589
Crail 1152
Kilrenny 1592
Anstruther E.1583 & W.1587
Pittenweem 1541

CENTRAL

Clackmannan – 1164
Stirling – 1127 ■
Dunfermline – 1126
Culross 1592 B
Airth = 1203 ■
Inverkeithing – 1162
Dysart 1594
Kirkcaldy 1644
Kinghorn – 1172
Burntisland 1541
North Berwick 1425

FIFE

LOTHIAN

Inveraray 1648 B
Dumbarton 1222 ■
Tarbert 1329 ■
Rothesay 1401 ■
Renfrew – 1147 ■
Glasgow 1611 B
Rutherglen 1153 ■
Hamilton – 1549 B
Queensferry 1636
Linlithgow c.1138
Edinburgh – 1328
Haddington – 1153
Dunbar 1445
Lauder – 1328
Ber– – 1

Lanark – 1153 ■
Peebles – 1153
Selkirk 1328
Jedburgh – 1153
Roxburgh – 1124

BORDERS

STRATHCLYDE

Irvine 1372 ■
Campbeltown 1700 B
Ayr – 1206 ■
Sanquhar 1598

DUMFRIES & GALLOWAY

New Galloway 1630 ■
Lockerbie 1440 B
Dumfries 1188
Annan 1532 B
Stranraer 1617 B
Wigtown 1292 ■
Kirkcudbright 1330 ■
Whithorn 1511 ■

seem to transgress this rule, which obviously became difficult to enforce on a sloping site. In masonry, rubble walls with ashlar dressings give way to the droved (horizontally tooled) ashlar which was to become standard in Georgian Edinburgh. At first only the very grandest houses were faced with ashlar that was 'polished' perfectly smooth, and most of these were in Queen Street where an aristocratic owner might feel (but temporarily as it turned out) monarch of all the northward view he surveyed. Of these No. 8 is the finest; designed by Robert Adam in 1770 for Baron Ord, it spurns a basement area, and its seven-bay frontage has a columnar doorpiece in the centre of a rusticated ground storey – another sign of status. It is a work of extraordinary reticence and refinement which outclasses all its rivals with the least possible architectural show. Other and later developers exploited the possibilities of paired bow windows, as in the north part of Hanover Street or more elaborately in Castle Street, where Sir Walter Scott lived at No. 39 (1793, pl. 15c); and of the long and graceful pilastered frontage, like that of the Tontine building at 122–4 George Street. But none could equal the *gravitas* of Adam's work for Baron Ord.

As for the rest, the standard house was of three bays with its door to one side, occasionally distinguished by individual features like the columned porches of Princes Street. Was this a rather ordinary street, with almost a mile of middling Georgian houses all the same height? If you only looked at the houses it undoubtedly was. Was it dull? Emphatically not. To householders like Robert Craig of Riccarton it offered the wonderful advantage of light and air; the same air that the promenading ladies tacking up-wind thought it worth while to defy with the skirts, hats and parasols they had bought in the luxury shops which were the first to move into the adapted ground floors of the main streets. Above all, Georgian Princes Street deferred to the prodigious scale and craggy outline of the Castle.

Diversity within unity is thus the keynote of Edinburgh's First New Town. As regards unity, it is especially interesting that one particular feature persisted from end to end; the returned corners of every end house of every block had a perfectly plain chimneyed gable. Inconsiderable in themselves, these gables marked time up and down Craig's gridiron plan. The last complete set of them, in North Castle Street, was broken in 1969 after the Secretary of the Royal Fine Art Commission for Scotland had been obliged to choose between a holiday and nervous prostration. It is better to destroy a house than a man, but there must have been something wrong with the system in which they could not both survive. As to diversity, the same plan that was originally built up with a modest variety of plain Georgian houses was to prove just as effective when half of them were replaced by the architecture of Victorian commerce [pl. 14b].

Edinburgh itself, as feudal superior, decided to introduce architectural uniformity for the last stage and in 1791, the year before he died, Robert Adam was appointed their architect for the proposed church and for the external elevations of the houses in Charlotte Square. It was not quite the first time the Edinburgh developer had conformed to an overall design, for this had been the case at St James's Square, laid out in 1773 on ground immediately to the east of the first new town and still outside the city boundary so that it was for the time being (like George Square) neither rated nor serviced by the town council. This Square, whose three- and four-storey frontages suggested at first that all the accommodation was in flats, in fact consisted partly of houses, their front doors distinguished by delicate classical doorpieces. At intervals a slightly projecting section of wall indicated a common staircase and excused the functional placing of its windows, out of line with the rest in order to light the landings within. The doors to these staircases were set in much plainer arched openings, and led up to the flats which occupied the higher levels.

James Craig made the plan that accompanied the prospectus issued by the superior of St James's Square (Mr Walter Ferguson, a lawyer). Assuming that he designed the frontages as well, he achieved a union of Edinburgh's old and new life styles – tenement and main-door house – in a way that was just as effective and influential as the plan he had made for the first new town. When the latter became a business quarter, it was this Square's unhappy fate to become its backyard workshop

82

and printing office. The problems of preserving the square would have been great, but far smaller than those caused by its unworthy successor. Something like its plain, unfanciful authority can still be seen at Gayfield Place in Leith Walk, built by James Begg twenty years later.

By contrast the effect of Adam's Charlotte Square (1791, pl. 15a) relies on a type of variety which is in a sense entirely superficial. The north side, for example, is basically just a long row of houses; it would not make the slightest difference to their interiors if the modelling of the stonework were the same all the way along – or for that matter if the windows were uniform, for the slim additional sashes at ends and centre are blind and it is doubtful if these tripartite windows could ever have been expressed inside the houses even if Adam himself (had he lived) had been given the job of designing any of them. Externally he has treated them with a ceremony far more elaborate than that which John Wood senior applied to Queen's Square in Bath, a pioneer work of its type. In Charlotte Square the heavy masonry of the basement graduates into ashlar which is rusticated on the ground floor, perfectly smooth above. Ends and centre are accented with slight projections; the end pavilions with their flat pilasters are given a stylized touch of life by their crowning sphinxes gazing inwards to the columned centrepiece whose pediment is the climax, and which has a pair of supporting columns on each side. All this incident contrasts with the calm horizontals of the intermediate house fronts. Only slightly garbled when it was carried out in the second decade of the nineteenth century, the remainder of the Square sustains this level of invention, the main difference in the shorter blocks to east and west being the omission of the centrepiece; for the emphasis here is on the entry from George Street and the final climax in the dome of St George's Church. As designed by Robert Reid in 1814 this building serves the Square less well, but the George Street vista probably better, than Adam's version would have done; the latter maintained the scale of the houses, and had a smaller dome for which, characteristically, two little flanking domes were the visual preparation.

The two other great works which Robert Adam contributed to

Edinburgh are in two different moods again. First there is the Register House (1774) which gives you, as you cross the north bridge from the old town, precisely the sort of welcome to the new one which you might expect from a senior civil servant dressed with maximum elegance and minimum show – indeed from Adam himself as Surveyor of the King's Works in Scotland. Then the front of the Old Quadrangle of Edinburgh University (1789) sees him transformed from this polite mood into the heroic role of his ambitions. Yet the great monolithic columns of this Roman frontage are still street architecture, a roll of drums not at the end of a vista but on one side of the sloping, elevated street known as South Bridge, for which the necessary act of parliament was passed in 1785. In similar imperial vein, Adam's grandiose scheme for other buildings lining the nineteen-arch bridge and spreading east and west along the valley would have classicized, had it been carried out, a large part of the romantic prospect of the old town seen from the north which we now take for granted. Although it might have been hard to live up to his majestic porticos on the bridge, or tolerate what would have been a row of dreary north-facing courtyards, it is also worth while to speculate on whether this huge development might not have come into its own as a business centre in the following century; the head offices of the banks and insurance firms might then have been sited on the south or old-town side of the valley, and even in the Royal Mile itself. In the event Craig's town became the business quarter and only the head office of the Bank of Scotland stayed, majestically enough, on the slopes of the old city [pl. 32a]. South Bridge was built up with perfectly good effect in a thin bread-and-butter Georgian manner, an asset which any less architecturally rich city would have taken more seriously. Adam's Old Quadrangle (he actually intended a double courtyard) was finished in 1834 in a fussy parody of his own late style, and in 1876 Sir Rowand Anderson placed the long-delayed dome over the entrance front, much larger than that which had been intended; it is topped with a gilded figure of fame.

Despite these reverses and the demolition of his late master-piece, the Bridewell on Calton Hill (1791), Adam left his mark more durably on Edinburgh than on Glasgow. He sensed the romance of Edinburgh, advising James Craig that his observatory on the Calton (1776) should have 'something of the castle air', and even the romantic classicism, for he has left a sketch that foretells the Regent Bridge. But most important of all, in Charlotte Square he supplied an architectural source which was to be quoted over and over again in the elevations of Edinburgh's subsequent new towns.

V. NEW TOWNS OF THE EIGHTEENTH AND NINETEENTH CENTURIES

There are three aspects of Georgian achievement in Scotland in which it would be wrong to separate the eighteenth century from the first part of the nineteenth century; agricultural and industrial improvement, the building of an inland transport system of roads and canals, and the birth of new towns and villages. All are primarily functional and are closely connected with each other. The *Statistical Account* (p. 65) is a progress report on them, but their story cannot in any sense be brought to an end until the 1830s, which saw the partial reform of local government, the beginning of the railway system as the product and the servant of centralized industry, and the accession of Queen Victoria. The *New Statistical Account,* published in the 'forties, conveniently marks the point after which the old partnership of rural industry, road transport and paternal management were no longer particularly significant as forces for change in the face of Scottish towns.

ROADS

Where transport is concerned, it is easy to forget the supreme importance of sea and river routes (and therefore of seaports) up to and indeed right through the eighteenth century, when they began to be logically supplemented by canals. The first sign of national concern for internal communication by road had been an Act of 1587 which appointed commissioners to oversee roads, bridges, ferries and other public services. In 1667 this function, and a share in the expense involved, was handed over to the Commissioners of Supply in each sheriffdom, whose original job had been the collection of land dues for the Crown. Drove roads at least partially opened up the central highlands, and the Turnpike Act of 1751 made possible the building of hundreds of toll roads, mainly in the lowlands. Further north General Wade began his military roads in 1724, converging on Inverness from Crieff and Dunkeld, and up the Great Glen from Inverlochy on the west coast. The Commissioners for Highland Roads and Bridges were appointed in 1803, and for them Thomas Telford rationalized Wade's network (designing for example the much needed bridge across the Tay at Dunkeld, one of the southern entries to the highland region) and extended it to the far north coast. More than a thousand bridges were needed over some 730 miles of road. By 1859 there were 5768 miles of turnpike road in Scotland, with toll points at an average of one every five miles; these were only abolished in 1883.

This inland road system was not only useful to existing towns. It made possible the foundation of new ones, at road junctions, at the crossing of one or more rivers (these might be harnessed to drive mills), or simply at staging posts like Dalmally or Spittal of Glenshee. Short-haul transport, modest in speed and capacity, served and even demanded frequent small towns in which, as far as the traveller was concerned, the inn was the most important building, often financed by the landowner. The Adam brothers designed an inn (as yet unidentified) for the government roads in the highlands, and the lodge which was formerly the inn at Dalnacardoch, Blair Atholl, was built on the site of General Wade's road-building headquarters, to a design by John Baxter.

The local function of the roads was to link farm and village, village and market town. William Cobbett, on his *Tour* in 1832, resented even this degree of centralization;

. . . a regular cavalcade of carts, each carrying about twelve English sacks of corn, and all going to Dunbar, which is a little sea-port (though a large town) apparently made for the express purpose of robbing Scotland of its produce, and of conveying it away to be squandered in scenes of dissipation, of gambling, and of every other vice tending to vitiate man and enfeeble a nation.

But even Cobbett could be impressed by town life, as we shall see (p. 125). The roads and bridges he used on his travels were essential to the formal enlargement of older towns as well as to the creation of the new ones which are the main subject of this chapter.

THE NEW TOWNS: THEIR PURPOSE AND CHARACTER

Some two hundred new towns were founded, sometimes supplanting or supplementing older communities, in the eighteenth century and the first forty years of the nineteenth. All were planned in an economic and some in a formal sense, and in both these respects they followed eighteenth-century principles. This is also true of their buildings; even after 1800 they tend to bear the solid stamp of eighteenth-century good sense, without much of the suavity that the late Georgian age brought to the established towns.

Why and how did these places come into being, and how did they differ from those which already existed? In his *Analysis of the Statistical Account* published in 1826 Sir John Sinclair gives the following description of an old-style village, which can be taken as applying (regardless of size) to baronial burghs in general:

Villages were originally established, for the personal objects of powerful families, able, notwithstanding the turbulence of the times, to protect their retainers, and disposed to encourage settlers, by fairs, markets, and other advantages, that they might have assistance near them, on any sudden emergency.

He later quotes a description of their actual appearance:

They generally originated in accident – were put down at

random – and the form was often absurd, irregular and inconvenient; nor was uniformity in the houses built, scarcely ever attended to. The whole was erected in confused groups, with a total want of taste. Dunghills, coalhills, or peatstacks were put up in front of their houses, and often gutters filled with putrid water, either in the front, or in the rear of the house.

The new villages were regular and disciplined. Sinclair, a great pigeon-holer, divided people into three classes; the productive or labouring class, the useful class who offered professional skills and services, and the unproductive or useless class. The old burghs had been made, with royal licence, by the useful class – that is by the merchants. The new villages and towns, though in some ways they represent a continuation of the old baronial burgh principle, were the direct creation of the landowner for the profitable accommodation of the productive class, who built the houses and worked at village industries, or in the surrounding farms. The main profit was of course to the landowner himself, from increased rents and feus.

Agricultural progress was the mainspring of the system. The farmer, now enjoying the benefit of an enclosed holding on a long lease, used better methods to produce more food, whose price was steadily climbing, for marketing in the town. Problems arose from the unemployment caused by more efficient farming, and that was where manufactures came in – or so it was hoped. The town labourers' houses (or at least the feuing plans for them) were there on the ground, but capital and management did not always materialize and this nice equation of town and country life did not then work out. A new personage, the industrial entrepreneur, became indispensable for larger industrial projects and in due course began (sometimes in partnership with a landlord) to make his own sort of new town.

Even when they prospered, the importance of the new centres was limited by the specialized function for which they were intended. They helped to fill up the back-log of town building in Scotland, but the majority are so uniform in purpose and design that they lack on the one hand the diversity of class, scale and use which we associate with towns, and on the other, the small-scale, cosy informality we connect with villages. Comparison with English villages is hard to avoid. Cobbett, passing through the village of Roxburgh Park (presumably the Roxburgh Newton named on the gravestone of the centenarian Andrew Gemmels in the churchyard) noted that the people were 'very hearty', but there was:

> no such thing as a little garden before the door; and none of those numerous ornaments and conveniences about labourers' dwelling, which are the pride of England.

Likewise the Revd Micah Balwhidder in John Galt's *Annals of the Parish* (1813):

> Her [Mrs Malcolm's] house was sold, and is the same now inhabited by the millwright, Mr Periffery, and a neat house it still is, for the possessor is an Englishman and the English have an uncommon taste for snod [pretty] houses and trim gardens.

The general rule by which houses were built right on the street undoubtedly originated from the desire to avoid the sort of unpleasant frontdoor dumps already mentioned, though the discipline of the baron-bailie was still required to deal with this problem when it arose. But this is a thing of the past. Today's visitor, if he bothers to stop in one of these villages, may find it enjoyable in quite a new way, especially if he compares its discipline with (for example) the monotonous diversity of a twentieth-century shopping centre. Visually there is much to be said for having all one's eggs of the same size and colour and all in the same basket. But functionally a town built on these lines, even after it is established, is extremely vulnerable to changes in work pattern or economic demand. As soon as the railways began to open up new options in work-places and market-places, the days of this sort of town seemed to be numbered. The return to a road-based transport system which allows purely residential towns and villages came in time to their rescue, giving the survivors at least a temporary reprieve.

For some of them the increased petrol prices of the 1970s may be the final death-warrant.

TRANSPLANTED TOWNS

The most successful of the new towns were undoubtedly those which continued the traditions and constitution of an established burgh, even if they did it on a new site. One of the first transplants was that of Kinross [pl. 12d], which Charles II gave to his courtier-turned-architect Sir William Bruce as a burgh of regality in 1685. Having founded his splendid house very near the site of the old village by the shore of Loch Leven, Sir William encouraged the building of the present town along the road to Perth, entered by a bridge (now replaced) over the Queich. In 1706 the historian Sir Robert Sibbald commented:

> Kinross has been much enlarged of late with several new buildings, and some tradesmen of several employments have been brought to it by Sir William Bruce.

Indeed two years later he had disposed of 47 plots at initially reduced feus, an incentive often to be given to settlers in these new towns. By 1724 there were 35 cutlers, 10 in the iron trade, 22 shoemakers and no less than 320 weavers. The knife trade flourished almost to the end of the century, but the *Statistical Account* reports:

> Cutlery, for which this place has been famous, has of late been much on the decline, owing to the general use of Sheffield wares.

The traditional, virtually medieval, ribbon layout of the burgh of Kinross is in contrast with the picturesque formality of the house and its grounds. At Inveraray [pl. 18c] this principle was applied not only to the new gothic castle that displaced the old royal burgh, but to the new town as well. Founded in 1743 by the third Duke of Argyll, Lord Justice General under the Union since 1710, it was laid out on a basically simple one-street plan by John Adam (Robert's elder brother) and Robert Mylne, athwart the peninsula that juts out into Loch Fyne just before it

91

branches into Loch Shira. From the north approach it appears water-borne, Mylne's arcaded screen wall (1786) offering a frontage of Venetian promise across the loch. First of the units thus linked together are a lodge and a modest house disposed round the curve of the shore, after which the parade of official welcome begins; Adam's Argyll Arms Hotel to greet the guests of the town, an avenue seen through the arches for those of the Duke (the castle is otherwise quite separate) and then Adam's town-house, followed by the entry to the main street. This is lined with three-storey tenements of the utmost plainness leading up to Mylne's church portico with its tall columns (1795). Their austerity is of another kind, the extreme refinement of the turn of the century when the town was still building; moreover they are of stone, as against the abstraction of harling all around. But disastrously, to anyone who can remember or imagine it, the central spire that once united the double church and its two vistas was taken down as a crazy precaution against damage in the second world war – and the pieces then lost. Between church and loch stands the urbane frontage of Gillespie Graham's court-house, built in 1816; the reverse side with its jail and seaward ramparts is grimmer, the only perceptible echo of Hanoverian fife and drum. Inveraray is without equal among small British towns in having achieved by deliberate planning just that balance of man and nature, function and ceremony, which is the essence of townscape.

In 1775 the burgh of Fochabers was similarly displaced by Gordon Castle and resited on the main Elgin road which trans-fixes the central square of its grid plan. Well planted with syca-mores, the square is overlooked on its cross axis by the portico and spire of the Bellie Kirk and its flanking house fronts, all of dressed stone, the work of the duke's architect John Baxter. The focus and hierarchy thus established give point to the disciplined rows of harled houses with which private builders completed the layout over the next thirty years. They are just what we miss in New Scone, just north of Perth. Resited at the beginning of the nineteenth century, it left its symbolic centre behind and never found a substitute; the mercat cross of what had been the ancient capital of Scotland is now an ornament in the palace park. Many a burgh has lost its cross, but here, as at Preston in East Lothian, a cross has lost its burgh.

REVIVED TOWNS

Many burghs were given a new lease of life on their old sites as Georgian new towns. An early example was Thornhill in Dumfries-shire, where in 1714 sites were feued on a cross-roads plan with a heraldic town cross at the intersection. Dorothy Wordsworth was unfavourably impressed when in 1803 she

> passed through the village of Thornhill, built by the Duke of Queensberry, the 'brother houses' so small that they might have been built to stamp a character of insolent pride on his own huge mansion of Drumlanrig, which stands in full view on the opposite side of the Nith.

But she was not quite fair. The comment of the *Statistical Account* is that

> the whole village belongs to the Duke of Queensberry, who receives 5s 4d of yearly rent for every house-stead and garden. The villagers build their houses entirely at their own expence.

This simple system applied to the great majority of these agricultural-industrial villages. But her general criticism seems to have been taken to heart, for Thornhill as it stands today, complete with heavily lopped ducal avenues of limes down each street, shows signs of the extensive improvements of some thirty years later. Langholm in the same county, whose baronial burgh status goes back a little earlier to 1621, was much more ambitiously replanned in 1788 to take advantage of its position on the main road. It has a fine main street widened at the end to provide a market area in front of the town-house, and again half way down for the roccoco-pedimented Crown Hotel.

Some towns of course, like Edinburgh and Aberdeen, carried out ambitious expansions on their own initiative and are thus beyond the scope of this chapter. Other extensions such as the planning of New Stonehaven in 1797 (as it was then called) over the grounds of Fetteresso Castle, were in the nature of a partnership between town council and landowner. But of newly constituted burghs there were few indeed; Lord Gardenstone procured this degree of independent status for the town of Laurencekirk which he had founded in 1770, and the last creation of a burgh of barony was in 1846 when the Earl of Eglinton, faced with the collapse of his hopes for Ardrossan (founded in 1805 as a canal-head seaport), prudently handed over the superiority to the ratepayers. To them alas neither its draughty open plan, nor more recently its overpowering smell of oil, have commended it [pl. 19e]. The earlier Eglinton foundation of Eaglesham (1796) never aspired to higher status than that of a wearing village. But its layout is uncommonly spacious and imaginative, with the broad mainstreet running downhill towards Polnoon Lodge on each side of a rough central green. It now prospers as a quiet residential refuge from Glasgow.

THE DIVERSIFIED VILLAGE

In East Lothian, a county which gave a lead to Scotland in the years just after the Union, three families built villages which reflected their ambition both for themselves as improvers and for the nation under the new regime. It is noticeable that two of them also look back to the old order, for they boast the quasi-burghal symbol of commercial status, the mercat cross. In 1710 the Fletchers of Saltoun made the farm hamlet of West Saltoun into a productive centre by building mills for pearl barley and Hollands weaving, both as a result of an industrial espionage expedition by Mrs Henry Fletcher. One of the barley mills is still standing and is now being restored. Otherwise a short row of eighteenth-century houses, recently supplemented by some very respectable new ones, is the only relic of the village whose importance has passed entirely to its early-nineteenth-century agricultural satellite of East Saltoun.

It was probably at the village of Yester (now Gifford pl. 18a) that formal layout made its first appearance. Here in 1708 the second Marquess of Tweeddale built an austere T-plan kirk at the junction of three roads, and he and his successors feued off development sites to produce a close-knit, formal L shape, its stalk leading up to the church and its already existing bottom bar (a single row of houses and an inn overlooking a green) to the main avenue of Yester House itself. At the junction, though Gifford never had formal burghal status, stands a town cross.

The third and most famous East Lothian example is Ormiston [pl. 18b], where John Cockburn succeeded to the estate in 1714, revolutionizing its methods and reordering its fabric until his bankruptcy in 1747. In the village, houses were built to the strict standards he laid down. He wrote to his gardener in 1742:

> I can give my consent to no houses being built in the Main Street of the town but what are two storys high. None who thinks justly and well to it can wish to have it disfigured in that particular, or any other that can be prevented.

The general layout has survived well enough, with the cross in the centre of the long main street, but there is only a handful of houses from Cockburn's time, and all afflicted by the curious Scottish attitude to masonry in recent times. The manse, promoted to three-storeys by the addition of pointed dormers in the early nineteenth century, was given an even more antique appearance when its harling was stripped off in the twentieth. The house opposite has been religiously encased, all but the skewputts, in coloured cement 'rubble' of the sort that was applied to so many old houses all over Scotland in the 'twenties; and another to the west of the cross, with low wall head and a central bullseye window, has more recently been stripped of its harl and heavily altered. But there is still an effective entry at the east end, and best of all, the street is still lined with trees. Indeed it is evident from many of these early villages that the idea of regular street planting, an extension of the avenue in the landlord's park, came before the principle of full regularity in house design and persisted as a mark of special prestige.

Cockburn's other ambition, to establish a diversity of crafts which would service his village and provide a saleable surplus, did not prosper. The *Statistical Account*, which also noticed the trees, reported that:

> This is chiefly a farming village. Though attempts have been made, the linen manufacture never succeeded here.

Ormiston is one of the earliest examples within the time-limits of Professor Smout's *The Landowner and the Planned Village 1730 to 1830*, in which he introduces the history and theory of the subject as the key to its practice. This essay appears in a valuable collection, including two by its editors Rosalind Mitchison and N. T. Philipson, under the title *Scotland in the Age of Improvement*. John Dunbar's *Historic Architecture of Scotland* goes further in explaining the layouts and buildings themselves. All that can be attempted in the present account is to spread the net a little further on in time (as it has already been stretched a few years backwards) and to concentrate on the townscape of the planned villages – or towns. What should they be called?

'Village' is obviously suitable insofar as it implies a place under the wing – and equally the thumb, of its landed founder, who may well be the occupant of the neighbouring *villa*, or country house and estate. A more obvious criterion is size. Today a population of about 600 marks the borderline between village and town, though of course many old burghs with their own tolbooths or town-houses, and till recently their town councils, fall below that figure. Cockburn, as we have seen, described Ormiston (population 5–600 in the *Statistical Account*) as a town, and other landlords had similar ambitions. It was realized that a new village, just as it had grown from a hamlet, might grow into a town. The Revd Robert Rennie, in an essay which won a prize from the Highland Society in 1803, recommended a regular layout so that this would happen in an orderly way. It did indeed happen at Keith in Banffshire, a near-defunct settlement of uncertain status greatly enlarged on formal lines about 1750 by the Earl of Findlater, which is today (together with the later eighteenth-century extension of Fife Keith on the other side of the Isla) a town of about 4000 inhabitants.

A NORTH-EASTERN GROUP

'New' Keith is built entirely of pinky-grey granite. Its gridiron plan is of an apparently simple type with four parallel streets running along the built-up frontages of six rows of garden plots,

96

back-to-back with walls between, the biggest about 50 m. deep. This is a highly practical arrangement which avoids the conflicts of back-land planning associated with the fully built-up gridiron. But the suspense grows as you walk southward along the barely interrupted Mid Street, until at last the gap comes – a relatively huge, tree-lined oblong some three plots wide and three deep. Out of the east end there is an open view of the Balloch Hills, or would be, if quite a pleasant little public lavatory had not been sited plumb on this tremendous new axis (if you resent this, compare the examples at Peterhead and Fochabers). On each side of the elongated square the scale mounts up the gentle slope from one storey to two, then narrows and becomes even grander, the big houses at the second intersection turning their gables to the next long street and thus declaring it subsidiary; at the very top an extraordinary vision, the baroque front of the Roman Catholic Church of 1831 shows how to close a vista in style.

Keith has been lucky. It was a place of sufficient importance for the railway not to exhaust but to nourish it, bringing (among other things) the different granites of the north-east to adorn the front door frames of the tall Victorian houses that have taken over half the sites in Mid Street. It is good that so much of the original building survives on the great cross-vista, for it supplies much more than just two limbs of a traffic junction – in fact neither end continues out of town; it is, for Scotland, an early expression of ideal planning.

It was also highly influential. From Speyside eastward to Strathbogie and the fertile, undulating lands of Buchan, gridiron planned towns were established by owners who were now realizing the capabilities of this hitherto wild and undeveloped region. A string of them in their various local shades of granite extends from Tomintoul (the 4th Duke of Gordon, 1779) to Grantown-on-Spey (Sir James Grant of Castle Grant, 1766), Archiestown (Sir Archibald Grant of Monymusk, 1760, but largely rebuilt after a fire in 1783) and Keith, where you can either turn north to Fochabers or south to Huntly, refounded about 1765 by the same Duke of Gordon.

Perhaps it was its existing burgh status that encouraged or

allowed Huntly's feuars to build an unusually wide range of eighteenth-century types within the framework of the plan, including a curly chimney gable (possibly the latest of its kind) on a three-storey tenement in the square; the early nineteenth century continues the development of this universal Scots feature at No. 1 Gordon Street, which imitates the monumental chimney of Archibald Simpson's Clydesdale Bank in Aberdeen (p. 218). Simpson himself contributed the symmetrical gothic Gordon Schools at the end of the Gordon Street vista in 1839. It is an axis so strong that it can afford to be challenged by the Brander Library (1885) and its dissimilar counterpart, standing on each side of the entry from the square. And its basic geometry is further emphasized by a twentieth-century master-stroke, the slim needle of the war memorial designed by Frank Troup.

IDEAL TOWN PLANS

All these layouts aspire to the conception of the ideal town, but this is an absolute term which really applies only to a perfect example. Such a town needs to have a plan transcending its function; symmetrical (preferably in both directions), self-contained and complete, this last qualification contradicting Rennie's idea of indefinite growth. It may also have symbolic associations. Craig's plan for the first New Town of Edinburgh [pl. 14a] has all these attributes; Aberdeen's Union Street on the other hand, despite its symbolic name, cannot properly be called an 'ideal' layout (p. 129). Inveraray (p. 91), doubly symmetrical on the axes of its double church, is a very near approach; the more so because its screen wall, though only built on the side facing the water, itself achieves symmetry by reflection in the loch. So is Sir John Sinclair's own new town of Thurso [pl. 19c] started in the last decade of the eighteenth century. Newcastleton, founded by the 3rd Duke of Buccleuch in 1793, is the ultimate development of the idea of linear symmetry, its main street traversing three squares, small, large, and small again [pl. 19d]. A degree of symbolism is obvious in those towns or streets which bear the names of their founders, and Charlestown on the north coast of the Forth carries the principle to an ideal conclusion, being planned as a giant letter E after its founder the Earl of Elgin, whose house is close by at Broomhall. Curved layouts like the crescent of Garliestown on the Wigtownshire coast (Lord Garlies, 1760), are very rare, but in 1780 James Playfair designed a completely circular layout for Dunninald at Buddon Point on the Angus coast. This conception, though rather less surprising in view of the circular steadings at Prestonfield, Leith Hall and Gordonstoun, all in Scotland (not to mention the famous saltworks town by Ledoux at Chaux) represented the ideal village *par excellence*. But it was never carried out.

SPECIALIZED TOWNS: THE ESTATE CONNECTION

Most of the places so far mentioned are 'general purpose' villages whose houses (externally at least) give little idea of the trades that were plied in them, and whose industrial buildings, where they existed, have mostly disappeared. There are some, however, that still owe their special character to their chief means of livelihood, even though this may have declined or faded out altogether.

The close connection between agricultural improvement and village building has already been noted, but of the few eighteenth-century villages intended specifically for workers on the land the majority were for smallholders rather than estate employees. Professor Smout (p. 96) gives Athelstaneford in East Lothian as an example of a village where the new farming methods were deliberately grafted on to the old farmtoun system in order to make the village efficient and self-supporting; this is confirmed by Sinclair himself, but it should be noted that the *Statistical Account* also records the success of the village in weaving striped cloth; the search for industrial opportunity seems to have been universal. Smout then describes the hopeful paternalism of the Commissioners of the Forfeited Estates (following the risings of '15 and '45) in establishing what they called *coloniae* in Perthshire. The colonists, in the sense of incoming cultivators or pioneers, were ex-soldiers who were given small-holdings and cottages. But few of these places made good. Kinloch Rannoch (1763) alone has survived more or less unchanged, and Callander

(1730) eventually succeeded in quite a different way – through tourism, which was boosted by the coming of the railway. The main street has been gaily Victorianized, but in the square many of the plain-fronted houses bear dates from the 1770s.

Kenmore, founded by the Earl of Breadalbane in 1760 [pl. 20b] is one of the few villages which have an obvious visual relationship with their owners' houses or at least, as in this case, with their entrance gates. Occasionally however a neighbouring landowner established a vicarious but effective connection with a nearby town. The triumphal arch (1822) at the gate of Springwood Park, looking across Rennie's Tweed bridge of 1800 into the town, gives the old burgh of Kelso one of the most splendid entries in Britain.

Most of the surviving estate cottage developments belong to the nineteenth century. Two of the smallest that come within the scope of this book, having at least village names, are Balnagard, a neat group of cottages and steading on each side of the road seven miles down the Tay from Aberfeldy, and New Winton in East Lothian (Lady Ruthven, about 1840), a charming half-square of one- and two-storey cottages whose layout was effectively mirrored about a century later by the local authority houses on the other side of the road. In both these places the houses themselves are of workaday design, but where such villages closely adjoined the houses of the landowners, who were generally their builders too, they were often given a deliberately picturesque look. The cottages, the inn and other buildings at Kenmore were clothed with craggy dormers and tree-trunk porches in the estate-rustic style that became familiar in the highlands during the period of Queen Victoria's benign patronage. Its air of primitive fancy was rightly judged to match the royally approved scenery, and it was soon adopted as a Scottish type hardly less evocative than the Scottish baronial, especially for inns, from the Invercauld Arms at Braemar to the Eskdale Hotel in lowland Langholm.

Other estate villages were treated in a more conventionally romantic style that would not look out of place in England. Lamington in Lanarkshire has a single village street that jaywalks across the main road south of Culter in such a way that

Lamington Hill looms over its northward end. The earliest inscribed date is 1843, and its hood-moulded, deep-eaved manner, with spikes on the gables of the village shop, is obviously influenced by the cottage designs of the Edinburgh architect George Smith. Sinclairs Hill on the Kimmerghame estate just outside Duns was built about the same time, and its Tudor gables are carved with what were once the trade symbols of the occupants, probably influenced by similar conceits in the estate villages of Stobo and Dunmore. Fortingall, not far from Kenmore, is a highly successful marriage of the English and Scots vernacular near the turn of the nineteenth century, but the half-timbering of the Edwardian village of Rosebank on the Clyde (1901, for pensioners of the Mauldslie estate) is unashamedly English. All these places, it will be noticed, give front gardens to their tenant cottagers.

FISHERTOWNS

The development of the earlier harbour townscape is best seen on a tour of the East Neuk of Fife, which takes a good two days if you want to see everything. Fishing boats shared the harbours, of course, with merchant ships, and similarly on dry land the fishermen's houses jostle the compact merchant townscape. Generally of one storey, and more concerned with the communal net-drying space in front than with private gardens at the back, they perch on difficult sites at the end of the town or are jammed into gaps, singly or in groups.

The north of Scotland also has a number of early fishertowns. Stornoway was established in the seventeenth century and so were a few, like Buckie and Portknockie, along the coast of the Moray Firth; Fraserburgh, a new town at the furthest point of Aberdeenshire, goes back a hundred years earlier to its foundation by Alexander Fraser of Philorth in 1569. In the eighteenth century, fishing was the basic industry of most of the new villages founded by north coast landowners; on the east side, where they prospered, their intensive development continued right through the nineteenth century. Stornoway has been a special favourite of the paternalist improver. An ambitious scheme of improve-

101

ment is outlined in the plan of 1821 drawn by John Wood
(p. 123) with a note that 'The feus are held in perpetuity under the
Seaforth Family'. However in 1844 the island of Lewis was
acquired by Sir James Matheson, who built the vast castle in
1856. What he had done for the agriculture of Lewis Lord
Leverhulme attempted to do for its industry, but with smaller
success.

The coast from Nairn, which has its own fishertown, to
Burghead and on to Fraserburgh is lined with new or expanded
fishing villages, but unless you have at least a week to spare it is
necessary to be selective. As in Fife, each visit involves a detour,
but here it is much longer. One of the few places penetrated by
the main coast road is Portsoy, and this is a good starting
point.

Being an old town largely redeveloped on the existing plan in
the eighteenth century (the houses near the harbour recently
restored) Portsoy contrasts with what may seem the cramped
regimentation of later, more specialized fishing villages. One
of the earliest of the new generation is Findochty, founded in
1716 by a group of fishermen from Fraserburgh. Its seaward
face is of the mid nineteenth century and is a standard one, with
rows of chimneyed gables belonging to the ends of parallel
single-storey terraces, overseen by a granite kirk on the green
hump behind. But the old centre survives, a narrow, wandering
street in which the cottages, though sheltering behind each
other, push out for a better look at the passer-by; he in turn has
something to look at, for this is one of the most surprising of the
coloured fishertowns of the north-east. The older, rubble-walled
cottages are more commonly painted than those built of squared
granite, which indicates that the paint was originally applied
for weatherproofing. Quoins and surrounds are picked out,
and often the entire surface except the actual glass of the
windows, but including the chimney and even the pantiled
roof, is thickly covered in glossy oil-paint. The harshest and
most brilliant of colourmen's palettes is exploited to produce a
result as far from the gentle pastels of the south-west as from
the self-conscious taste of a street improvement scheme. The
villages of Pembrokeshire, where there is the same need to

keep out furious wind and driven rain, have a similar tradition but with less inclination to violent colours.

The first eighteenth-century landowner to set up fishing villages in these parts was Alexander Garden of Troup, who founded Gardenstown and Crovie in about 1720. The latter is found down a hairpin road at the bottom of a cliff, so isolated by modern standards that in 1962 it narrowly escaped withdrawal of all public services and consequent closure, but was rescued by the oft-maligned class of holiday-cottage owners. On a very narrow tapering shelf the end cottages face the sea, while those in the middle are in parallel rows sometimes building up to two storeys before they run into the rock at the back. Some of both types appear to be of the original date. Over the remainder of the century almost every similar opportunity on this far northern coast in the shape of a buildable site, a fresh-water stream, and of course the universally excellent stone, was taken up with success. On the more constricted sites the 'fishermen's rows' point their gables at the sea. In the more spacious and diversified towns the plan is the conventional gridiron. The old and now splendidly painted village of Buckie was expanded in 1723 and again, much more formally, in 1797. Its superiors, the Gordons of Cluny, invested £70,000 in the reconstruction of the harbour as late as 1874. Row-houses were still being built in Portknockie at the end of the century and in Cullen at the beginning of the twentieth.

Fishing was thus not only the most permanent of all the new town industries, but the first to create its own type of housing. The boom extended, of course, down the coast to Aberdeen where, from the Edinburgh train, kipper kilns can still be seen across the warehouse roofs; where in 1809 the City Architect John Smith laid out a new sort of fishing colony in the shape of the two squares of Footdee (pronounced *Fitty*), now considerably altered; and where the early morning fish sales are hardly less a tourist attraction than those of Venice. Likewise it reached Arbroath, whose High Street built its continuous story of nineteenth-century prosperity on the fishing industry, and whose harbour still has its long sheds for curing 'smokies'. And to the Forth by Edinburgh, where the fishwives and their famous choir have outlasted the old main street of Newhaven with its forestairs.

It also went still further north; first to Cromarty (1772) diversified both in industry and layout, with tight-packed, parallel fisher rows fronting the shore. Then on the Sutherland coast comes Helmsdale, a gridiron-planned fishing town founded and fitted out by the first duke in 1814. In Caithness there is Pulteneytown, a new suburb of Wick developed from 1803 by the British Fisheries Society, and by far their most successful project. After access had been provided by Telford's bridge in 1808 the great engineer also produced a layout, and elevations for two classes of house, of one and two storeys. The long central 'square' of the grid, built up with first-class houses, is unusual because its canted corners make it almost into an octagon, a pleasing variation which also makes for easier house planning. Ullapool over on the west coast was a less (but by no means the least) successful enterprise by the Society. In a spot whose natural advantages had already begun to be exploited, they began work in 1788 on a modest gridiron layout of the Keith type (traversed by lanes between garden walls) with two sides to Loch Broom. It was not the first or the last time that the planners' hopes have been disappointed in the western highlands, and today Ullapool, like its contemporary Shieldaig, survives mainly as a holiday place.

INDUSTRIAL VILLAGES

Thriving cottage industries were the aim of every small town in eighteenth-century Scotland, old or new, with or without the mills and warehouses that the landowner or the in-coming investor might provide. Two exceptions already noted were the more specialized fishing and farming villages, and to these must now be added the industrial and mining villages, in which the housing is there to serve the industry rather than the other way round. A place on the borderline, and one of the very first to incorporate a factory as a deliberate element in its layout, is Spittalfield near Caputh in Perthshire (1767). It has a half-courtyard formed by single-storey terraces, a two-storey mill forming the centre of the long side.

Perthshire was part of the large east midland area in which the nation-wide linen industry especially flourished, whether in new towns like Keith or old ones like the close-packed, red stone town of Kirriemuir; a cottage industry first challenged by the factories of Glasgow and Paisley, then ousted for good by those of Dundee and Dunfermline. But Perthshire was also to be one of the two main centres of the water-powered cotton industry. In 1785 the Duke of Atholl and a group of other investors joined with the engineer and entrepreneur Richard Arkwright to establish the village and mill of Stanley, on the duke's estate. Although not architecturally related to the mill, which is some way downhill on the bank of the Tay, the village is none the less impressive, with parallel rows of houses built at three main periods. The oldest are harled, the next are of black and brown whin with red sandstone dressings, and seem to date from after the reopening of 1823 that followed the post-war slump; and finally there are some pleasant Edwardian blocks. All conform to a general discipline of scale, and all make more or less use of local red brick, a conspicuous rarity in Scotland. But what mainly distinguishes the housing at Stanley from that at most of the new villages is that its houses seem to have been rented to the workers, not built by them, and this now became the general rule for the factory village or colony. Stanley's Mill is now closed and the village a half-occupied dormitory, with many gaps and derelict houses. Deanston, founded in the same year on the Teith near Doune, has fared better [pl. 19a]. A distillery occupies the splendid late Georgian building that replaced the original mill, and two rather later rows of cottages have been carefully restored by the County Council.

It was also in the 1780s that another important series of factory villages was built by the cotton magnate and first Glasgow agent of the Royal Bank of Scotland, David Dale; New Lanark and Blantyre, both on the Clyde, and Catrine on the river Ayr not far from Boswell's seat of Auchinleck. Blantyre [pl. 19b] would have disappeared completely had it not been for the chance that the explorer David Livingstone had worked in the mill as a boy, his family living in a one-room flat in the tenement that has been partly preserved and restored in his memory. The setting is strangely isolated except for the tourist buses, and still quite rural although today this is mining country. What has disappeared, together with most of the buildings, is the sense of a large, literally enclosed community with its gates and lodges, its parallel rows of tenements, and the manager's house behind its own high wall. Of Catrine there is rather more to see, though its success in its original role and also as a more diversified town has led to much haphazard alteration. The landowner, Claude Alexander of Ballochmyle, had a direct interest in the mill, a monumental building distinguished by ranks of Venetian windows lighting the staircases, and the focus of the whole formal plan. This, together with most of the two-storey houses, has now been replaced, and the layout itself considerably obscured.

New Lanark is still virtually entire [pl. 20a]. It lies just over a mile south of Lanark town, the last part of the road zig-zagging down towards the river. There are four mills, of which the two earliest have Venetian windowed stairs. Slightly above them, tenement housing is strung out along the lower contours of the densely wooded hill down which you have come. In the middle, opposite the mills, are the 'new buildings', a four-storey block the same size as the north side of Charlotte Square, but at no pains to disguise the repetitive pattern of the windows. A plain pediment marks the centre of the frontage and is also (helped by the little bell-house overhead) a sufficient focus for the whole composition; the bell itself is supposed to have been brought to New Lanark from their wrecked ship by a destitute party of would-be emigrants.

In 1799 Dale sold New Lanark to his future son-in-law, the Welsh cotton-master Robert Owen. It was already acknowledged as a model of its kind, but Owen made it world famous as the successful proving ground for his system of enlightened management. His ideal community of Orbiston (i.e. *world town*, begun near Bellshill in Lanarkshire in 1827 but now totally vanished) was a failure because it was created by Owen the theorist, not Owen the business man. At New Lanark he had built success on success, and plenty of evidence of his humane authoritarianism

can still be seen; the 'nursery buildings' for the pauper appren-
tices whom in due course he ceased to employ though they were
an accepted source of cheap labour, the schoolhouse, the
'Institution for the Formation of Character', and the village
shop, part of whose limited profits went towards the educational
programme. He also knocked each pair of flats into one two-
roomed dwelling and paved the streets, which then had to be
kept clean.

Owen played a triple part at New Lanark. As manager he
contributed to his own success as a shareholder, with a share of
close on £400,000 profit over twenty-five years. His various
partners had little reason to complain, but complain they did,
and in 1809 (the year before the Nursery Buildings) he was
obliged to take over the village as a separate concern at a cost
of £84,000. Only four years later he was forced to put it up for
sale, and bought it in at £114,000. He was thus cast in a third
quite distinct role and a traditional one, that of the improving
landlord, concerned for his property and his tenants. After he
left for good in 1825, New Lanark underwent the gradual decline
that allows the physical survival of a town and at the same time
puts off the final day of reckoning, the population falling from
nearly 2000 to about a third of that number by the end of the
century. The Gourock Ropework Company, having nursed both
village and mills through a difficult period, and having offered
the former to Lanark Town Council for £250 (and been refused),
had to cease operations there altogether. Starting in 1966 the
specially formed New Lanark Association reconstructed 22
houses to the modern equivalent of Owen's standards in Caithness Row and the Nursery Buildings, but in default of any
initiative by the housing authority so far, the prospect is bleak.

Of all the new towns and villages, none have been so vulnerable
to change – indeed to improvement in housing standards and
transport – as those that were founded for miners. The charming
terraced rows built about 1840 at Lugar in Ayrshire were demolished in the 1950s and now there is only the village shop of
the same period. Penicuik, planned by Sir John Clerk in 1770
as a mining town, has fared better – thanks largely to the
subsequent rise of the paper industry. Yet very few of the

original houses are still to be seen. The most remarkable survival is that of the ancient mining village of Leadhills, whose promotion by the eighteenth-century Earls of Hopetoun just entitles it to a place in this chapter. Straggling down from a height of some 450 metres above sea level in the Lanarkshire hills, its vernacular logic defies the rules of orderly planning, of conservation and even of survival itself. But it lives on; as did John Taylor (1637–1770), a lead miner for a hundred years, who now lies in the churchyard.

VI. THE EARLY NINETEENTH CENTURY

August, around, what PUBLIC WORKS I see!
Lo! stately streets, lo! squares that court the breeze.
See! long canals and deepened river join
Each part with each, and with the encircling Main
The whole enlivened isle.

from *Liberty, part V; The Prospect*

James Thomson was born in 1700 at Ednam, Roxburghshire, and finished his long poem *Liberty* in 1736. Thirty years later his nephew James Craig inscribed these lines in the cartouche at the head of his prizewinning plan for Edinburgh's New Town [pl. 14a], and by the end of the century the streets, more stately in plan than elevation, were complete. Of breeze there was plenty, and in his *Picturesque Notes* R. L. Stevenson was to refer affectionately to the New Town's 'draughty parallelograms'. As to canals, by 1822 the Union Canal had linked the Forth and Clyde to Edinburgh where it stopped at Lothian Road, not far short of the valley between Princes Street and the old town; here Craig had hopefully shown a canal on his plan.

More lines from the *Prospect* appear at the beginning of *Metropolitan Improvements* (1827) in which the architect James Elmes takes an imaginary party on a series of townscape walks in London, with much attention to the work of John Nash:

Lo! numerous domes a *Burlington* confess:
For kings and senates fit, the palace see!
The temple breathing a religious awe;
E'en framed with elegance the plain retreat,

109

> The private dwelling. Certain in his aim,
> *Taste,* never idly working, saves expense.
> Lo! the proud arch (no vile exactor's stand)
> With easy sweep bestrides the chasing flood.

All this came true. The ceremonies of town life in Georgian
Britain took place in an urban theatre remarkably like Thomson's
vision. His idea of *Taste* is perceptive. Going further than Pope,
he practically identifies it with sense and moderation, a standard
nicely observed by Robert Adam when he 'framed in elegance'
the frontages of the Adelphi and Charlotte Square (p. 76)
possibly less so in Nash's vicariously regal schemes for the
Prince Regent in London, and the palatial terraces of the last
phase of Georgian Edinburgh.

Bridges certainly became flatter, the level roadway of Kelso
superseding the humped profile of Perth or Dunkeld; and the vile
exactor eventually stopped collecting tolls (p. 87). Only in his
description of harbours was Thomson a little optimistic:

> Lo! ports expand
> Free as the winds and waves, their sheltering arms.

In fact the customs house has an honoured place in Scottish
townscape. At Leith, where harbour improvements to Rennie's
design were the main cause of Edinburgh's civic bankruptcy in
1833, Robert Reid's massive customs house of 1812 is seen
obliquely across the Water of Leith bridge from the end of
Bernard Street, terminating one of the finest urban prospects of
early-nineteenth-century Scotland. In contrast, that at Fraserburgh (*c.* 1810) stands at a built-up intersection above the
harbour. Curving round the corner, its domestic scale is dignified
by a screen of little Ionic columns on first floor level. William
Burn's Doric masterpiece at Greenock (1818) is the grandest
customs house in the British Isles, exceeding even that at Dublin.
A solemn, solitary monument of the exchequer, it looks northward to the Clyde over a great area of granite setts.

If something of the idea of the Georgian town can be traced
back to this early prophecy, what was new about the urban
scene at the beginning of the nineteenth century, and who were
the main actors on the stage? Thomson had not been specific

on this point, but by 1800 the answer was becoming clear. They were the middle classes who had profited from the first stage of Scotland's industrial revolution, either directly or by providing the services and professional administration that went along with it. Their first aim was to establish themselves and their families in a life style of leisure and culture, and the result was a transformation in the aspect of the town. The merchants and manufacturers of Glasgow had already achieved a tidy, cumulative development north of the Clyde; Edinburgh's professional men and traders had eventually followed the aristocratic exodus into the formally planned New Town, and Adam had designed Charlotte Square in 1791. But it was not until the beginning of the nineteenth century that the residential terrace, often designed as a single unit, became the accepted convention for town houses. Before long even the vocabulary of urban design was changing, from Robert Adam's neo-Imperial Roman and its aftermath, to the civic conventions of neo-Greek; this, though it represented a Regency norm, was to have a special importance in Scotland.

EDINBURGH: THE LATER NEW TOWNS

In 1801, before Charlotte Square was complete, Robert Reid and William Sibbald designed Edinburgh's Second New Town downhill from the first, whose householders were placated with the intermediate green belt of Queen Street Gardens. Like its predecessor it had a central street. But Great King Street, as it was called, was designed in four great palace-fronted sections; their centrepieces and end pavilions consisted of flats or superimposed houses, with ranges of single houses linking them together. On the cross streets produced northward from those of the earlier town, huge flatted blocks stepped downhill towards the Forth [pl. 25a]. Before its continuation into London Street, Great King Street's vista is interrupted by the trees of Drummond Place in which the eighteenth-century country house of Bellevue was retained till 1844 as the focus of the whole plan. Their well-grown state today takes some of the edge off Lord Cockburn's bitter criticism in the *Memorials*:

All that art and nature had done to prepare the place for foliaged compartments of town architecture, if being built upon was inevitable, was obliterated.

The Heriot Trust, as feudal superiors, not only echoed the plan of the First New Town but developed the idea of a hierarchy of parallel streets providing different classes of accommodation. At the opposite end of the scale from the first-class houses of Heriot Row and Great King Street were the artisan tenements of Cumberland Street, some of which have four front doors to each landing on the common stair, each flat having windows to one side only. Curiously but effectively, in the intermediate Northumberland Street there was a relaxation of the rule that all feuars, whether building for themselves or as a speculation, must conform to an elevational design supplied by the superiors' architects. Beyond the central grid the plan was more adventurous, with outward-looking crescents to north, south and east. To the west the extraordinary difficulties of terrain and street alignment were solved in William Playfair's Royal Circus (1820).

In spite of deviations in Heriot Row, the piecemeal building-up of monumental terraces worked remarkably well. But there were obvious difficulties in applying the same principle to causeyed (cobbled) roadways, pavements and sewers as required in the contract of 1806 which is quoted by Professor Youngson. Great King Street eventually acquired a complete sewer but it was part of a system full of sharp bends and uphill runs. George Smith, in a paper read to the Architectural Institute of Scotland in January 1852, tells how 'several hundred tons of solid soil' had been removed from under the roadway after a blockage in 1833, and a year after him the City Engineer condemned the arrangements of the town at large:

An enormity about the city of Edinburgh is, that the *cabinets d'aisance* are at present not connected with the sewage system, as they most evidently ought to be. If this were done they might be rendered comparatively *inodores*, and not be, as many of them now are, public nuisances.

Both architectural discipline and more mundane obligations

were better enforced in the Earl of Moray's scheme for which the feuing conditions were drawn up in 1822, just forty years after his father had acquired this odd triangle of ground between the First New Town and the valley of the Water of Leith. Some of the last houses to complete the layout (10 to 14 Great Stuart Street for example) were not built until 1855, but they still had to 'conform to the elevation prepared by the said James Gillespie'. The architect James Gillespie Graham of Orchil, to give him the prestigious name that he acquired on his subsequent marriage, here achieved a triple success. His scheme joined up with the street lines of both the First and the Second New Towns, so that to enter his scheme from Charlotte Square or Heriot Row is to experience a change of mood only, without a single awkward break. He planned a sequence of 'foliaged compartments' – crescent, oval, octagon – which is dramatic in its own right. And he relentlessly punctuated the walls of these urban rooms with identical pilasters and finally, in Moray Place [pl. 23a] with columns, thus securing an architectural unity well calculated to impress if not overpower the visitor. In musical terms the whole group has the repetitive quality of a chaconne, joined in the last section by a booming ground bass and by the whole orchestration of pedimented palace fronts (derived from Charlotte Square) which are contemptuously allowed to slip down the considerable gradient, and cruelly bent round the corners of the octagon. As a bonus, the cliff-like backs of the north side stand on the brink of a precipice that descends through the private gardens of Lord Moray's Feuars (as they are still entitled), through Lord Moray's Pleasure Gardens (to which they hold keys) down to the public walk along the bank of the Water of Leith.

This eighteenth-century riverside walk is now hemmed in by the later Georgian town. Past the Roman temple of St Bernard's Well (1789) and then over the river, you come to the estate that Sir Henry Raeburn began to feu for house building as far back as 1813. Its charm is noted by every writer and has never disappointed a visitor, but wherein does it lie? Ann Street is up on the hill and thus happily open – to the sky and to low-lying trees at one end, to the panorama of the Dean valley at the other. Nature, though here more domesticated, invades the street itself. Yet behind the front gardens, which are most unusual in Georgian Edinburgh, comes an unexpected formality. The terrace on each side, having started on a predictably small scale, rises with the ground to a big temple façade in the centre before dropping back again into the shrubs over the brow of the hill. Looked at head-on, these frontages are almost exaggeratedly formal. Seen obliquely, as of course they are, they have an almost casual look. Even the temple fronts in the middle are merely the light-weight tokens of grandeur, with shallow Ionic pilasters.

Another nice balance of formal and informal is achieved at St Bernard's Crescent in the next part of the same estate (1824, pl. 23b); its architect was James Milne who had probably been responsible for Ann Street too. Doric columns had appeared (cautiously, in pairs) on the latter's porches. In the Crescent they form a regular ground-floor colonnade, but at the centre they leap up to heroic two-storey scale, rivalling those of the Royal Institution building (now the Royal Scottish Academy) then in progress at the Mound [pl. 24a]. You come face to face with this domestic monument not at the end of a straight, pompous vista but round the calm, inviting curve of Danube Street.

These are only three of more than a dozen developments which are collectively known today as the New Town, though the name is still sometimes applied to the First New Town by itself. The other phases, distinct as they are, have no separate names in common use and merge into the unity of the whole square mile of the New Town at large. The greatest unifying factor is the hard yellow sandstone at Craigleith and the similar but often whiter stone of Hailes, two quarries to the west of the city which are both now closed. The face of these thousands of houses is predominantly a great expanse of ashlar, polished smooth or horizontally tooled (droving and broaching are alternative terms for the latter), and defined by the horizontal lines of plain string courses or continuous sills. Despite the notoriety of Auld Reekie, these surfaces are remarkably free of soot. The chimney stacks of Georgian Edinburgh, most of which have some importance as architectural features and have too often been badly rebuilt after the damaging stresses of their working life, no longer give out much smoke, and the rain is now steadily washing the stone cleaner again. What has taken place is the weathering or chemical discolouration of the stonework to a considerable depth, an entirely happy accident that has brought together the stones of Georgian Edinburgh into a lovely silvery grey, a good foil for the crisp lines of white astragals and the colours of front doors. 'Cleaning', even where it has not blunted the original form, has unfortunately broken the unity of many terraces and has sometimes also produced colours unpleasing in themselves. The only major cleaning operation that has justified itself so far is that of 23 Waterloo Place (1973), where the removal of an unusual amount of surface soot has revealed a consistent white stone free of the latent iron oxide whose stains have disfigured many similar jobs.

No other architect, with the possible exception of Robert Reid in his fussy refacing of Parliament Square (1808) was to emulate the decorative intricacy of Adam's Charlotte Square. Nevertheless in its general arrangement, with accented end blocks and pedimented centre, it was the prototype of many terraces in the city. When one of these facades met another at the angle of two streets, their two ends formed a solid corner which, like the centre, would be given the further emphasis of an attic storey. Whole blocks (today called super-blocks) would be built up in this way, sometimes in complex shapes like those of the Moray estate. The precedent of Charlotte Square was also followed in the general use of a two-storey order of columns or pilasters mounted over the ground floor, Palladian fashion. The more neo-classic arrangement of columns on pavement level had of course already been seen in the doorpieces of George Square and was charmingly incorporated in a terrace of Charlotte Square type at Forth Street by Robert Burn in 1800. But with the growing influence of the Greek revival it came into its own, not only for doorpieces and porches but continuous colonnades; Ionic columns were prettily paired in Major John Hope's development of 1825 between Haddington Place and Hope Crescent designed by Robert Brown but never completed, and the giant Doric order of St Bernard's Crescent (p. 114) was the most uncompromising of all essays in house-building for Modern Athenians. Elsewhere the rusticated ground storey persisted, but from quite an early stage the strong rhythm of round-headed doors and windows began to give way to the placid horizontal line of flat-topped openings. Long, flat stretches of smooth masonry and even horizontally proportioned glazing (the astragals corresponding with the stone joints) were employed to emphasize the air of Grecian repose and its deference to the vertical prerogative of columns.

William Playfair was the master of the Edinburgh terrace, subjecting all stylistic doctrine to his appreciation of each site and of the essential quality of the flat stone surface; it was not for his personal charm alone that he enjoyed the admiration of Lord Cockburn. In the principal triangle of the Calton scheme of 1819 he treated each of the outward-looking terraces on the merits of its situation. The north-facing Royal Terrace with its magnificent view he took by storm, interrupting the stretch of plain masonry with bursts of huge columns, but keeping up the rhythm of the ground floor with powerfully channelled arches from end to end. Having rounded the eastern extremity with the modest houses of Carlton Terrace he achieved his greatest success in Regent Terrace. These houses which look southward, down onto Holyrood and the back of Canongate [pl. 2a], are no mere improvised adjustment of a formal composition to a gradual slope; they come to terms with it, building up in successive blocks along the gradient, formality restricted to the Doric doorpieces. At Royal Circus in 1820 he showed the same flair, reducing the giant order of the conventional elevation to a plainness which accords (where in other hands it might have contrasted) with the main surface of the wall.

The comparison with Bath is irresistible. In 1767, when Craig laid the foundation stone of the first house in his New Town, John Wood's Gay Street had already climbed the hill from Queen Square to the Circus and his son was just starting on the second part of the great sequence, Brock Street and Royal Crescent. Most of the remainder of Georgian Bath was finished in the eighteenth century, on a generally looser plan than

Edinburgh's subsequent development. The formally enclosed spaces of Bath, including the incomparable townscape of the old centre, are almost all on level sites. Crescents enjoy the sunny hillside above the Avon, not rigidly linked, but often approached up stepped streets of smaller houses. Edinburgh, by contrast, is dogmatic and introverted. Having successfully devised the most formal layout in Britain on the George Street ridge, she went on to develop the possibilities of geometric enclosure, only grudgingly accepting the fact that much of the ground was on a steep slope, northwards towards the Forth. Her architects drove a much harder bargain with nature, and the contrast between monumental stonework and romantic terrain is all the more poignant, as when colossal façades are obliged to pick up their skirts and step suddenly downhill, and when trees, sky or sea are glimpsed between them. Playfair's more subtle approach brought something new to Georgian Edinburgh.

The city's late start in the eighteenth century was the main reason for her ability to fill this huge, densely planned area in the first part of the nineteenth. But it was only in the year of Waterloo that the growth of this great stone dormitory began to be complemented by civic architecture and churches on a worthy scale. Lord Cockburn made the point with his usual candour:

> Peace, with its other blessings, wrought no change more striking or more necessary in Edinburgh than the improvement of our architectural taste. Europe was immediately covered with travellers, not one of whom . . . failed to contrast the littleness of almost all that the people of Edinburgh had yet done, with the general picturesque grandeur and unrivalled sites of their city.

Waterloo Place immediately followed (1815, pl. 24b), providing government offices, a hotel and theatre. A direct challenge to Nash's London equivalent, Elliot's porticos frame the prospect of the Calton Hill, Edinburgh's acropolis. Between them and over the Regent Bridge (Robert Adam's conception now realized), then between sombre Doric screen walls dividing the

Scottish Townscape

Calton cemetery, the road sweeps round a shelf blasted from the side of the hill by Robert Stevenson, till it finally gains an open view of the old town to the right and Thomas Hamilton's High School of 1825 piled up on the slope to the left; this, with its romantic deployment of classical elements, set the seal on Edinburgh as one of the main centres of the international Greek revival. In the preface to his *Antiquities of Athens* (1762) the architect James Stuart had already remarked on a natural similarity between that city and Edinburgh. By 1829 the title *Modern Athens* was sufficiently well deserved for Thomas Shepherd to use it for his book of Edinburgh views, the sequel to *Metropolitan Improvements*. Gifted with a mature second generation of architectural talent, the city was fulfilling her opportunities; and nowhere more brilliantly than at the Mound, about whose very existence Cockburn's feelings had been strong:

> The creation of that abominable incumbrance, the 'Earthen Mound' by which the valley it bridges and deforms was sacrificed for a deposit of rubbish, was not merely permitted without a murmur, but throughout its progress was applauded as a noble accumulation.

The encumbrance was itself exploited by the building of Playfair's two galleries on the Mound, cutting across the valley on the hitherto inviolable south side of Princes Street [pl. 24a]. Cockburn's subsequent approval is expressed in a footnote:

> Scott's Monument has since been erected on Princes Street [George Meikle Kemp, 1840]; the Art Galleries are rising on the Mound; and a railway pollutes the valley. But the last of these perfidies was irresistible; and the other two abatements of the strict exemption that was obtained were consented to, and were quite right.

The Scott Monument and the National Gallery (1845) are of course Victorian buildings. The former adorns one of the prospects of the old town from the new, and appropriately, for it was to Scott that Shepherd had dedicated his Edinburgh volume. The latter actually incorporates the railway tunnel in its foundations. Right up on the ridge of the old town [pl. 32a]

118

and precisely on the Hanover Street axis are two more proofs of the continuing passion for picturesque improvement; Playfair's own double-towered building originally designed for the Free Church College (1846), and the more truly medieval spire of the Tolbooth Church by James Gillespie Graham (1841). At the west end Melville Street, the latter-day equivalent of Bath's Great Pulteney Street, ends not with a discreet Georgian hotel but with the three spires of St Mary's Episcopal Cathedral (begun 1873). Edinburgh's gothic revival had actually started long before the reign of Queen Victoria, in two earlier Episcopal chapels; decoratively at St George's in York Place by James Adam (1793, much altered as a shop), and with impressive correctness at William Burn's St John's Church at the west end (1816).

Visiting Edinburgh in the course of his *Tour* of 1832, Cobbett sat down and wrote his 'First Address to the chopsticks of the south':

> I think little of its streets and rows of houses, though all built of stone, and though everything in LONDON and BATH is beggary to these; I think nothing of Holyroodhouse; but I think a great deal of the fine and well ordered streets of shops; of the regularity which you perceive everywhere in the management of business; and I think still more of the absence of all that foppishness, and that insolent assumption of superiority, which you meet with in the fashionable parts of the great towns in England.

The only formal provision for shops in the First New Town had been in Rose Street and Thistle Street which lie between the main residential thoroughfares. Here lived the people who serviced the big houses (other than resident staff who lived in their basements); coachmen, craftsmen and the shopkeepers themselves. In the mews lanes behind were not only horses and carriages but cows and hens whose produce would be delivered at area doors. Coal went into the cellars under the pavements, often through a sloping trap in the kerb such as may still be seen between the mounting blocks on the north side of Charlotte Square.

119

In Rose and Thistle Streets the first shops simply established themselves in the ground-floor flats of the working-class tenements, a practice which of course continued. But in the later (westward) parts of the First New Town's development, a distinctive type of shop front began to emerge and soon became standard throughout Scotland. It had larger windows separated by stone pilasters which were carefully placed in relation to the wall above, so that a row of shops formed a sort of flat colonnade with a continuous fascia and cornice overhead. The fascia and often the pilasters bore painted lettering. This type persisted in the more formally designed tenements of Edinburgh's later New Towns, and rows of them can be seen still fairly intact in William Street (West End), Deanhaugh Street (Stockbridge) and in north-west Circus Place just up the hill. Sanquhar is one other Scottish town with a good number of them, and also happens to have the oldest post office in Scotland (1763), with a very rare example of a projecting bow window which is probably slightly later in date. The 'suppressed' bow window between pilasters, not sticking out beyond the line of the wall, used to be much more common. One of the very few survivors is in Dumfries High Street (p. 229). Of the standard, flat fronted type, many still survive in Ardrossan [pl. 19e].

Middle-class Edinburgh at the beginning of the nineteenth century still did its household shopping at the markets, which extended northwards from the Tron Kirk vegetable market. But by the 1830 pattern was already beginning to change. Some sorts of shopping had become socially respectable even in the First New Town, where books and stationery, clothes, wines and even groceries (from 'Italian Warehousemen') were now obtainable from mainstreet shops. The ground-floor flats or tenements were naturally the first to be converted, and when shops were formed in houses the upper floors were usually made into offices, either quite separate or, as at Blackwoods the publishers at 45 George Street (1829) connected with the business below.

The main streets of the First New Town, and of almost all its successors, had sunk areas in front of the building line. The 'ground floor' was some two feet above the level of the road, which was formed by piling up the earth excavated from the house foundations. A bridge, with steps and platt (doorstep) connected the pavement to the front door. It was easy enough to treat the existing pattern of door and windows to give the look of a shop, but of course the windows (even if they were enlarged to attract attention) could only be seen by people craning their necks across the front area. This difficulty was often solved with iron balconies leading off the platt, to give them a closer view; or if more window space were needed a pilastered or arcaded shopfront could be substituted for the original ground floor. The Dean of Guild records for the first three decades of the nineteenth century are full of graceful, fashionable designs for these conversions, virtually none of which now survive; though the great variety of attic or storm windows which form the other main subject of petitions for alteration at that time (all with slate-hung sides, and some charmingly bow-fronted) are still a feature of the First New Town skyline. The wine merchant's frontage at 45 Frederick Street, with its Ionic colonnade, has escaped alteration except to its glazing. Like Blackwoods, it has steps and platt extended over its full length, blacking out the basement windows. In both cases the colonnade stands a little way out from the wall face, foreshadowing the Victorian shopfront which projected right out to the edge of the pavement. In the later New Towns, as at Playfair's Elm Row in the Calton scheme (called after this formerly tree-lined section of Leith Walk) main street shopfronts were incorporated in the original design as a continuous arcade. But in this case all the arches, except those on the corner and those serving the common stairs to the tenements above, have been altered to the more modern plate glass convention.

Street corners, with their opportunities for picturesque emphasis above and commercial advantage below, were seized upon by architects and shopfitters alike. One of the most impressive is on the angle of north St Andrew Street and York Place designed in 1824 by David Paton who subsequently, in the building slump of the 'thirties, went to Raleigh (North Carolina) where he designed and executed the State Capitol building. The York Place corner has a continuous pilaster-colonnade not only on the ground storey but extending down-

121

wards, with the fall of the ground, into a lower range of shops; and even more surprisingly upwards, so that the round corner tower and its flanking walls are as near to being continuously glazed on all these levels as the technology of the time would permit. The link with the traditional galleried treatment of the old town is also recalled by a number of late Georgian two-storey shopfronts in the High Street (pp. 231-2).

With houses and shops, with public gardens, with churches, schools and institutions, the early nineteenth century left its graceful stamp on so many Scottish towns that no mere catalogue of new building types can convey what is really important, the townscape quality that results from their coming together in one place. It was less an age of great architecture than of notable townscapes deliberately created (though often piecemeal) in the fluent architectural idiom of the time. For the government, for town councils, for private benefactors and speculative developers alike, the aim was to gain prestige by contributing to the excellence of the whole. It was in fact the age of townscape *par excellence*.

Stemming from such unanimity of purpose and architectural language, the results might have been dull and uninspired, and it is only fair to admit that some critics have so judged them. Pugin in his *Contrasts* (1830) attacked such work as symptomatic of the architectural and social decline of Britain in general; Ruskin in his Edinburgh Lectures (p. 138) condemned them particularly in that city. How he hated the endless flat-topped windows of Georgian Edinburgh, and what was his delight at seeing the danger signs already apparent in the structure of St George's Church! Neither man had any time for the reach-me-down classicism of the Regency, and they had very little more for the cardboard gothic that was one of the available variants. Yet within its manifest limits this was an ideal town style. Thanks to the flexibility of its language there was nothing so uniform that it could not be suitably enlivened, no site so difficult that it could not be turned to pleasing advantage. It could compass all functions, any degree of scale or importance. Despite the almost universal use of stone, early-nineteenth-century architecture in Scotland could always maintain a light touch, unless something more portentous were required. And it is partly due to its very superficiality, complained of by purists, that a style in which pretension and privilege were so important has stood the test of time. Remarkably adaptable within, externally it now clothes many a different function and altered way of life without absurdity. Had it never happened, most of our towns would be incoherent.

WOOD'S TOWN MAPS: GLASGOW

John Wood's *Town Atlas* (1809–28) a collection of detailed maps of the 53 most important places in Scotland, provides a comprehensive view of Scottish towns at this time. Most of them have retained their medieval centres. Some have laid out neat extensions while others have hardly expanded at all. Seen with hindsight, they are a picture of technological innocence, of bland progress which took little account of the great changes already on the way. The wonder is that so much has survived.

Of all these towns, Glasgow has altered most since Wood's map was published. Before the American war the eighteenth-century tobacco city had diversified into the import and manufacture of cotton, of whose raw material the former colony was not yet a producer; its native industry dates from the break with Britain. Glasgow's cotton industry contributed to the demand for ships and plant, and quite early in the century a technical break-through was made in two crucial directions. In 1801 David Mushet succeeded in smelting the blackband ironstone of the Clyde valley, and in 1802 William Symington launched his steam-powered stern-wheeler *Charlotte Dundas*.

In the same year John Laurie began to develop the suburb of Laurieston. Wood's map shows it as one of four parallel gridiron developments south of the Clyde, Kingston, Tradeston, Laurieston, and 'Hutchesonton', but architecturally it is much the most distinguished. Peter Nicholson, author of the *Student's Instructor* and many other books which helped to spread the theory and practice of classical architecture throughout Britain, designed Carlton Place (1802, pl. 22b) with which it confronts the river. Superbly plain, its two long façades were restored in 1959 by a

Civic Trust improvement scheme and they are now impaired only by one stupid Edwardian intrusion whose red sandstone colour was sensibly acknowledged in the painting of their long-suffering stonework. In Nicholson's design their absolute identity was no doubt the reason for his use of an odd number (seven) of pilasters under each of the central pediments, which are themselves a rarity in Glasgow terraces as compared with those of Edinburgh. Laurieston has another distinguished street in Abbotsford Place (*c.* 1820). With its unusually tall houses repeated indefinitely down the long vista, it marks (for all its elegance of detail) the climax of Glasgow's Georgian austerity. Sometimes called the Harley Street of the city, it was built for professional families, few of whom ever lived there; indeed its wall-head chimneys foreshadow the tenements into which it was soon to be wretchedly adapted. Conceived for Glasgow's middle class, this whole area was to become a warren of dwellings, more or less makeshift but never well maintained, for the workers in Glasgow's new industries; in short, the Gorbals.

North of the river, Wood shows that the western extension founded in 1800 had not got very far. The new line of Sauchiehall (literally 'meadow of willows') Street had as yet no houses, and the whole rectangle down to Argyle Street was bisected only by St Vincent Street (named like its Edinburgh equivalent after the naval victory of 1797), where but two feus had been developed on a line that ran hopefully up Blythswood Hill and down the other side. The entire area was to be built up gridiron-fashion soon afterwards and it fared better than the southern suburbs, Glasgow's iron age transforming it not into slums but offices. Converted Georgian houses still stand shoulder to shoulder with later commercial buildings, among them the long palace frontage of Adelaide Place (1839) which keeps its footing with some difficulty on the slope of Bath Street. As if to hurry you past the pedimented centrepiece, it is given a median pilaster in the manner of Carlton Place. A much more usual Glasgow treatment is to be seen atop the hill in Blythswood Square, whose four identical sides have no centre break at all; even the central porches are a later addition. But the Square must date from the 'twenties. In the late 'thirties, when Edinburgh was still recovering from her Georgian exertions, Glasgow was developing and enriching the idea of the Georgian terrace. By 1839 the city had spread to the west as far as Woodlands Hill, and here the rigid gridiron at last came to an end; the south-facing slope is lined with terraces which show no sign of their Victorian date, other than a slight thickening of detail and an extra enjoyment of stonework texture (p. 158).

But Glasgow was not wholly committed to the Georgian norm. Back in the centre, churches and public buildings continued to be inserted in the already tight layout, and in a virtuoso range of style. Much architectural history was made in these cramped surroundings, and continued to be made right up to the end of the century, as a walk through the central area will show. But the Georgian contribution restricted itself to exploiting the classical situations of the gridiron. William Stark at St George's Tron church (1807, pl. 37c) pioneered the sombre revival of the English baroque, and in the same year designed what was probably the first Greek Doric portico on a public building in Britain – that of the Courthouse in the old Salt-market, looking out over Glasgow Green. In 1802 David Hamilton designed the charming new building for Hutcheson's Hospital in a clever summation of the whole *fin-de-siècle* vocabulary, and then turned his back on it to achieve his own neo-classic triumph at the Royal Exchange (1827), tightly packed into the square from which its temple-topped portico looks down Ingram Street [pl. 37b]. William Cobbett greatly admired the Exchange, despite his aversion to 'the politics of the persons generally assembled' in such buildings, and devotes nearly three pages of his *Tour* to a description of its setting, its external grandeur, the excellence of the basement coffee-house and the splendour of the News Room, 'quite free for the admission of all strangers gratuitously'. This great room still forms a brilliant indoor extension of the city's townscape and still fulfils the same function as a free library, though now maintained not by subscribers but by ratepayers.

The success of the Glasgow Exchange as a commercial and social centre contrasts with the lack of enthusiasm for that in

Edinburgh, to whose building Lord Provost Drummond had attached so much importance. Glasgow was predominantly a city of merchants dealing in goods, Edinburgh a city of professional men whose less tangible specialities were money and the law. Besides, the latter's mercantile concerns were concentrated in Leith, which (though administratively a part of Edinburgh since 1920) remains physically distinctive to this day. Leith built its own new Exchange and Assembly Rooms in 1783.

Professor Smout in his *History of the Scottish People* points out the difference between the character of the manufacturing towns which took after Glasgow and the professional towns which more or less consciously modelled themselves on Edinburgh. Buildings and layouts afford plenty of evidence of this, though very few places (with the obvious exception of the Georgian new towns) belong exclusively in either category. The manufacturing towns were quick to show their worth with fine steepled town halls like that of Falkirk by David Hamilton, but the industrialists themselves did not live gregariously; moreover their direct contribution to the central area townscape through churches, halls, libraries and the like, does not become evident until the second half of the century, a much more individualistic period. The professionally biased towns were quick to embrace and exploit the shared benefits of urban life; the palace-fronted terrace, the assembly rooms and prestigious academies of learning, and in time the museums. Commerce, as a formative influence in town-building, was an important link between the two types. Glasgow had early produced its aristocracy of trade, and for its leisured class Adam had designed the Assembly Rooms in Ingram Street in 1792 (p. 76). But for their houses even the wealthiest Glaswegians tended to avoid vicarious splendour of the Charlotte Square variety, preferring the detached villa, the single front or a more anonymous – even monotonous – type of terrace. Commerce also brought to towns the important activity of retail shopping, which is no respecter of persons except insofar as they benefit the shopkeeper. Very often the shops were the pioneers of Georgian improvement, though they did not always succeed. Embedded in the middle of Coatbridge is a tenement block of great refinement whose bowed end stands on an Ionic colonnade of twelve bays of shops, an act of faith in the elegant trade which this town of coal and iron was never to produce. It is now overlaid with thin catchpenny facias.

PERTH

This town, whose nice balance of industrial and professional interests is noted by Professor Smout, is also a representative masterpiece of the early-nineteenth-century art of town improvement. First a ferry town on the west bank of the Tay and then for a time a bridge town, Perth was again without a bridge for 150 years until the opening of Smeaton's bridge in 1771. This was the year before the completion of Edinburgh's North Bridge, and Perth, like Edinburgh, was given its George Street; it curved round from the bridge into the High Street, one of the two main thoroughfares of the medieval town. A link into the other was formed at the turn of the century and named after the old burgh kirk of St John, past which it ran. By 1800 Perth was established as a manufacturing town, famous for its gloves (the Glovers' Hall still remains), its linen and, significantly, its printing. George Street had been built up with stolid traditional tenements, and some elegant houses stood in Charlotte Street, which also ran up to the end of the bridge.

The town's expansion and improvement, shown in progress in Wood's map of 1823, took a most unusual form. To the north and south are two large commons, called the Inches or islands because they were formerly surrounded by water. On these, as on the river, the streets had so far turned their backs. The new face of Perth looked outwards, enjoying the view, defining the town, and presenting to the approaching traveller a happy collusion of natural and man-made which is unique in Britain.

First came the loose string of terraces facing over the North Inch to the river; the very simply detailed Atholl Place and Atholl Crescent, and finally Rose Terrace which is highly original in two ways. Its end elevation is enriched with fluted pilasters, thus marking the first house in Atholl Street. And its monumental centre by Robert Reid of Edinburgh was designed to accommodate the Perth Academy which had been the first of these establishments for liberal education to be founded in Scotland. All this was in hand by 1805, the terrace of Barossa Street and detached villas of Barossa Place soon following.

The southern development was much more formal in plan, resembling the simple gridiron of Edinburgh's First or Second New Town (pp. 77, 111); indeed Robert Reid, the architect of the latter, turns up here too as the designer of the most important frontage, Marshall Place. Not much of it had been built when Wood made his map, but as completed soon afterwards it faces the South Inch in a manner which immediately recalls Reid's work in Edinburgh, skilfully scaled down; a double terrace like Great King Street, but relying for its effect (as in London Street) on simple planes and characteristic semicircular windows in the attic storeys of the end blocks.

Follow the line of Marshall Place to the river [pl. 21a] and on the corner where they meet stands the big drum of the Waterworks, completed in 1832 – and not before time, for this was the year of a cholera outbreak in the town. They are a master work of abstract townscape (shaft and cylinder), of architectural literacy (Trajanic column and domed Grecian rotunda) and technical ingenuity (pumping house chimney and cast-iron reservoir), and all to the credit of Dr Adam Anderson who was Rector of Perth Academy. Another dome, this time with a portico, stands in the bend of George Street, a focus for the view from both directions including the approach to the town over the bridge [pl. 21b]. It was designed in 1822 by the Perth publisher David Morison, for the combined role of Museum for the Literary and Antiquarian Society of Perthshire and a memorial to Provost Marshall, who had been mainly responsible for the direction of the town's improvements.

Hardly an opportunity was missed. The sign and triple ballroom window of the Salutation Hotel look down St John Street. Canal Street (the canal had fed the town's moat) ends with the Italian arcade of St Leonard's church by the city architect William Mackenzie (1834), the High Street with the improbable gothic of St Paul's by Adam's pupil John Paterson (1807). On an awkward acute angle by King James VI Hospital an early-nineteenth-century corner block bulges out not in the accustomed single bow, but in three. Most important of all, in 1818 Sir Robert Smirke's County Buildings (that is the county hall and courthouse), with their noble Greek Doric portico, were boldly sited to face the river across what was to be Tay Street; Wood shows this merely as 'proposed street', tentatively cutting through the old back lands. It was many years in completion and not every building is worthy of the site, but Perth's Victorian developers understood the Georgian message. John Honeyman's tall church spire of St Matthew's (1871) supplies a valuable marker for Tay Street, while J. J. Stevenson's crown-spired church of St Leonard's-in-the-Fields (1885) does a similar service with even greater sophistication for Marshall Place. These two architects, a Glasgow and a London man respectively, thus supplied two townscape elements which would have been quite outside the abilities of their predecessors fifty years before.

ABERDEEN

The site is important as a double river-crossing, the name signifying the coming together of the Dee and the Don. It is a university city in which printing and publishing have flourished since the early seventeenth century; the Spalding Club was founded there in 1839 for the publication of learned papers relevant to north-east Scotland. Wood's map of 'the Cities of Aberdeen' (they were not united till seventy years after) was made in 1821. At that time there was a well-established range of textile industries together with fishing, shipbuilding and brewing. Specialized exports included stockings, salmon, meat and granite.

All the city's late Georgian improvements are subsidiary to the opening up of two great new thoroughfares, to the north along King Street and to the west along Union Street, both of which are described elsewhere (p. 216). These and other streets which cut over and through the byways of the old town were laid out at the turn of the century, to be supplemented in 1840 by Market Street which takes the shortest way from Union Street to the harbour.

Based on the need for better communication to and through

the centre, this ruthless redevelopment was realized in the most uncompromising of all building materials, the pale grey granite of Rubislaw quarry whose mechanical dressing was introduced in 1800. Its hardness favours the simple line, penalizing ornament but guaranteeing the effect of the slightest projection. Granite obliges buildings to be serious, and that is why early-nineteenth-century Aberdeen has more in common with the other neo-classic capitals of northern Europe, Helsinki most of all, than with the easy charm of most of its contemporaries in Britain – even with the splendours of Edinburgh. Gravity is here a necessary rule, not merely an attitude to be assumed on appropriate occasions. Aberdeen's two great designers, Archibald Simpson and John Smith, simplified the contemporary language in accordance with the demands of granite. But their contribution was actually far more positive. While never relaxing in classical correctness, they had a real sense of the possibilities of their material from the start; not only the abstract quality in which it excels, but the avoidance of dullness which is its obvious pitfall. Both, for example, were conscious of the effectiveness of detail high up on a building, where simple enrichment appears as comparatively delicate. The North Church in King Street (1829) converted internally to an Arts Centre in 1961 (p. 211) is Smith's masterpiece – the ultimate simplification in Grecian terms of the favourite British theme of the steepled and porticoed church, which another Aberdonian, James Gibbs, had established at St Martin in the Fields just over a century before. Towards the end of his life Gibbs himself designed the West Church of St Nicholas, but this has a different, more Roman, austerity (p. 43).

Simpson's own talent for imaginative simplicity, like Smith's, is well displayed on a walk down Union Street and into King Street. Here more than in most towns, a nicely calculated building loses much of its reality by inconsiderate change of use, and none so much as Simpson's Athenaeum club house which stands at the eastward narrowing of Castle Street, overlooking the city centre from the big windows of its first-floor reading room. This is splendidly columned with an Ionic order which matched that of the interior, but it was later blacked-out, subdivided and altered beyond recognition as a restaurant. Following the serious fire of 1973 it awaits internal rebuilding as an office.

It is characteristic of Aberdeen that with this one exception none of these monumental buildings is formally placed in relation to the layout, so that in this respect the comparison with its European contemporaries is a misleading one. There are in fact only three modestly formal domestic layouts beyond the main streets; Silver Street and Golden Square to the north of Union Street (1810) and Bon Accord Street, Crescent and Square to the south (1822), while Albyn Place to the west (1819) is shown in Wood's map with a mere handful of detached villas. Simpson was the architect of the first two and eventually of most of the third scheme, for which a much more extensive layout by Elliot of Edinburgh was soon dropped. Smith's masterly screen in front of St Nicholas's churchyard is one of the rare signs that anybody in early-nineteenth-century Aberdeen was thinking about the formal handling of space. But this, like the grandest of the houses, is in Union Street, whose bold straight line embodied the city's aspirations. Elsewhere, in the placing of buildings even more than in their design, Aberdeen wilfully turned her back on the suavity of the late Georgian age.

DUNDEE

Baldly titled 'Dundee, surveyed 1821', Wood's map is unusually sketchy. Possibly no great sale was expected, for there are few signs of civic or private improvement. This was still a seventeenth-century town with some eighteenth-century marks of status, modestly prosperous on the strength of the home-based linen manufacture that was carried on in its teeming centre and straggling outskirts. Middle class development likewise straggled out of town, mainly to the west. Dundee's record of epidemics increasingly stimulated the building of detached villas, of which the finest was to be the Vine, a monumental Graeco-Egyptian bungalow designed in 1836 for the display of the owner's works of art. This and many others in Magdalen Yards Road can be seen, if you are lucky, from the train just before it draws into Tay Bridge station. Wood shows only one connected group of new houses, the charming terrace of South Tay Street and its associated Square which the local architect David Neave designed for Provost Riddoch. One of the very few that were to follow was Springfield, laid out on the garden of an earlier detached villa of that name.

In the year following that of Wood's map, William Baxter built the town's first steam-powered mill in Lower Dens (1822) and the first cargo of jute was unloaded at the docks; once its processing had been mastered, it became the staple (though specialized and acutely subject to fluctuating demand) of nineteenth-century Dundee. The Improvement Act of 1825 having established, and in considerable style, the necessary requirements of the centre, nothing else was done about the old town until the later Act of 1871. As squalid as it was picturesque, it became the makeshift dormitory of thousands of mill workers; the population of 63,000 in 1841 had more than doubled in thirty years.

Reform Street (1828, pl. 22a) survives as the main civic achievement of the earlier Act and, potentially at least, the finest Scottish example of the street in which shops and tenements are combined. Four regular blocks, whose only emphasis is the slight projection at their ends, make the flats quite anonymous; sills and cornices establish a bland horizontal line. On street level however the shop fronts were pilastered throughout, and in the course of this uniformity (now alas superseded) the entrances to the common stairs are still marked by Ionic columned doorpieces of the utmost correctness. The father of this perfect hierarchy, and likewise built in 1828, was George Angus's own High School, whose Greek Doric portico looks down the street. This was also the year of the Exchange Coffee House at the harbour by the Edinburgh architect George Smith, who used it to solve a tricky but very real stylistic problem of the day. Given the larger unit (the reading room) above, and the smaller units (the shops) below, the obvious monumental treatment was the Palladian one: tall columns on a lesser basement. What then was the proper arrangement in neo-classic terms? Most architects were content to compromise, retaining the

Palladian base and merely making it as simple as they could; Elliot at Waterloo Place and Simpson at his Athenaeum had both used a perfectly plain arcade. But Smith manages to include the ground floor in his columnar system, making up for its lack of height by twinning the pilasters (or strictly, *antae*) on this level. No such pedantic curiosity was to trouble the designers (James Leslie and John Taylor) of the nearby customs house in 1842. Neo-Greek in detail, it is blatantly and indeed impressively Palladian in composition. Perhaps the happiest compromise solution of this stylistic problem had been reached two years before at the much smaller customs house in Clyde Street, Glasgow.

AYR, AND THE BEGINNING OF HISTORICISM

In his contribution to the *New Statistical Account*, dated 1837, the minister of Ayr proudly describes the town's recent progress:

> Few places have undergone a greater change for the better than this town has done, within the last twenty years. During that time, it has made greater advances in architectural and other improvements, than it had done during a century before.

But he later makes it clear that this was not due to any sudden expansion in industry:

> It has often been a matter of surprise that Ayr has not been more benefited by manufactures and public works, possessing, as it does, so many advantages for this purpose.

On the other side of the river Newton-on-Ayr, a fourteenth-century burgh of barony, had more than doubled its population to 4020 in the thirty years up to 1831, when its coal mines began to be worked out. Ayr was larger with about 6500 people, but had only increased by about a third in the same period, having declined from its seventeenth-century peak of prosperity in trade, and then survived in quite a modest way by the home-based industries of weaving and shoemaking. Expansion was to come with James Templeton's introduction of the carpet industry, with the improvement of the docks in 1832, and finally

133

with the rail link to Glasgow in 1840. But what explains its previous nineteenth-century growth and the exemplary civic design that went with it?

In the first place the credit goes to Provost John Ballantine who inspired the building of the new bridge in 1786. To Ballantine Burns dedicated his poem *The Brigs of Ayr* (p. 218), an imagined dialogue between the old and the new bridges which is the best account ever given of the interaction of two buildings in the town scene. But in practical terms the new bridge (until flood damage led to its replacement and thus fulfilled the auld brig's prophecy) gave Ayr a vastly improved river crossing and opened it up to Glasgow. The appreciable boost to the weaving industry was less important, in terms of town growth, than its stimulus to Ayr as a centre of road communications and a well-placed seaside resort. In 1826 the old tolbooth with its nineteen steps and 'drowsy dungeon clock' was cleared away, so that having crossed the river and entered the town with great architectural ceremony, the road has a clear sweep down Sandgate, past separately redeveloped shops and houses and out of the old town, after which it becomes the main spine of the new development. Barns Street opened out to the left at the beginning of the century and was followed six years later by what was to be known as Wellington Square to the right, their south sides nicely in line. Wood's map of 1818 shows the domed and porticoed County buildings just complete on the west side of the Square, which lines up with the axis of Cromwell's citadel, soon to be bisected by Eglinton Terrace and ultimately half-filled with villas. But Ayr's best terraces lie south of Barns Street, in Alloway Place, still on the line of the main road; or rather just back from it, for Barns Terrace, probably built in the late 'thirties, has a deep forecourt (unfussed by gardens though today obstructed by parked cars) along its entire front.

Ayr built its Academy in 1810, but it has since been replaced on the same site. The Relief Church built to supplement the old parish kirk in 1816 still stands, albeit at present disused, in Academy Street. In contrast with these quite prosaic buildings, Ayr was to have the tallest of all town-house steeples, and easily the finest of the distant landmarks that advertise the approach of Scottish towns. Designed by Thomas Hamilton of Edinburgh in 1828, it is a lively offspring of that marriage of neo-classic and baroque which was often characterized by a strange, deliberate deadness. In Edinburgh Playfair's St Stephen's Church (1827, pl. 25a) and Hamilton's own Orphan Hospital (1833) at the Dean are examples of the latter phase, which might be thought of as the senile paralysis foreshadowing the death of classicism. But in fact it is no such thing. Both these buildings are dynamically related to their settings, and moreover classicism did not die with the Georgian age, or for a very long time after, as is proved by the completely convincing Grecian extension to Ayr's town-house by James Sellars of Glasgow, architect of the St Andrews Halls in that city. It was built in 1880.

Complementary to his great steeple both in style and in outline, Hamilton also designed Ayr's Wallace Tower in 1833. Built on the site of an earlier tower (possibly that of a friary church), and jutting out into the High Street like some true medieval totem preserved amid modern improvements, it is a sign of Scotland's growing consciousness of her history – though obviously not as yet of the precise forms of her historic architecture. In Aberdeen the title of Wallace (wall house?) Tower was attached to the little turreted house on the corner of Netherkirkgate; it was a public house, and a battered, unidentified and formerly recumbent effigy was set up in a niche to make a very convincing Wallace, as a sign (p. 59). Ayr's Tower has a suitably primitive statue by the local man James Thom, best known for his Tam o' Shanter figures at Kirkoswald nearby. Stirling's Athenaeum at the head of King Street (1816) was similarly a place of instruction and entertainment. It has no pretension to medievalism, but in 1859 a highly realistic and competent figure of Wallace by Handyside Ritchie was mounted on it. At this time also J. T. Rochead's astonishing Wallace Monument was nearing completion outside but in full view of the town, and acting as an external town-mark. In the best of the native historical revival that was to come, enthusiasm and scholarship went hand in hand.

CUPAR

The enlightened self interest of the Georgian town developer, the happy manipulations of the provosts and other members of unreformed town councils, are typified by the story of St Catherine's Street in Cupar (p. 226). In 1809 Provost John Ferguson, a local banker, acquired the necessary land by purchasing and demolishing the old house of Balgargie on the edge of the town. Having improved the site by straightening out a bend in the river Eden, he extended it through to Crossgate by further acquiring, free of charge, the site of the old town hall. In exchange for this he built in 1815 the new town hall with its dome and lantern for a nominal charge of ten pounds, but retained the ground floor which he developed as a shop, extremely well placed on the corner of Crossgate. The design was the work of its builder Robert Hutchison, but for that of the County Buildings in St Catherine Street, which he constructed entirely without charge, Ferguson engaged James Gillespie Graham of Edinburgh in 1820. Wood's map shows this side of the street almost complete but the north side only partly built up, two of the vacant sites belonging to Hutchison. In retrospect at least, the propriety of this sort of deal (comparable on a very much smaller scale with the operations of Dobson and Grainger in Newcastle) is unquestionable, for private gain and civic design had not yet become separated.

VII. THE VICTORIAN TOWN

Neat, square, plain, regular, box-like, Grecian; these words are used in Victorian guidebooks to describe the Georgian buildings and Georgian townscape whose merits are to us so clear and enviable. All are terms of faint praise, not explicitly damning, but suggestive of reaction and an awareness of other possibilities. It is with the realization of these that we now have to deal.

We are now further in time from the Victorians than any of them were from the Georgians, but misgivings about Victorian architecture persist. The Georgians, from the accession of the first George in 1714 to the death of the fourth in 1830, worked out a townscape language which we regard as consistent and universal. There followed a surprisingly distinctive period of seven years which can bear the name of William IV. William Mackenzie of Perth was one of its local masters; his Parish Church of St Leonard's in King Street (1834) and his Infirmary (1836, now the County Offices) in South Street are typical. Both have a dry, Roman gravity that prefers the heavy arcade to the graceful facility of columns, as if architecture were solemnly marking time. What came next, if we are looking for another period of easily identifiable style and aspiration, is extremely confusing. The sixty-three-year Victorian period, exactly half as long as the Georgian, seems to have nothing of its discipline and consistency. It is easy to put it down as an era of muddle, its products as a series of intrusions on the happy Georgian scene.

ATTITUDES

The oddest achievement of the Victorian age was to supply the language of moral indignation in which itself would one day be

unfairly indicted and wholly condemned. John Ruskin was a
professed anti-Georgian, and the second half of the nineteenth
century was pervaded by his seductive blend of aesthetic and
moral judgement. He sanctified the bay window and the pointed
arch, the leafy capital fresh from the craftsman's chisel, and in a
curiously unreal way he sought to connect architecture and life.
He hated the plain, flat-headed Georgian windows that in his
view so lamentably failed to express this connection, and actually
made a count of them on his way along Picardy Place, York
Place and Queen Street to deliver the first of his four *Lectures on
Art and Architecture* in Edinburgh on a November evening in
1853; the total was 678, and nothing has since happened to
alter it. His ideas, including what amounted to a programme for
gothicizing Georgian Edinburgh, were not very warmly received. But his bigotry lived on, and the twentieth century
condemned Victorian architecture in the moral terms it had
learned from this most popular – and in some ways most influential – of Victorian critics. George Scott-Moncrieff ends his
book *Edinburgh* (it is otherwise an exemplary study of the city
and its buildings) with some nicely aimed but ill conceived
pot-shots like this one:

> After William Burn came David Bryce, and with him Scottish
> architecture plumbed the depths of meaningless ostentation,
> derivation in which every source is arrogantly misunderstood.
> Most of Bryce's work was done at country seats, where he
> ruined many a fine old castle, and not infrequently its fine old
> family as well. However, in 1868–70 he reconstructed the
> Bank of Scotland on its prominent site at the top of the
> Mound . . . when Bryce had finished with it everything about
> it was bad, and it remains to this day a hideous conglomeration
> of architectural fatuity.

Nobody who has seen this [pl. 32a] and Bryce's other bank
buildings in Edinburgh, or visited the country houses which he
was commissioned to restore or extend (from Blair Castle and
Cullen House to Robert Adam's Newliston) will take this
knockabout comment very seriously. Yet now that not merely

the reputation but the survival of a building may hang on a critic's word, such sweeping generalizations are dangerous.

CONTINUITY

It is misleading, for a start, to think of the Victorian town as making a sudden break from the Georgian tradition, either by thoughtless replacement or wilful contrast, though both were to become apparent towards the end of the century. By the 1830s most Scottish towns had established their identity, and were quite content to extend and enhance it. Flat-fronted terraces continued to be built, as at Montrose [pl. 25b] and St Andrews, betraying their late date only by a certain thickening of detail. The feudal superiors of Edinburgh's principal New Town developments continued to insist on conformity with Georgian elevations where these had been started, or where gaps remained to be filled (p. 113). The unbuilt expanses of the west end were developed, on the Georgian plan, well into the 'eighties in a manner which had the best of both worlds, combining Georgian discipline with Victorian opulence. The principal vista along Melville Street was completed in the 'fifties and then terminated in 1873 by a strange but effective bonus in the shape of Sir George Gilbert Scott's Cathedral; its conscientious gothic is altogether at home in these straight-laced surroundings, where its cluster of three spires is alternately brought to life by the morning sun and thrown into grand evening silhouette. Another church by Scott, subsequently promoted to cathedral, contributes one of the two spires that punctuate the long stretch of Glasgow's Great Western Road; Union Street in Aberdeen is similarly marked (p. 216). Dalkeith owes its distinctive silhouette to a pair of spires by Burn and Bryce respectively (1840 and 1851), and two gothic spires of superlative quality mark the town of Montrose and the geographical climax of Edinburgh's Castlehill.

These last are both the work of James Gillespie Graham. A fluent classical designer with a particular flair for effective siting (p. 113), he also purveyed the reach-me-down gothic frontage for the Georgian town church (most notably in his

Scottish Townscape

pioneer design for the Catholic chapel of 1816 which is now the
cathedral in Clyde Street, Glasgow), and for more isolated sites
the cardboard gothic tower like that of the parish church of
Dunbar. But he moved on from this primitive stage of the
gothic revival, and the spire he added to Montrose parish
church in 1832 is a landmark in British architecture as well as
in the Angus landscape, showing that a serious and scholarly
revival was a Georgian aspiration inherited, not invented, by
the Victorians. This design was in fact closely based on that of
Louth parish church in Lincolnshire; Sir Joseph Banks's lecture
about the Church to the Society of Antiquaries in 1790 had been
published, with a well detailed engraving, in the following year.
At Tolbooth St John's Church in Edinburgh, the first great
monument of the Victorian gothic revival (1841) Gillespie
Graham's collaborator was none other than the fanatical
gothicist A. W. N. Pugin, whose most eloquent memorial may
not be the dressing up of Barry's new Palace of Westminster,
not even his own Catholic churches and cathedrals, but this
spire for the Gaelic branch of the apostate church in Scotland.

The same continuity may be seen in the work of other architects of Gillespie Graham's generation. To take only Edinburgh,
there were Thomas Hamilton, William Playfair and William
Burn. All these were late Georgian architects who found their
first opportunities in the early-nineteenth-century growth of
the city, but continued to practise well into the 'fifties, Burn
indeed remaining prodigiously creative (though latterly from a
London office) till his death in 1870. David Bryce, Burn's pupil
and for a short time his partner, started a little later but shared
his master's understanding of the Georgian idiom. It was he
who established the strongest of all architectural links between
the Georgian and Victorian townscape – the Italian palace
front, rich and regular. Starting with Burn's New Club, (1834,
demolished 1966) and brilliantly developed by Bryce for banks
and insurance offices in the other streets of Edinburgh's First
New Town, the Italian palace became an accepted type for
bank buildings all over Scotland right up to the end of the
nineteenth century, most of all in J. M. Dick Peddie's graceful
frontages for the Royal Bank of Scotland's offices [pl. 27c].

140

It was also Bryce who led the breakaway from the classical tradition as a founder member of the Edinburgh Architectural Association in 1857. This date, which also marks the death of Thomas Hamilton, is more significant than 1837 (the year of Victoria's accession) as the beginning of a new age, for it opened the door to a serious Scottish revival, in town no less than in the country where its fame – to some people its notoriety – is of course much greater. One of its most accomplished practitioners was Peddie's partner C. G. H. Kinnear, so that a further point of interest comes to light. Victorian architecture in Scotland was not subject to sudden changes of style; the main stream continued and prospered along with the innovations. In this period of Scotland's tremendous expansion there was room for everything.

SWEEPING CHANGES, LIMITED REFORMS

Meantime a real revolution had taken place in the social structure and constitution of the town. Basically it was a change from a feudal to a managerial system, with the large industrial towns dominating the economy of the southern half of the country. In these towns the nineteenth century provided an employer's and a landlord's market from start to finish, and literally (as we now see) with a vengeance. From its earliest years the independent textile worker was obliged to consider, however reluctantly, seeking work at the mills that had thrown him out of it. The mechanized wool industry was set for long success and so was linen, despite the removal of the export bounty in 1832. By this time the cotton-weaving industry of Scotland was fast giving way to that of Lancashire, but the industries it encouraged – thread spinning, machinery and shipping – were about to become giants in their own right. Jute was becoming the staple of Dundee (p. 132). Yet in spite of this prodigious growth and limitless opportunity, it was not the demand for labour but the demand for work that proved insatiable; to the former small-town craftsmen were added Irish immigrants who by 1851 were supposed to have formed about a quarter of Glasgow's population, evicted tenants from highland estates,

141

and finally, after the withdrawal of protection for the home agricultural industry in 1846, surplus farm workers from all over Scotland. The increase in the country's population from 1,608,000 in 1801 to 4,472,000 in 1901 was heavily concentrated in what is now called the central belt, the industrial areas of the seven counties of Ayr, Renfrew, Lanark, Dumbarton, Stirling, West and Midlothian. In these parts and in the similarly mush-rooming towns of the east coast the long overdue Burgh Reform Act of 1833 and the further measures of the next hundred years were in the nature of emergency operations.

The older order, in which private (even paternalistic) enter-prise had usually made up for the feebleness of authority, and had struck a nice balance between public and private benefit, was played out. One of its last monuments was Telford's Dean Bridge of 1829 across the Water of Leith. Though now taken for granted as part of the main road northward out of the city of Edinburgh, it was largely paid for by Lord Provost Learmonth in order to provide convenient access to the land he was feuing on the other side. In its primary purpose however its success was delayed by the twenty-year recession that followed. Pro-fessor Youngson describes how in 1833, on the very day after the Burgh Reform Bill was enacted, the city was declared bankrupt. Nor was it the only burgh to get into this scrape. Aberdeen was already broke, partly thanks to the sale of town land at far below its development value, and Dundee and Dunfermline followed. Values of course continued to rise as exploitation became more intensive. In *Economic Developments in Victorian Scotland* W. H. Marwick gives a dramatic example from Glasgow, a city which managed to remain solvent. In 1787 the Corporation sold an acre of ground to Robert Smith for £645. Less than a century later they bought it back for £173,000 as the site for the new municipal buildings on the east side of George Square.

Soon after the accession of William IV in 1830 the Grey administration came to power, pledged to a programme of national and local reform. In Scotland Francis Jeffrey as Lord Advocate and Henry Cockburn as Solicitor General set them-selves to do their part. The Reform Act of 1832 gave the parliamentary vote to any householder worth £10, and Scotland gained eight more seats at Westminster. The Royal Burghs were represented with greater fairness in relation to their size, Paisley and Greenock were to return their own members as 'Parliamentary Burghs', and other towns to whom this title was given were included in the reorganized voting districts.

The Burgh Reform Act of the following year was less radical. With hindsight it can be seen as a minimal, almost defensive measure which gave vast social responsibility to local authorities, but without the positive powers that have since been added and which we now take for granted. As far as municipal elections were concerned, it merely regularized the position that had arisen out of events in Montrose in 1817. In that year an election had been successfully challenged at the Court of Session and the burgesses had been allowed to elect a new council. Many other burghs had followed suit. Accordingly the Act gave £10 householders the municipal vote. As to the functions of the elected councils, it allowed existing burghs to become 'Police Burghs' with responsibility for lighting and cleansing, roads and water supply, as well as keeping order. In 1847 this provision was extended to the Parliamentary Burghs, and subsequently to other centres of population; the new steel town of Motherwell was given the status of Police Burgh in 1850. Meantime the councils in many burghs of barony continued to be nominated by their superiors, and the Royal Burghs, though democratized, remained intact. In his article on Scottish Administration at the end of the 1895 edition of Groome's Ordnance Gazetteer of Scotland, H. A. Webster reflects that if the inhabitants of Glasgow (population 658,193) were to enjoy the same proportional representation on their town council as those of Culross (population 380), they would need to have 15,000 councillors. Financially it cut the other way, Glasgow's £50,000 annual revenue comparing with the £52 with which Culross had to look after itself. These particular anomalies survived the piecemeal adjustments of the nineteenth and twentieth centuries, though the Scottish Local Government Act of 1929 went as far as to differentiate between 'Counties of Cities' (Edinburgh,

Glasgow, Dundee and Aberdeen), 20 other Large Burghs and 170 Small Burghs.

THE ARCHITECTURE OF LOCAL GOVERNMENT

With what zeal did many burghs express, in the new generation of town halls, their democratic sanction, their traditional status and their Victorian prosperity! Some of course, like Culross, were by-passed by progress and still found their old tolbooths perfectly adequate for meetings, the actual administration of the burgh being carried on in his own office by a local lawyer acting as town clerk. Others like Fraserburgh (1855) and Irvine (1859) built themselves fanciful versions of the classical town hall. Paisley's sumptuous example (1879) continued the same tradition; designed by Lynn of Belfast, it used to bear the name of the George A. Clark Town Hall, having been paid for by the American branch of the family of J. and J. Clark, thread makers. It was not surprising that Glasgow made such an obvious effort to outdo it in 1883, and thus Greenock had to show that it was in the running too (1886). Stylistically these buildings represent classicism run to seed, but not through ignorance or carelessness. Theirs is the language of superabundant wealth, the language of the banks in fact, but stretched upwards and sideways so that the effect is not of reassurance but of astonishment. Thus with a degree of architectural licence far less common in Victorian Scotland than is often supposed, the great and growing towns were to identify themselves with commercial progress in the late nineteenth century.

Much more typical is the Scottish baronial town hall. The subject of many caricatures (including the affectionate portrait in Osbert Lancaster's *Pillar to Post*), it must at least be given credit for being indigenous to Scotland. Yet the romantic tolbooth revival began, like its equivalent in country houses, with types other than Scottish. James Gillespie Graham's perpendicular gothic town-house at Duns was unfortunately demolished in the 1960s, and Glasgow's old tolbooth has also disappeared (except for the tower) along with the battlemented Tudor refacing which David Hamilton gave it in 1814 [pl. 13b]. So

144

one of the earliest survivals is the staged Flemish tower at Forres which breaks charmingly forward at the centre of the long main street (1839). Among the first truly baronial town halls is that of Rutherglen, an older burgh than Glasgow and perhaps for this reason asserting itself in traditional style – but a highly original interpretation of it; the medieval market space is dominated by its strangely gabled tower (1861, pl. 26a). In the dozens of examples that followed, clock-towers were common and were generally spired like that of Aberdeen (1868) or Hawick (1887). The old town hall of Castle Douglas was given a clock tower of medieval Italian form in the town's vernacular of white granite with red sandstone dressings, presumably before 1862 when a new hall was built on another site. A similar tower at Gatehouse-of-Fleet a few miles across Kirkcudbright-shire (1871) plays a Montague to its Capulet. More frequently a light admixture of foreign detail enriches the baronial town hall, but hardly weakens the case for seeing it as the continuation of a native type. The idea of the castle come to town is not so far fetched when one considers the old tolbooths of Tain, Canongate and Musselburgh (p. 61). The main problem with this gawky, turreted family of buildings is its functional obsolescence now that the duties of town councils have in some cases increased, in others disappeared altogether.

The same problem faces an even less regarded Victorian type, the county buildings, which are often less suitable than their Georgian predecessors for adaptation to new social uses. Until 1889 their principal and ever-growing function was as court houses, but in that year the county councils were set up, taking over from the county road trustees and the Commissioners of Supply, and assuming many new functions in the smaller towns of their county areas. Their job was subsequently extended to include planning (they and the town councils being empowered to draw up town planning schemes from 1909), and education, for which each county including the 'counties of cities' became responsible in 1918. Most of the new generation of late Victorian county buildings were fussily classical, and one of the first was at Paisley in 1890. Like many others it was on a lonely site beyond the centre. The position of Stonehaven's county buildings, now long disused, is an ideal one, outside the town on the road from the south, but facing into it. This however is the Georgian court-house site, redeveloped by the new county council. One of the few county buildings to have adapted itself successfully is that of Haddington, where William Burn's Tudor gothic court-house of 1832 has been tactfully enlarged with each successive growth in the county's administrative powers. The latest extension, by Peter Whiston in 1955, provided for the new functions of the post-war era, including development control, in which the county of East Lothian has been conspicuously successful.

Certain other types of public building, many of them now superseded and forgotten, begin to appear in the late 'forties as a result of national provisions entrusted to local authorities. The poor-house (resulting from the Scottish Poor Laws of 1845) was seldom a feature of the town centre, but among the best was that which served the Edinburgh parishes of St Cuthbert's and the Canongate from 1866. Designed by Peddie and Kinnear with a Dutch steeple to make it worthy of its position on the flat northern outskirts, it still stands as the nucleus of the Western General Hospital. The Board later built its office in a proud position on the corner of Castle Terrace; it was designed by the famous architect-historians McGibbon and Ross, and looked (until it was burnt out and demolished in 1974) exactly like one of the line drawings in their great work, the *Castellated and Domestic Architecture of Scotland.* Glasgow was notable for the architectural distinction of its public wash-houses in the early Victorian Italian style with appropriate towers for water storage, but all have now disappeared. Cattle-markets and slaughter-houses (the provision of the latter was a perpetual challenge to nineteenth-century town councils and a constant source of complaint to those who did not build them) were sited conveniently near to the railway and often designed with considerable pretension, featuring the stone heads of cattle; they were (and still are, though banished to the outskirts) part of the essential mechanism of feeding the population of the large town, as well as safeguarding its health. Edinburgh's Victorian slaughterhouses in Fountainbridge have disappeared, but the

146

meat market (1852) is at present a gaily painted discotheque. Large slaughterhouses are found, as at Turriff, in the towns of the great cattle-raising areas. Another important type, the corn exchange which is likely to have been built in the years following the repeal of the Corn Laws that had protected the home producer at the expense of the hungry urban consumer, has fared better; redundant in its original function, it still provides many towns like Haddington (p. 237) with their largest covered space for public use. Leith has one of the finest, by Peddie and Kinnear, with a finely scultpured frieze (1860).

The trouble with useful monuments is that they may cease to be useful. Fettercairn commemorates Victoria and Albert's visit of 1861, and equally celebrates the entry of all and sundry to the little baronial town, with a pretty stone archway across the road. Edzell followed suit (in memory of the Earl and Countess of Dalhousie) in 1888. Their address of welcome is entirely convincing in its provincial rhetoric. They have no other purpose; long may they stand.

SCHOOLS

Education remained till 1872 a church responsibility, the parish schools being supplemented in town by the 'Society', 'Sessional' and 'Assembly' schools provided respectively by the Society for the Promotion of Christian Knowledge, by the collaboration of kirk sessions and (in areas of special need) by the General Assembly of the Church of Scotland. There were also the endowed schools, many of them in Grecian buildings of Georgian foundation. George Heriot's Hospital (begun in 1628) which itself became a school in 1885, had already used its financial prosperity for the public good by establishing throughout Edinburgh from 1835 twelve elementary schools under the management of the town council. All these buildings, of which the best preserved survivor is at the top of Easter Road, were charming designs by Alexander Black in the image of the Jacobean original. But the generally accepted style was gothic, in keeping with the general association of church and school. Such was the school of 1838 in Great Junction Street, Leith, founded and endowed by Dr Bell whose statue stands in a gothic niche on one of its flanks, though again it was administered by the city. Gothic too were the first of the 'normal' schools for adult education, like the original Stow College in Cowcaddens Street, Glasgow (1846) and the Mechanics' Institutes which provided lecture halls and libraries for evening study; a large one of these confronts the visitor on the fork of the southern entry to Brechin; it was endowed by Lord Panmure. The industrial or 'ragged' school, the sensible innovation of Sheriff Watson in Aberdeen and Thomas Guthrie in Edinburgh in the 'forties, made little contribution to the townscape; the Duchess of Atholl's Girls Industrial School at Dunkeld is an exception – a storybook gothic pile to which, though it is now a tea-room, the weathering of its soft stonework has given an aspect of hoary age [pl. 32d].

The Scottish Education Act of 1872, which made education compulsory for all children between five and fourteen and replaced the old parish system with that of school boards elected by the ratepayers, produced its own characteristic type of building. This was the board school, almost always a tall symmetrical block with two entrances – for boys one side, girls the other. Such schools have been the particular butt of recent educational campaigners, but it is hard to see the reason. In their own time they represented a victory for democratic enlightment, and expressed it in their design. Simple and ingenious in planning (they are seldom difficult to modernize internally), they brought prestige and even gaiety to the idea of public education. Each of Edinburgh's original board schools bore a roundel in a gentle della Robbia spirit (an allegorical figure of Education and a pupil) and the date and name of the school board responsible. The Stockbridge School by Sir Rowand Anderson (1876) exploits the large unit of the board school to create a major work of gothic street architecture. Other architects gave the drab streets colour with the newly available red and yellow sandstones from outside the city, and liveliness too, with Flemish crowsteps and central lanterns. The chief functional shortcoming of these schools today is not in themselves, but in the lack of green playground space round about, for the majority are on cramped, asphalted sites in the middle of congested housing areas, and the acquisition of more open space has never been considered.

PUBLIC HEALTH MEASURES

By the year of the Reform Bill (1832) all the more important town streets were numbered and paved, and many were lit by gas; its first appearance in Scotland was at a coppersmith's shop in Bridge Street, Kelso, in 1818. Glasgow had its main streets lit by gas in the same year, Edinburgh, Aberdeen and Dundee soon following. But 1832 was also the year of the first and most terrible of nineteenth-century cholera epidemics, when of 20,203 cases in Scotland more than half were fatal. The 'police' acts of 1833 and subsequent years required local authorities to see to water supply and drainage, but money was lacking and only in the face of the most urgent need did they take the initiative. Deficiencies in the public water supply were made up (at a price) by private companies, and Glasgow was the first town to recognize the need for a public service supply of unpolluted water from outside; Queen Victoria inaugurated the pipeline from Loch Katrine, thirty-four miles away, in 1859. As to sewage, Glasgow had a rudimentary Georgian system but the real problem (aggravated by a vast output of industrial effluent) arose after it had all gone into the Kelvin and the Clyde. Only in 1892 did the corporation embark on its first sewage processing project, with a works on the north bank of the befouled river between Dalmarnock and Rutherglen bridges. They showed more enterprise in their takeover of the city's whole gas supply from the many private gasworks in 1867.

Edinburgh's water supply was taken over by a public trust in 1869. The city's earlier sewage problems have already been mentioned (p. 112). By 1865 sewers had been laid on the lines of all streets and thereafter, by the happy accident of geography which placed it up-hill from an estuary rather than astride a river, it has calmly discharged most of its sewage into the Firth of Forth. A processing plant at Seafield is now under construction.

The rescue of the Victorian town from its own filth and the

public supply of water were both put on a formal basis by the
Public Health Act of 1867. This put mandatory powers and
government aid in the hands of local authorities, and also
required them to appoint Medical Officers of Health. In Edinburgh the job went to Dr H. D. Littlejohn, who had recently
published his *Report on the Sanitary Conditions of the City of
Edinburgh*. This in the Victorian sense of the term included
housing as well as sanitation, and in both respects it shows the
quantitative worsening of a situation already exposed in a
similar report in 1838. In a typical tenement at No. 8 Cowgate,
consisting of five storeys over shops, Dr Littlejohn found 38
families; 155 people, including 24 children under five, in a
total of 60 rooms. There were a W.C. and two sinks on first
floor level, where two families accounted for twelve of the rooms.

HOUSING CONDITIONS

There were two sources of supply for Victorian workers' housing,
the old and the new. In Edinburgh a large number of Georgian
artisans' flats still existed, and there are still many today. They
play their junior part in the great Georgian layout, and behind
the bland face which has greatly helped their survival, the
standard of accommodation (but not always of craftsmanship) is
of course lower than in the grander streets between which they
are interspersed. The flats are 'single ends', facing only one way.
In Cumberland Street (1822) there are generally four front doors
on each landing. In St Stephen Street (1825) there are often six,
the common stair being embedded in the middle so that the
fullest use is made of front and back walls for windows to light
the rooms. The stair tower to the back is sometimes seen in
Edinburgh, especially in the more vernacular parts of the south
side which reflect common Scottish practice, but was particularly
tenacious in Glasgow; the most celebrated example is seen at
the backs of the majestic tenements of Abbotsford Place (1825)
which were intended for middle class owners but soon broke up
into single room occupancy. For every better-off owner-occupier
who decided to go elsewhere, or who failed to materialize at all,
there was a handful of worse-off families ready to move in, and

150

often to sub-let a room to another family or a corner to a single lodger. Single room living was not always an economic necessity, but it was a way of life inherited from the rural housing from which many of the workers came.

The most shocking thing about these conditions is the slowness with which they improve. In 1861 27 per cent of Scotland's whole population lived in 'houses' of one room and another 38 per cent in those of two; the one-room cottage and the but-and-ben, or their urban equivalent. Fifty years later the combined total for both types was still very nearly 50 per cent and the census of 1951 showed that it had only been reduced to just under 30 per cent, the better areas being balanced by such figures as that of 85 per cent for Hutchesontown, which embraces the Gorbals.

THE NEW TENEMENT

For those who needed housing and could afford to buy or rent it in new buildings, from skilled artisan to clerk and lower salaried professional man, the choice lay between the different areas of tenement development on the edge of every town. These were built throughout the last forty years of the century (with hardly a break in the depression of the 'seventies which slowed down so many other kinds of investment), and wherever land values were high or sites were scarce, the tenement was universal. By 1900 few towns, even the smallest, were without their quota of at least one large, metropolitan-looking flatted block; some of the latest examples, built in 1897, are called 'Jubilee Buildings'. More typically, built up along indefinite lengths of street on the edges of larger places, they provide the most characteristic experience of Victorian townscape. Round Edinburgh they form an almost continuous ring, well built in the main, and regularly planned. Functionally, the main difference between these and their Georgian predecessors was the segregation of each type, according to status and ultimately cost, in distinct areas. Thus the working-class tenement proliferated along the main traffic routes to north and west (Easter Road and Leith Walk, Dalry Road and Fountainbridge), and the better sites at Marchmont (south of the Meadows) and Bruntsfield were developed for the middle-class owner, on much the same lines but in all respects to a higher standard. The king of tenement developers was James Steel, subsequently Lord Provost, who in the 'seventies built a large section of the cheerless artisan suburb of Dalry, and later acquired land from Col Learmonth's feuars on which he constructed most of the middle-class tenements of Comely Bank.

The finest of the Edinburgh tenements are noble in their own right. Concentrated round Bruntsfield Links to the west of the Meadows, they have the large scale splendour that can speak from a distance, with carefully composed elevations and majestic corner towers, sometimes of baronial outline. More usually these buildings confront not an open space, but each other, and such pains as were taken by their designers to avoid monotony and exploit the architectural quality of the type are in direct relation to the status of the area concerned. Apart from the intermittent wall-head chimneys which betray the juxtaposition of two long-fronted flats served by the same stair, their only elements are the windows. These are dominated by stone, and their uniform height transgresses the Georgian custom of reduction towards the top. A regular pattern of grouped windows and bay windows gives evidence of individual flats, but its effect overall is of remorseless verticality indefinitely prolonged, whether on the flat, up-hill or down dale. These are the fortresses, comfortable within but anonymous without, into which the mass of Edinburgh's middle class abdicated from participation in the city's townscape.

MODEL HOUSING

It is worth staying in Edinburgh (since the subject is better documented than in Glasgow or elsewhere) to look at the charitable and co-operative building agencies who were the other, though far smaller, suppliers of new housing. One of the earliest sources (1858) is the *Report of a Committee of the Working Classes of Edinburgh on the Present Overcrowded and Uncomfortable State of their Dwelling Houses*. Of Ashley Buildings (1849, since demolished), a warehouse-like tenement to the north of John

Knox's House, named after their reforming founder to whom (as the Earl of Shaftesbury) the Eros memorial was erected in Piccadilly Circus, the Committee's opinion was low; ill designed and built, it had already become a slum. Chalmers Buildings in Fountainbridge (*c.* 1853) earned their better opinion; the scheme's builder Mr Matheson named it after the famous minister who had led the Disruption of 1843 and whose tireless support of the principle of voluntary poor relief was based on his earlier experience in Glasgow. Its boldly inscribed gable still fronts the street, appropriately next to the gable and spire of the former Fountainbridge Free Church (unhappily neither building is likely to last much longer). Here for an annual rent of £6 10*s* a worker could get a kitchen, bedroom, scullery, coal cellar and water closet, besides the use of a communal drying green. The architect was Patrick Wilson, who will be heard of again in this field.

By this time also certain innovations had been introduced from the south, where Henry Roberts's tenement in Streatham Street, London (1849) had set and indeed still sets a remarkably high standard. The most notable was that of balcony access, which broke away from the unhygienic tyranny of the common stair; even the model plan put forward by the Working Classes Committee, and followed more or less closely in hundreds of speculative tenements, had followed the Georgian practice of ventilating the water closets straight on to the stair, and in tenements less well provided the stair itself became filthy; not until 1900 did the law require an outside window for the closet. Curiously this rule no longer holds, but the balcony survives – sometimes for access, always for baby-airing. Two of its earliest appearances in Edinburgh were at Rosemount Buildings, a hollow, brick-built square of three storeys with continuous access balconies round the inside, and Patriot Hall, Stockbridge; this is in the same red and white brick with similar fireproof detached stairs leading to balconies, but is only a half square, open to the north-west. Both developments date from about 1860.

CO-OPERATIVE HOUSING AND THE
FLATTED COTTAGE

These pioneer efforts were not followed in the official housing built under the City Improvement Acts of the 'sixties, admirable though this was in many respects; unfortunately it was its sheer architectural quality, commended elsewhere (p. 196) that put the rents beyond the reach of all but the most skilled and industrious worker. The motives for clearance were altruistic and so was the excellence of the officially sponsored design; not so the rents, which were simply those charged by the speculative builders. So the main effect of the scheme was to push the real problem elsewhere. Nevertheless it was its joint architect, David Cousin, who in a paper to the Architectural Institute of Scotland in 1861 drew attention to a valuable precedent for self-help, the workers' co-operative which in 1826 had built six tenements (now gone) in Canning Street, Causeway-side. In the same year the Revd Dr James Begg addressed a meeting to encourage the sale of shares in the Edinburgh Co-operative Building Society. In his book of 1866 *Happy Homes for Working Men and How to Get Them*, he explains that the purpose of the society was to break the landlord's monopoly; 'the houses are planned, built, purchased and tenanted by the working men'.

The Society did not build tenements. Low-rise artisan housing had already been pioneered by the Pilrig Model Dwellings Company with Patrick Wilson as its architect (1849). This semi-philanthropic venture, which like others of its kind paid a respectable dividend to its shareholders, had been coolly noticed by the Working Classes Committee; the water closets were outside the flats on both levels, for in fact this was a sort of tenement, though a low-rise one. The vital modification of this type was made by James Gowans, the remarkable railway contractor turned architect who was knighted for his working-class housing achievements, but is hardly less to be admired for his other works like the astonishing middle-class tenement of 1868 on the corner of Castle Terrace and Spittal Street; its townscape triumph is largely due to a quality which it expresses more strikingly than any other building in Britain – the joy and pride of working in stone, free from the professional inhibitions of the architect. He did however in 1857 employ an architect (Alexander MacGregor) at Rosebank Cottages, which were built for railway staff, and of them he said to the Royal Commission on Scottish Housing:

> The idea that I had, was to get working men into small self-contained houses, where they would have their own door to go in by, every room being independent of the others, having a door from the lobby for privacy, and having a little green attached to each house, and having everything arranged in a sanitary way, with the closets to the outer wall, and plenty of light about them; and those houses have been fairly successful. On one side were the entrances to the ground floor dwellings approached through small gardens; on the other, an elegant external stair in cast iron, at right angles to the terrace, led up to a short balcony giving access to a pair of dwellings on the first floor.

This was the clever compromise adopted by the Co-operative Building Society in 1861 for what are now called the 'Colonies' [pl. 27a] between Glenogle Road and the Water of Leith. The eleven parallel blocks and their upstairs-downstairs arrangement look back, as Elizabeth Filor has said, to the vernacular of the Georgian fisher-town. Their names demonstrate a fine combination of loyalties; Balmoral Place, Hugh Miller Place, Kemp Place (Miller and Kemp the type-figures of masons made good). Craft emblems carved on the gable keystones carry the message of the three-month builders' strike for shorter hours in 1861, when Sir Hugh Gilzean Reid of the *Edinburgh News* had urged just such a venture, and earned his name on the first of the rows, Reid Terrace. Yet in the *Builder* two years later it was reported that twenty-seven of the houses had been bought by an investor. So much, it may well be said, for the dream of the working-class owner-occupier. Originally sold for between £130 and £250, these houses now change hands at close on £10,000. Their value was in the lead they gave to similar organizations in the other major towns, and indeed to the cause of humane standards in publicly owned housing, when that came. A heavy premium was placed on speculative tenement building in 1910, another Royal Commission reported on Scottish Housing in 1917, and the Housing Act of the first Labour administration in 1924 changed the whole pattern of responsibility for providing housing for those who could not or would not get it for themselves. At least it did so in theory; in fact, it gave to local authorities a task with which, after a slow start, they have never caught up.

THE ARCHITECTURAL QUALITY OF THE GLASGOW TENEMENT

For all their bad reputation, Glasgow's tenements were and are finer than those of the capital. Edinburgh's long (and in this context unfortunate) affair with the bay (or bow) window may have been influenced by what Ruskin had said there (p. 138):

> You must surely all of you admit the delightfulness of a bow window; I can hardly fancy a room can be perfect without one. Now you have nothing to do but to resolve that every one of your principal rooms shall have a bow window, either large or small.

Glasgow did not embrace this idea so quickly, and from the 'fifties almost to the end of the century tenements were built whose prodigious length is modulated and civilized by nothing more than the bold grouping of windows and the continued use of simplified Georgian detail to emphasize some parts and merge others in the whole. Such are the blocks at the west end of Bath Street (*c.* 1860) and their late Victorian descendants in Pollock Street, Kingston (*c.* 1880). But it should also be noted that one of the most consummately detailed of all Victorian tenements, Walworth Terrace in Kent Road (1858) shows an early use of bay windows in Glasgow. They are used with cool intelligence, in pairs, bracketed out as oriels over a firm horizontal base. Their regular rhythm brings the wall to life, and into a new sort of relationship with the tall, six-light windows.

156

'GREEK' THOMSON

The partnership of wall and window as plane to plane, rather than their opposition as solid to void, is the keynote of much of Glasgow's Victorian and Edwardian architecture. Alexander 'Greek' Thomson was fascinated by it. He reduced the finality of the wall surface by cutting back into it, sometimes with fine punched out ornament and sometimes more deeply, to discover part or whole of a structural member hidden within (a refinement in the top floor windows at Walworth terrace which probably owes something to his example). His tenement masterpiece is Queen's Park Terrace in Eglinton Street (c. 1857), but it is to his grander terrace houses and to their contemporaries that we must now turn.

All of Thomson's terraces are based on the theme of the flat, polished surface of Giffnock stone (a material that has not lasted well, but that is another story). Great Western is the most famous, but its achievement is backward-looking in that it says the last word on the subject of the neo-classic terrace front as it had been understood. His Moray Place (1857), charmingly monkey-puzzled in the southern suburb of Strathbungo, is likewise a final statement on that subject as he himself saw it – walls, doors and windows subjected to the discipline of the Greek *stoa*, the two-storeyed flat colonnade that lined the classical market place. Walmer Crescent (1857) and Westbourne Terrace (1871, pl. 26b) are brilliant reconciliations between his own obsessive classicism and the growing fashion for the projecting bay.

Walmer Crescent, with its square projections of two storeys, is comparable with the deft but much fussier treatment of Peddie and Kinnear's terrace at Drumsheugh Gardens in Edinburgh (1878). Most of the other terraces of Edinburgh's west end, cramped perhaps by the preconceived layout, are more in the nature of Georgian postscript than pure Victorian townscape. It was to the west end of Glasgow that the latter came into its own, each development characterized by a stunning confidence only equalled by its stylistic logic and discipline. At Queen's

Crescent (1840) John Bryce does it by nothing more than a grand layout, supported by competent detail which is now being progressively enfeebled with 'masonry paint'. Thomson's terraces excepted, the later Victorian developments are superbly Italian, culminating in the infinitely prolonged Venetian arcades of J. T. Rochead's Grosvenor Terrace (1855).

CHARLES WILSON ON WOODLANDS HILL

No experience in Scottish High Victorian townscape is matched, however, by that of Woodlands Hill, the domestic masterpiece of Charles Wilson [pl. 28]. His also, in the following year, are the triple Italian towers of the former Free Church College which announce it to approaching visitors to the west of Sauchiehall Street. The prelude, on the lower contours, is a series of early Victorian terraces strung out rather in the Bath manner, and mostly the work of other architects. Then between them an arduous climb on to the plateau, up the stone stairway overlooked by the vast scale of the College. Park Circus, once reached, turns out to be a pair of huge, inward-facing crescents confronting each other through trees; except that the centrepiece of the opposite side is flat and square between its curved wings. A similar combination of grace and dignity is seen in the detail, which is uniform from end to end, and totally subservient (for all its richness) to the effect of the whole. But this hill-top composition looks outward too. Through the triumphal westward exit between the crescents you can walk out on to the platform that overlooks Woodlands Park, laid out by Joseph Paxton who was Wilson's collaborator on the scheme, and thence descend into the trees. Here the architectural crown of the hill (it is Wilson's own word) looks down on you, but in a totally different guise; not now the classical but the romantic face of the High Victorian – bay windows, dormers and iron-crested mansards leaping into the air. This is Park Terrace, the obverse of the Circus, round whose concavity it forms a bold convexity. Even Glasgow today does not live in this style, and it is hard to be censorious of the haphazard and sometimes seedy conversions that have enabled it to survive, if not unscathed. Though inevitably destined for office and hotel use, it now has a life-line in the shape of a town-scheme (the first to have been started in Scotland) providing a trickle of grants towards essential restoration work (p. 203).

VILLA DEVELOPMENTS

The self-contained retreats of the great figures of Victorian industry and commerce – veritable country houses sheltered by miniature parks – are outside the scope of townscape. Moreover any mention of them, as for instance of the palaces of the jute barons once strung out along Tayside from Dundee to Broughty Ferry (but few of them destined to survive for more than a century) must be by way of obituary. A handful may still be seen round each of these towns of great industrial growth, swamped by the sort of reality from which they were once a refuge. Naked and forlorn, they do duty more or less cheerfully as road-houses or welfare centres.

Multiple villa developments however are a real part of the Victorian townscape, evolving from the Georgian terrace to the detached and semi-detached villas such as line Inverleith Row in Edinburgh (from 1823); then to the sort of architectural diversity seen in the nearby district of Trinity, and finally to the Victorian individualism of Murrayfield and Merchiston. What they and their like have in common, though this becomes increasingly less obvious, is that they were planned; garden plots and villa sites were laid out, and the whole of each development was feudally controlled, on a system precisely similar to that which had applied to a typical Georgian scheme. The difference of course is in character. In a formal Georgian layout you can immediately see where you are, but in a Victorian suburb (the word now begins to imply a dilution of urban character) the intention seems just the opposite; you may well enjoy a walk between the trees along a sinuous road, and the houses half hidden behind them, but you may find it difficult to find the house to which you have been invited. In Edinburgh the gridiron layout died hard; the Grange, for example, lines up most of its villas in time honoured fashion. And everywhere the smaller terraced house remained in demand till the end of the century; a compromise that made it possible to live economically in a good neighbourhood, with bay windows, porches and gables making up for the loss of individuality. Eskbank, to the west of Dalkeith, is typical, feued from about 1840 in villa plots from the little estate of the Georgian house which still stands in the middle. The higher the status of each villa, the more curvaceous is the road that serves it, and the less likely you are to glimpse it among its now mature trees. But adjoining this select area, and even within it, the little bay-windowed terraces enjoy its 'good address' and other amenities.

GLASS

Two great advances in building technology came to the fore in Queen Victoria's reign, each affecting the other; the iron or steel beam that could span wide openings, and the glass with which the latter could be filled. Both tend to be camouflaged by the Victorian fondness for historical styles whose original authors had not known either of these devices, and it was generally in buildings erected for new purposes that technological progress was exploited and expressed.

Until 1845 the use and manufacture of glass had been influenced not only by style but by statute. In that year the United Kingdom tax on glass, which doubled its prime cost and doubled it yet again in the period of the Napoleonic war, was finally removed. *Crown* glass (the spun disc cut into rectangles) had been used for virtually all Georgian windows because of its natural clarity, and a smoothness and brilliance that needed no polishing. Even the 'defect' of its slight curvature was put to advantage; each of the small units of a Georgian window, well matched with those of the wall, took on a life of its own thanks to the slight bow which was invariably placed outwards, partly no doubt to resist the wind pressure. *Broad* glass (the blown cylinder slit open, unrolled and polished) was ousted by crown quite early in the eighteenth century but was steadily improved; in 1778, the year after the foundation of the famous glassworks that gave Dumbarton its landmark of three bottle-shaped

Regions

	Counties (Former)
	Regions (under the Local Government (Scotland) Act 1973.)
■	Royal Burghs

ORKNEY & SHETLAND

Kirkwall 1486 ■

(ISLANDS AREA)

WESTERN ISLES

(ISLANDS AREA)

CAITHNESS

SUTHERLAND

HIGHLAND

ROSS & CROMARTY

NAIRN   MORAY

BANFF

ABERDEEN

GRAMPIAN

INVERNESS

KINCARDINE

ANGUS

TAYSIDE

PERTH

ARGYLL

CENTRAL

K

FIFE

C   FIFE

DUNBARTON

STIRLING

EAST LOTHIAN

LOTHIAN

STRATHCLYDE

RENFREW

W   MIDLOTHIAN

BUTE

LANARK

BERWICK

PEEBLES

SELKIRK

BORDERS

AYR

ROXBURGH

DUMFRIES

DUMFRIES & GALLOWAY

KIRKCUDBRIGHT

WIGTOWN

C = CLACKMANNAN
K = KINROSS
W = WEST LOTHIAN

V. NEW TOWNS OF THE 18TH AND 19TH CENTURIES

18 **(a)** Gifford: from the cross to the church (p.94). **(b)** Ormiston: the main street and cross (p.95). *New Towns in Argyll.* **(c)** Inveraray before the demolition of the steeple (p.92). **(d)** Lochgilphead, founded in 1822, from the loch.

19 *Two cotton villages of 1785.* **(a)** Deanston, still in industrial use, with newer housing (p.105). **(b)** Blantyre: the counting house of the ruined mill, and Livingstone's tenement (p.105). *Geometrically planned towns.* **(c)** Thurso (p.98); **(d)** Newcastleton (p.98); **(e)** Ardrossan (p.94).

a

b

20 (a) New Lanark on the Clyde (p.106). (b) Kenmore at the gate of Taymouth Castle (p.100).

a

b

VI. THE EARLY 19TH CENTURY

21 Perth: **(a)** The South Inch, with Marshall Place and the old Waterworks; Kinnoull Hill in the background (p.128). **(b)** The entry over Smeaton's bridge of 1766 (p.19) with the domed Marshall Monument of 1824 and the late 18th century houses of Charlotte Street.

22 (a) Dundee: Reform Street, terminated by the High School of the same date (p.132). **(b)** Glasgow: Carlton Place; the westward of the two terraces between which the suspension bridge of 1851 crosses the Clyde (p.123).

23 Edinburgh: (a) Roman magnificence in Moray Place (p.113); (b) Grecian pomp in St Bernard's Crescent (p.114); (c) Dollar Academy by Playfair, 1818, with adjoining villas. (d) Stirling: Allan Park; an early development of detached and semi-detached houses, about 1810 (e) Hawick, on the Teviot; Dickson & Laing's water-powered mill was established in 1811. (f) Kirkintilloch: chimney-gabled workers' houses (p.71).

a

b

24 Edinburgh: (a) Princes Street, with the Royal Scottish Academy, Scott Monument (p.118) and North British Hotel (p.169); (b) Waterloo Place, the eastward extension of Princes Street, with the Nelson Monument and the National Monument (p.117).

a

b

25 (a) Edinburgh: down St Vincent Street, past the entry of Great King Street to St Stephen's Church (p.111). **(b)** Montrose: the Museum and Panmure Terrace, with footbridge leading past the Parish Church to High Street (pp.139-40).

VII. THE VICTORIAN TOWN

26 (a) Rutherglen Town Hall and High Street (p.145). *Glasgow; development and redevelopment.* **(b)** Westbourne Terrace (p.157); **(c)** the 'Hatrack' in St Vincent Street, with surviving Georgian neighbour demolished in 1974 (p.164).

27 **(a)** Edinburgh: the 'Colonies', Glenogle Road (p.155). **(b)** Glasgow: demolition of tenements with rear stair towers in the Gorbals (p.124). Stirling: **(c)** the palace-fronted Royal Bank of Scotland (p.140); **(d)** the cemetry near the Castle. Inverness: **(e)** late Victorian shop in Academy Street; **(f)** the Market (p.165).

28 Glasgow; Woodlands Hill. (a) the approach, with Park Church to left and Trinity College to right; (b) Park Circus, looking west; (c) the view from Park Terrace westward to the University of 1866 and towered Library of 1968 (p.158).

opposite

VIII. THE 20TH CENTURY

29 *Edwardian Commerce*. (a) Edinburgh; Forsyth's in Princes Street (p.173); (b) a wall of painted advertisements in Elgin. *Housing*. (c) high-rise at Hutchesontown-Gorbals (p.190); (d) low-rise at Torryburn (p.189). *Modern structure in Edinburgh offices* (p.21). (e) pre-cast wall sections at Argyle House, 1965; (f) curtain wall at the Standard Life extension, 1962, both by Michael Laird.

a

b

c

d

e

f

30 (a) Linlithgow: shops and houses at the town centre (p.181). (b) Glasgow: St Francis' School extension, Charlotte Street (p.188) beyond the McLennan Arch (p.76).

IX. CONSERVATION

31 Edinburgh: **(a)** St Mary's Street; the entry from the Canongate (p.196) and **(b)** the West Bow (p.57); **(c)** Victoria Terrace and West Bow (pp.194-5).

32 (a) Edinburgh: the old town skyline from Princes Street; from left, the domes of the Bank of Scotland (p.138), the twin towers of the Assembly Hall (p.119), the spire of St John's Tolbooth Church (p.140) and Ramsay Garden (p.15). (b) Thurso (p.204). (c) Montrose Supermarket (p.244). (d) Dunkeld (p.200): the Cross and entry to Cathedral Street, with the Industrial School to right (p.148). (e) Dysart: new housing round the Tolbooth (p.205).

kilns, the Royal Society for the Encouragement of Arts and Manufactures awarded a prize for the making of clear glass sheets whose size exceeded 30 ×26 inches – far greater than the maximum obtainable from crown – at Stourbridge. Yet its comeback as far as windows were concerned was delayed by the simple fact that it was thicker. Glass was taxed not by area but by weight. Thus crown, despite the wastage involved in the bulls-eye centre and round the edges of the disc, continued to dominate the market, and the shops and houses of British towns retained their sparkling small-paned image, till the tax was removed in 1845. The manufacture of sheet glass had already been perfected by Chance of Birmingham in 1832, and they provided the glazing for Paxton's huge conservatories; first at Chatsworth in 1839 and then at the Crystal Palace for the 1851 Exhibition. By coincidence it was in the latter year that the window tax was abolished. Introduced in England in 1695 and extended to Scotland under the Union, this had virtually been a rule-of-thumb tax on houses, with much less influence on their design than is sometimes supposed; the number of dummy windows on Georgian buildings is due to the need to maintain external regularity without over-lighting the interior. It was the lifting of the glass tax that decisively changed glazing practice. From the 'fifties onwards, one pane to one sash became the rule for new houses, while the astragals (glazing bars) began to disappear even from existing Georgian ones.

Scotland has its spectacular feats of glazing, most notably in Glasgow. The Kibble Palace conservatory with its curved eaves was built in England about 1863 and then re-erected ten years later at the Botanic Gardens, but as additions to the townscape proper, embracing complex functions of transport and distribution under sheltering canopies, the stations and market halls are more significant. In 1878 James Carsewell designed the most graceful of Britain's glazed train sheds at Queen Street station with a span of 52 m, and Sir John Fowler of Covent Garden fame collaborated with James Blair at St Enoch which has a main span of 60 m (1875). The florid façade of the fish market by the river conceals a vast hall whose top glazing is supported on slim iron columns (1873).

COMMERCIAL ARCHITECTURE IN GLASGOW

Glass and iron, glass and stone; these are the themes of the warehouses, shops and offices that jostled first the original houses, then each other, along the frontages of Glasgow's Georgian gridiron. Of all of them the most deservedly famous is the 'Iron Building' of 1855, (Gardner's furniture shop and warehouse, as it still is) in Jamaica Street, the work of an ideally balanced partnership of engineer (R. McConnel) and architect (John Baird). John Honeyman's Ca d'Oro building, less refined in structure but more obviously designed for architectural – and commercial – effect in the rollicking arcades and circles of its iron external frame, was originally a furniture warehouse too (1872). It stands at the corner of Gordon and Union Streets, and in each of these streets 'Greek' Thomson exploits the possibilities of another new type, the speculative office block. Both the Grosvernor Buildings and the Egyptian Halls (1859 and 1871) are mounted on a row of ground-floor shops whose long facia and cornice (now entirely distorted by new and deeper facias) act as a base line for two different solutions to the extraordinary problem Thomson set himself; how to give everything its own clear identity and still relate it to the whole – each bay to the whole length, each storey to the next one and ultimately to the full height. The effect is that of a sculptural drama built up on the prosaic theme of a wall pierced with rows of windows. The means are architectonic, that is to say the wall is transformed into a complex structural system with the aid of his whole far-fetched but basically classical vocabulary. The top storey or eaves-gallery of the Egyptian Halls, his latest surviving office building, is in fact completely structural – a free-standing stumpy colonnade with the windows set back behind.

The group known as the Buck's Head Building (1849) began with his first major work, and this states and solves the problem far more simply. The first and second floors of the Dunlop Street frontage are united by tall pilasters; by no means a new idea, for it goes back to the theme of the old town-house (p. 75).

What is new, however, is that by the time they reach the second floor these pilasters, so plain that they look like an interrupted wall, stand free once again, with only glass between them. With the second phase (1863) Thomson swept round the corner into Argyle Street, and on these same two levels he deputed the whole structural theme (though not the whole load) to pencil-thin iron columns standing forward from the main stone piers. They spread into florid capitals and then dissolve into intricate cresting, but the masonry pushes up behind them to reappear in a massive eaves-gallery and attic.

It was the earlier theme, featuring the integration of the upper storeys, that was finally to re-emerge in Glasgow, especially in the work of Sir John James Burnet, as part of the mainstream of the international architecture of commerce. Burnet also developed, but with an ease that suggests the penthouse flat rather than the rooms full of toiling clerks, the motif of the eaves-gallery. Yet Thomson happily remains, despite a handful of buildings designed under his influence in Dundee, Edinburgh, Perth and Inverness, an isolated prodigy. Virtually everything was tried in Glasgow in this great age when architecture was the very coin of commercial prestige, but seldom without a solid backing of scholarship, and never without the desire to spend money in putting on the best possible show on each site. Adaptations of the Italian palace theme were bolder than in Edinburgh and were sooner followed, in this city where conformity was not of critical importance, by brilliant improvisations in other styles. It would be wrong to suggest that complexity became a criterion of excellence. It was more a matter of rivalry and contrast, and simplicity also had its say. Burnet's father had designed the French gothic Stock Exchange and thus broken the classical ice at the head of Buchanan Street (1875, pl. 37c). He himself could revert to the cool, bare classicism of the Athenaeum round the corner in St George's Place (1886, now the College of Dramatic Art) and then once again join in the scholarly free-for-all with the astounding red sandstone Charing Cross Mansions, at once huge, intricate and charming, the improvisation on French themes with which he turns in a generous curve from Sauchiehall Street into St George's Road (1891).

The dominant late Victorian motifs of gable and corner tower are not of course peculiar to Glasgow, but here they developed as nowhere else, and always with an eye to their culmination on the skyline. Gables suited the narrow frontages of new office buildings on the city's Georgian sites, but one of Glasgow's special tricks was to recess the centre of such a front and then push out a tall bay window or oriel into the gap. It was pioneered by Burnet and John Campbell in 1891 with their new Athenaeum at 191 Buchanan Street. In James Salmon's famous ten-storey 'Hatrack' (1899) at 144 St Vincent Street the bay window, pressing forward to catch the light, supplants the gable completely; in fact this is a cluster of three bays, the centre one rising behind the other two to crown the whole frontage with the hooked dormers that give the building its name [pl. 26c]. Likewise there are dozens of skilfully treated corner towers to show that when Charles Rennie Mackintosh designed the Glasgow Herald tower in Mitchell Street (1893) he was not raising his standard in an architectural desert; carried by a scholarly and adventurous tradition, he was able to go beyond it – and also beyond the art nouveau with which his reputation is often too closely associated. His winning design for the School of Art (1896) achieved the one feat of which his older contemporaries were never quite capable – he turned his back on style for style's sake and rediscovered the abstract values latent in materials, construction and function. Late Victorian to the east, Edwardian to the west, the School is timelessly modern.

ARCADES AND SHOPS

For many people it is the Victorian shop that conveys the most real experience of the townscape of that period. The supreme examples are the big emporia like James Smith's store for Trèron in Sauchiehall Street (*c.* 1860), some having the multistorey interiors (galleried round a covered light-well) like that of Wylie and Lochhead in Buchanan Street. Its Edinburgh counterpart is William Hamilton Beattie's masterpiece of 1893 at Jenners whose exterior is equally impressive, its renaissance opulence humanized by caryatid figures whom it is easy to cast in the role of dutiful providers, furnishing the good things of the world to be viewed, selected and placed on charge account. In a sense these stores are great covered markets, but it was also possible – and still is – to bring a multiplicity of separate shops under the single roof of an indoor street. Glasgow's Argyll Arcade (1827) is light and airy Georgian by John Baird of 'Iron Building' fame, though its shops without exception have been garishly altered. The Inverness Arcade (1870, pl. 27f) is particularly interesting because it is based on an area already used as a stock market since 1720. This was roofed over as a market hall and two butchers still have their permanent stalls there, while four dealers in fish (three fishmongers and one seller of live specimens) have theirs in the fishmarket built to adjoin it. The new Arcade makes its way into the main hall from Academy Street, where it is entered through the charming triple arcade opposite the station. There are also narrow pedestrian links with Church Street and Union Street, and a shop-lined walk was later formed to join up with Queensgate.

The Inverness Arcade seems to have been financed and managed by shareholders in partnership with the town council. That at Stirling (1878) was only vicariously linked with the local authority. Built as a private investment by Councillor William Crawford, on plots of ground he had gradually acquired between Murray Place and King Street, it was known for some time as Crawford's Arcade, but the splendid theatre at its centre was grandly if not quite properly titled 'The Town Hall'. At the Murray Place end the development includes the former Arcade Hotel, and the King Street entry has a commercial frontage in a similar manner, which its architect John McLean described as the 'Tuileries Style'. Its shop fronts and internal fenestration are much more ambitious than those at Inverness, and another point of difference is that for all its private ownership it has always been virtually a public street, with lighting provided by the Council. Owned and managed collectively by the members of the 'Arcade Association', it is still open twenty-four hours a day.

The design of the typical Victorian shop was subject to more constraints and more careful thought than is sometimes imagined. There was of course the limitation imposed by the available size of glass for the display windows; the huge sheets to which we are accustomed were hardly available before the 'nineties, and the regular intervals between the upright members of earlier shopfronts are a guide to the maximum widths available at the time of building. Such fronts were mass-produced in stone, with moulded mullions whose profile was continued round the top of each window. Modular shopfronts were also made in cast iron or wood. All of these shopfronts followed a general design whose purpose was to make the most of the available daylight [pl. 27e]; a window much taller than was strictly needed for display (its upper part acting as a clear-storey to light the body of the shop) and very often also more glazing under the window, or in the pavement itself, to give some light to the basement. A lettered facia ran along the head, and often matched that of the next door shop, as did the other finishings. This very generous height, incorporating three different lighting functions, is largely the result of the way in which such fronts had first been formed, as adjuncts to Georgian houses. When shops were built out over their front areas, their height included not only that of the original 'ground' floor but also the height by which the basement storey came up above pavement level.

Shopfronts are often criticized, especially when they have been added in this way, for the contradiction between their wide-span openings and the more solid masonry above; from the 'fifties onwards a clear opening of up to 9 m. (a generous Georgian house-width) could be spanned by an arched girder of cast iron. Modern shopfronts perform feats of support which are so much more startling that it is rather a surprise to see an occasional conscious attempt to minimize the effect of the wide lintel. One such attempt was made by MacGibbon and Ross at 92 George Street, Edinburgh (1879), where the lintel is interrupted by a succession of 'beam ends' which imply intermediate support even though they do not actually give it.

Today's shops and pubs are largely, by force of fashion rather than convenience, independent of natural light, and deep facias have clamped down on the airy clear-storey windows of many a

Victorian frontage. Hundreds of old shops survive and are increasingly enjoyed for their sensible as well as their ornamental features. But the majority are only shells. An occasional set of heavy wooden shutters (perhaps like some in Edinburgh's Victoria Street and Grassmarket they slide up like sashes from under the window); some mahogany-stained fittings in one or two of the more conservative minded shops (publicans and chemists have set the best example); these, and a shop-sign here and there, are the only reminders of the intricate fabric of Victorian life that filled and overflowed from these shops so that, for example, it was quite usual for every square foot of a commercial frontage to be covered with painted advertisements [pl. 29b]. With houses it is the same. Their plate glass windows were not made to look out so blankly as they do today, for in their time they were three parts filled with curtains and blinds and of course with potted plants.

HOSPITALITY

Except for a few lucky churches and rather more numerous shops, the pubs are our liveliest inheritance from the age before 1914. Like the churches, they offered – and continue to offer – an escape from the realities of wretched housing. Others are workplace pubs where, if you go in for a mid-day or early evening drink, you find yourself surrounded by men (yes, men only please, unless there is a little sitting-room set aside for ladies) of a particular occupation; postmen, for example, at the Guildford Arms in West Register Street, the far eastern end of the hospitable territory behind Princes Street. Immensely lofty, the single bar is crowned with a Jacobean ceiling that would not shame a baronial castle. Beneath it a counter and bottle-laden gantry of real or simulated mahogany, a brass rail for bar-propping feet, new plastic covered seats and a durable floor. The exterior promised all this, its windows not yet having been blocked with the simulated bottle-glass beloved of the brewery 'bar treatment' specialists; their tendency is to sever all connexion between inside and outside of a pub so that it ceases (in spite of bar lunches and carpets) to be the

167

place it was – a privileged indoor extension of the townscape.

The Guildford is an Edwardian pub; so is the famous Abbotsford in Rose Street (1902). Still going west, there is only one bar of palatial 'Victorian' character which is actually Victorian in date – and pretty late at that; the Kenilworth, whose tall frontage and tiled, palmy interior take up two storeys of one of the original Georgian houses (1893–9). The typical earlier Victorian bar, like the Georgian one, was simply a shop made over for drinking; Scott's at the far end of the street, though considerably refitted, is a fair example. Similar investigations elsewhere would confirm that the palace-pub is a late comer on the scene. Indeed outside Edinburgh the Edwardian pub is more often recognizable by its art nouveau detail, or what the modern bar-fitter has left of it. Least touched of all, but probably because it is under sentence of demolition for road-widening, is the Black Bull in Dalkeith. The Bull in Paisley has recently been dubiously up-dated 'in character', and so has the Crown in Bo'ness, though its exterior is still complete. Glasgow has a dozen of the finest quality, all vilely mutilated.

Round the corner from the Guildford is the Café Royal, surely a Victorian pub if ever there was one. But it is deceptive; designed in 1862 as a speculative block with ground floor showrooms for gas and sanitary fittings, it soon found a role to suit its festive image and opened in the following year as the Cafe Royal Hotel, with two storeys of richly finished public rooms, one more for bedrooms and finally, for the servants' garrets, a riotous Parisian mansard that originally boasted a cast-iron crest. The present public bar, certainly one of the finest in Scotland, was barely used as such before the end of the century. Its first architect, Robert Paterson, was later to design another hotel, the Windsor at 100 Princes Street (now a club); or rather he was to give the existing Georgian houses some grand rooms and an elaborate new frontage. Many a New Town house had been less drastically made over for hotel use, including the Roxburghe in Charlotte Square and even the great centre house on the north side. But by this time it was necessary to compete against the Victorian giants.

It was in the 'seventies that the grand hotels made their

appearance, impressing the visitor by sheer size, by serried ranks of complex palatial windows and by the promise of a variety of great public spaces within. Hotels like the Trossachs of 1852, with its famous turrets and candle-snuffer roofs, had already played at being country chateaux. Now it was the turn of the resort towns and their environs, for townspeople on holiday wanted the best of both worlds, touring from a comfortable centre. The eminently respectable hydropathic institutions (the taking of water being a blameless pretext for a holiday in their spartan halls) reared up in the wake of the hydraulic analyst. 1875 saw the building of two great hydros; the symmetrical, clock-towered institution above Dunblane with rooms for 200 guests and a recreation hall forty yards long, designed by Peddie and Kinnear, and Andrew Heiton's turreted masterpiece (now known as the Atholl Palace) beetling over the heights of the southern entrance to Pitlochry – the finest curtain raiser to any Scottish town. The baronial Marine at North Berwick was built in the same year (p. 172).

These were the rural resorts brought into easy reach by the railway. In the two distributor cities of Edinburgh and Glasgow there was bitter rivalry (as also in the very speed of transit from London) between the North British and Caledonian Railways. In Glasgow the former played first, with the conservative adaptation of houses on the north side of George Square; to be utterly beaten by the most princely of all station hotels surviving in that use, Sir Rowand Anderson's Central (1884). Many late Victorian buildings are equally confident – few so large, or architecturally so well educated. In Edinburgh the rivals made their entries at opposite ends of Princes Street, and both took some time over announcing the fact. The North British led off in expert but horrible fashion, Rowand Anderson losing the competition of 1895 to William Hamilton Beattie, the architect of Jenners' store. The horror resides not so much in itself, or indeed in its visual relation to the rest of the city (it is now as much a part of the customary landscape as Salisbury Crags), as in the combination of the two; standing at the hinge of Old and New Towns, it is coarse and obstructive at once – a caricature of Scots aggression which belies its internal calm and excellence [pl. 24a]. Peddie and Kinnear's Caledonian Station Hotel, rushed up so as to be ready in the same year of 1903, is relatively cool despite the red Dumfries-shire sandstone which gives a welcoming impression even if it is alien to Edinburgh. Entering at the north end (as if to the now defunct station) you are drawn up the easy stair to the long dining-room behind those anonymous, equivocal windows of the east face. Edinburgh, with its strange conspiracy of man and nature, lies open to view outside.

VIII. THE TWENTIETH CENTURY

What has the twentieth century contributed to Scottish towns? New powers of destruction certainly – but also of survival. A lot of rubbish undeniably, but enough good work to show that it can be done. In new building the final abandonment of the restraints and conventions that had hitherto governed the townscape has been followed by the slow emergence of new principles and the conscious revival of old ones.

More alarming than our heavy loss of urban architecture has been our usual inability to replace it well. It is reasonable to be shocked by any unnecessary losses, and we have recently learned ways of averting them; these are discussed in the final chapter. But we tend to forget that one of the blessings of progress has been the ability to adapt the existing urban fabric for new use. Hundreds of old towns, and the buildings within them, have been made over for different ways of life, thanks to the almost invisible infrastructure of public utilities begun in the nineteenth century and vastly improved (though in some respects still primitive) in the twentieth. Thus some people are able to enjoy the extraordinary luxury of living simultaneously in the past and the present – in old towns with all modern conveniences. Outside these preserved and interesting areas, the rest of life goes on in those territories of specialized use that form, in point of quantity, our century's main contribution to the townscape.

Power lines, water and drainage can all be slipped into and under the old fabric without showing. The ugly trail of telephone wires has almost disappeared from the scene and television aerials will doubtless follow. With modern road transport, however, it is another story. Cars, trucks and buses (until such time as they run out of fuel) have confirmed the dominance of towns, putting everything within their reach – and the towns themselves within reach of everybody. They are immensely flexible and convenient in use, and have come to the rescue of isolated places. But road transport has produced these limited benefits on its own very severe terms. Using existing roads and streets, it has changed their character and their very purpose. Streets that once united the buildings and activities on each side now make way for a stream of traffic which has the very opposite effect, keeping them apart both functionally and visually. Asphalt has taken the place of stone setts and the parked car has supplanted the market booth.

EDWARDIAN ESCAPE

But this is to anticipate the present situation. The Edwardian age with which the century begins, when the West Highland Railway reached Mallaig and the Lusitania was building at John Brown's Clydebank shipyard, was for those who could afford it a time of up-and-away, of escape into a sort of long vacation after the arduous Victorian term. But townscape? This was not what the escaping Edwardian was after, and the development of rural and seaside resorts followed what was by now an established suburban pattern. A good example is North Berwick, which had been a popular seaside resort since the early nineteenth century. In the words of the *New Statistical Account*,

> The geniality of summer and autumn is amply attested in the crowded influx of strangers for the enjoyment of sea bathing and perambulation among the beautiful scenery around.

Outside the old centre, which took like a duck to its new function, there are the long terraces (facing sea or one minute to sea) for those of modest means; and further out a great hierarchy of villas, from the grandest, well insulated by trees on their points of vantage, to the ever smaller ones crowding into the spaces between. Of a similar family of hotels, the eldest and largest is the Marine on the Edinburgh side of the town, its prosperous bulk combining the interest of advertisement with that of sea-viewing bedroom windows. Splendid hotels continued to spring up in highland towns and villages and these, developing the accepted image of dour frontage and romantic silhouette already established by their Victorian predecessors, are the most successful as well as the most typical Edwardian gift to the Scottish townscape; thus the Royal Hotel closes the view down the main street at Tain, and the villages of Aberfeldy, Birnam and Strathpeffer now owe most of their character to the architecture of tourism. So does the town centre of Inverness (p. 239), which offers the most complete spectacle of late Victorian and Edwardian townscape, thanks to its combined roles of highland capital and important staging post for the railborne traveller. He is shunted backwards into the clean and tranquil glass shed of the station, whence he may step into the finest (as internally it is still) of all station hotels, with its welcoming imperial staircase, huge trunks and rug-straps waiting in his room. The morning architecture of Union Street just across the square is masculine and (allowing for utter self-confidence) unaffected. At No. 18 Mr Ogston, chemist and perfumer, fitly greets him with a shop window whose angle is marked with a slim crystal column. This is indifferent architecture but consummate townscape, owing its meaning to the importance of Inverness as a regional centre as well as a tourist base.

THE EDWARDIAN IN BUSINESS –

In large towns, though more fragmentarily, the themes of leisure and prerogative are no less dominant, the genius of the age being embodied in the architecture of Sir John James Burnet. Kodak House in Kingsway, London (1910) is his most celebrated building, but his Scottish works like Forsyths in Edinburgh [pl. 29a] are a fine expression of the grandeur of Edwardian commerce. In contrast to the discreet adaptations of Italian palace fronts and the richly repetitive façades of earlier days, these are brilliantly and flamboyantly alive. The new technology of the metal frame, the concrete floor and the passenger lift is employed not only to raise a building to unimagined heights (often with the romantic implication of far prospects from

garret window or gallery) but to emancipate from their traditional architectonic roles the classical members with which
Burnet clothed the frame. Nor did any designer save Lutyens
have a better sense of the small scale detail with which these
great structures were relieved and made charming. Although by
our visual conventions of townscape they were presumptuous
in the highest degree, showing particular contempt for anything
like an established wall head level, these Edwardian giants
command our envious admiration for their sheet confidence,
and many of them (including Burnet's) for their architectural
mastery as well. As to their part in the townscape, they suited
the Edwardians who walked tall on the hard-won plateau (as
they believed) of human progress. Except for blatant sabotage
such as was committed by the redevelopment of one of the end
pavilions of Glasgow's Carlton Place, time and use have brought
their acceptance. Nor is the interest of these buildings always
limited to their fronts. Frequently their rear elevations, looking
on to lanes and light wells, have a satisfying functional quality
untrammelled by the demands of prestige and display. The
glazed-brick, bay-windowed backs of Lion Chambers in Hope
Street and the Northern Insurance Building at 84 to 94 St
Vincent Street are well known (1905 and 1908); both are in
Glasgow, and the former is the city's first building to be framed,
as it was also walled, in reinforced concrete. The back of Burnet's
Professional and Civil Service Supply Association, the gigantic
store at 80 George Street, Edinburgh (1905) is equally remarkable
in its exploitation of the fully glazed curtain wall.

— AND AT EASE

Of the late Victorian and Edwardian architecture of urban
leisure, Glasgow's supreme example is Miss Cranston's famous
series of tea-rooms. The only complete exterior is now that of
her Buchanan Street establishment (p. 236), (since acquired by the
Clydesdale Bank); a lovely French Renaissance gable front
gaily striped like a cake, in soft pink and cream sandstone.
Again the high standard of detail gives the lie to those who
would call this an age of architectural debasement. It is the

work of Sir George Washington Browne in 1896, not of Mackintosh, only one of whose Cranston tea-rooms survives – the eponymous Willow in Sauchiehall Street (1904) – and this sadly truncated as part of Daly's store. But it should be remembered that the high academic tradition of Glasgow's architecture, a tradition in which Mackintosh himself was proficient, was part of what enabled him to explore and understand the possibilities of historic style, and then devise a style to transcend it. His Glasgow Art School (p. 164) was indeed a pioneer building, anticipating in so many features the best of what was to come. Yet in its totality it is a lonely peak of intelligence and refinement, providing answers which neither architects nor civic designers find easy to understand; not about what they should design, but how they should design.

SCHOOLS AND LIBRARIES

This was also an age of continuing (and often competitive) altruism, in which board schools and branch libraries of great architectural merit were established in drab suburbs, and the former loomed large, with standard symmetrical mass, over many a small town like Dalkeith. Here, beside King's Park, is one of the gayest of them all in red and yellow stone, with curvaceous gables and a spindly central lantern (1903). In the following year Mackintosh himself designed his version of the typical board school in Glasgow's Scotland Street, and his distinctive mixture of flair and common sense is uncannily echoed in a number of schools by J. H. Langlands in Dundee, most notably at Stobswell. Here too the city architect James Thomson was responsible for public libraries at Blackness, Coldside and St Roque's; all charming classical essays which manage to achieve dignity without pomposity. Burnet himself, in his graceful Elder Library at Govan (1902), showed that he could achieve a dignity that was quite unpatronising. The new spirit of restraint in official architecture extended even to the post offices designed by what was then HM Office of Works. Among them are the miniature classical buildings at Dunbar and Banff, a type remarkable as one of the very few products of its age to be designed on a friendly scale with its surroundings.

LORIMER IN GALASHIELS

It was into this highly professional but scarcely popular architectural scene that Sir Robert Lorimer brought the message of the Scots revival, rugged and appealing. How far was he responsible for a general turning away from architectural expertise towards the worship of large masses of random rubble? One of the largest is at Galashiels. The first stage (1912) was the oddly pompous treatment of a hole in the roadway. In the middle of what is now of course a roundabout there stands a modern mercat cross, a sacred object which you cannot approach nearer than permitted by a ponderous stone balustrade. Craning over this (impossible if you are a child) you can look down the hole and see what has so far been laboriously concealed, indeed the reason for the whole thing – the thrilling confluence of what seem to be two small tributaries of the Gala Water. The second and more important stage came in 1924, partly as a war memorial. It is a large extension to the Victorian burgh chambers, with patriotic spirit implicit in its aggressively rubbly bulk and explicit in the warlike statue of a mounted moss-trooper, the whole composition being at most times in shadow for it points towards the north. In the summer the view is made charming by such leaves as are suffered to appear from the heavily pollarded trees round the hole, and by the wonderful municipal planting of flower-beds on the rising ground to the west, extending down one side of Bank Street. Discreetly visible among the flowers is a little Edwardian public convenience of terracota and brown glazed brick.

A WRONG TURNING

As the century proceeded, Edwardian grandeur was changed into something mechanical and charmless. The plateau having been attained, and architecture having reached for the sky and without difficulty touched it, where did one go from here? Glasgow had pointed a way ahead – and not in Mackintosh's

Art School alone; the back of John A. Campbell's Northern Insurance building has already been mentioned (p. 174), but its front elevation is no less exciting in its conscious enjoyment of plain surfaces. Yet this lead was seldom followed. Classicism reigned supreme in the prestige buildings of the inter-war years, ending most gloriously in the big extension to Glasgow's City Chambers (1923), most shamefully in hundreds of commercial buildings like Binns at Edinburgh's west end (1935), inspired by nothing except a curious belief that it was possible to have it both ways, up-dating the fruity Edwardian by reinterpreting it in the brittle language of art-deco. It was a terrible betrayal of the past, leading tradition into a dead end from which it has hardly emerged. Worse than this, it perpetuated the Edwardian faults of condescension and pomposity without their compensating qualities of confidence and fun. In this context, and with the dreaded naked bogey of modern architecture looming in the background, the tremendous appeal of Sir Robert Lorimer is not surprising. Here was a great architect prepared to come down to earth, and one moreover who could embody the spirit of the nation in modern monuments. For a long time he supplied the only link of confidence between Scotland and her architects.

Nevertheless architecture remained an esoteric art, and even Lorimer did little to move it down off its pedestal. *Building Scotland, A Cautionary Guide* by Alan Reiach and Robert Hurd, was published by the Saltire Society in 1948, but it gives a good view of the inter-war situation as seen by the eye of taste, and the missionary zeal of those who enjoyed both old and new buildings – and wanted other people to do the same. They are told what they ought to like (the simplicity of the old Scots vernacular and modern continental work), and what they ought not to like (the fancy dress of the baronial water-tower at Arbroath and James Thomson's elegant libraries in Dundee). The book is almost entirely about town buildings, but significantly few of the illustrations are properly identified; what is overlooked is that irrespective of their moral tone or architectural worth, these things are a valid part of some people's life and experience. They may not indeed have been good models for the architecture of a brave new Scotland, but this mandarin attitude is no less presumptuous than that of the Edwardian architects whose buildings are so consciously superior to their surroundings:

> Where . . . as in the case of this post office at Stuttgart, the adjacent buildings are bad, restraint and dignity arrest attention far better than strident vulgarity.

Thus the chasm between architecture and experience was widened and perpetuated, and thus the interest of townscape, which existed long before the word was coined and before architects were asked to contribute to it, was authoritatively set at naught.

THE VERNACULAR REMEMBERED

The aim of the Saltire Society is to keep Scottish traditions alive, and in one field their propaganda was outstandingly successful; that of setting a good example in the design of housing by a scheme of annual awards. Ever since the first award was given in 1937 to a small group of houses by Joseph Weekes at Milton in Dunbartonshire, a common theme has been recognizable in each year's prizewinning selection; not a mere reflection of progressive housing design in England or across the North Sea, certainly not a proliferation of crowsteps and wrought iron thistles, but something more fundamentally Scottish, a quality of straightforwardness that places this work – low and high rise, terraces and detached houses alike – in the direct line of the national tradition, of which the older members are recognized by similar awards for reconstruction (Cathedral Street in Dunkeld earned one of the first). Another and much more explicit principle of selection has been the quality of the houses and their surroundings as a whole. If more local authorities had taken their cue from these examples, and if more than a handful of private developers had thought about these criteria when the award scheme was opened to them in 1962, Scotland would be a better place to live in. The terrible division between the privileged and the unprivileged environment of the mid twentieth century need never have existed.

In their invective against superficial modernity, the authors of *Building Scotland* were of course rebuking their own profession, the architects who had reduced their art to a matter of skin-deep style. It is odd that for one of their good examples they chose Jay's store at 39 Princes Street (1938) though it certainly has a mournful interest in that its nicely contrasted textures mark the last appearance of hand-worked ashlar masonry on the Edinburgh scene. Otherwise this frontage is nothing more than a pattern in contemporary good taste, the functional implications of the vertically emphasized side bay having no more justification than the majority of the turrets on the derided mortuary chapel at Arbroath. In most of the flashy modernism of the immediate pre-war period there is no such earnest suggestion of purpose. The Odeons with their tall vertical fins, the Montague Burton stores 'in major towns', the fascist-looking picture windows hacked out of dozens of frontages like that of Woolworths in Inverness High Street, vitrolite shopfronts with jerky corners – all are meretricious, but all have a clear message; they want to be of their own age.

THE BEGINNING OF A NEW STYLE

To developers with this reasonable wish not much professional help was forthcoming. Few indeed are the inter-war buildings which represent anything but a blank assertion of modernism, and bother to take part in the townscape; one of them, opposite the Inverness Woolworths (*c.* 1936), has the wit to mark the corner of Castle Street with a curved and glazed staircase. Others are to be found on less conspicuous sites. The former Daily Express building of 1936 in Glasgow is a simple, classically modern envelope of a building in alternating strips of glass and black vitrolite, but unfortunately it is conducting an architectural soliloquy in the otherwise nondescript surroundings of Albion Street, five minutes east of Queen Street station. To the west in Renfrew Street the Cosmo cinema (1939), borrowing its idiom from the Netherlands architect Dudok, shows a complete mastery of its corner site. Most successfully T. W. Marwick, the designer of Jay's in Princes Street, gave a simple answer to the problem of how to fill a gap site with a less auspicious Edinburgh address in Bread Street. Between two co-op frontages, one workaday Victorian and the other (his father's work) rhetorical Edwardian, he stretched a glass curtain wall (1935). His clients lacked the courage of his convictions, for they subsequently painted the glass in pale blue and yellow, thus in effect up-dating (or rather back-dating) an advanced and acceptable design to forced gaiety of the Festival of Britain period.

PLANNING BY LAW

To a town-making system that was now in some disorder the Town and Country Planning (Scotland) Act of 1947 brought the rule of law. Its main principles were based, of course, on land use, and in this it represented a blunt but probably a realistic instrument; realistic because housing and commerce, industry and open space had all by now fallen out with each other, blunt and clumsy because diversity, as Jane Jacobs has pointed out in her studies of the American city, is part of the essence of town life. In existing towns its main instrument was development control to a degree far beyond anything previously undertaken by local authority officers like the Deans of Guild, whose main concern had always been with physical building standards. Thus the developer continued to hold all the positive cards, while the planning authority for each town or county held only the negative and restrictive ones. The Secretary of State for Scotland had a good view of both their hands and kept his own cards (the ultimate veto and the ultimate incentive) up his sleeve, because he might need them for all the other games in which he was engaged.

THE LOCAL AUTHORITY AS DEVELOPER

It was the statutory duty of all local planning authorities to produce development plans, but the term long remained a mere figure of speech. In the dozen lean years after the Planning Act the only towns that achieved even their former prosperity, let

alone any private development, were those which were essential
to regional trade. Public development in the shape of housing
was the first to get under way, and low density housing on the
outskirts was the general rule. Few indeed were the housing
authorities who took this opportunity of reviving their town
centres, and most of these, as related elsewhere, took a line that
was conservative rather than conservationist or frankly new.
However in Dalkeith the town council commissioned Sir Frank
Mears and Partners, who had hitherto followed a traditional
design policy there, to devise a new centre. Although it could be
said that they tried too hard and in too many different ways to
achieve modernity, the diversity of uses and their concentration
on the site set an admirable example. With its new burgh
chambers, shops and housing in 1960, and subsequently a
library in 1973, this is the most truly comprehensive redevelopment of its kind in Scotland. Much less successful is the way it
has drawn life away from the other, 'restored' end of the High
Street and from the intermediate area which, in the absence of
any clear guidelines for conservation or redevelopment, is
being rebuilt piecemeal.

Another council who took the future of their town seriously
was Linlithgow. In 1957 they appointed the firm of Rowand
Anderson, Kininmonth and Paul to modernize and extend the
existing town hall at the historic centre; this is in contrast with
Dalkeith, whose two previous town halls have been left as
irrelevant objects in the town scene. The same firm then carried
out a pilot scheme of high density housing at West Port, and in
1963 this was followed by a very large central redevelopment
based on an improved version of the same type [pls 1b, 30a].
The strong case for retaining a group of old houses and an inn
by the Cross was virtually ignored, but for once the gain has
demonstrably outweighed the loss. The new work is well related
to the roadway in front and the loch behind, and indeed to the
important group formed by town hall, church and palace. A
more controversial feature is the spiky golden crown by Geoffrey
Clarke on the church tower (1960), a modern version of the stone
crown taken down in the early nineteenth century. Whatever
doubts there may be about its precise form, it is a splendidly

clear and successful gesture, advertising to the traveller between Glasgow and Edinburgh (railway to the south, motorway to the north) the positive relationship between new and old which is the keynote of the whole scheme.

THE COMMERCIAL DEVELOPER AND THE SHOPPING CENTRE

These two towns are unusual because of the principal part played by their local authorities as town centre developers. Most authorities have assumed a subsidiary role, merely making central sites available to the commercial developer, who by definition is somebody more interested in realizing a potential than fulfilling a need; more in going to work on a happily flourishing centre where good things may be lost by rebuilding, than on a depressed or derelict one where trade has declined. He is seldom resident in the town himself, and his main obligation is to those who have put up the money – often the large insurance companies, backed by prudent investors. Those who deplore the result of the developer's operations, the anonymous rows of shop-shells tenanted by chain stores (the universal hermit crabs of the centres, each with his familiar plastic facia) and the displacement of local traders, do not always remember that their own insurance premiums have made it possible.

How desirable were these schemes to local authorities everywhere, as an alternative to stagnation and obsolescence! How tempting the prospect of vast increases in rateable value! One of the first to get under way was in Dundee's Overgate centre, whose relation to its surroundings (including the parish kirk and its medieval spire) is unusually good (1958). It was designed by Ian Burke and Hugh Martin, and the latter was mainly responsible for the appearance of Edinburgh's St James Centre (from 1958), the largest of its kind in Scotland, of which little good can be said. Replacing a noble, run-down square for which few tears were shed at the time (p. 182), it stands head and shoulders above Adam's Register House on the North Bridge vista and Sir William Chambers's Dundas mansion at the end of George Street [pl. 14b], looming enormous in the panorama from

Calton Hill or the Botanic Gardens. To Leith Street it presents a vast, grim backside, and to the former nodal point of town life and townscape at the east end junction it has been (if such a light term can be applied to the extra traffic load) the last straw. Moreover its errors were compounded by the Secretary of State for Scotland who is the tenant, and thus effectively the client, of its upper reaches; the fine bureaucratic monument of St Andrew's House (1936) is now a mere annexe, the seat of power having flitted to the grey commercial kremlin.

These developments have achieved their greatest success in the busy but hitherto under-privileged towns created or debased by the industrial revolution, especially in the sprawling urban wastes of Lanarkshire. Cambuslang has one of the finest new centres (1958), but once again we find that the credit for mixing shops and houses and excellent landscaping is due to the local authority (in this case the county council) who designed and financed it. Nevertheless two good centres have been made at Hamilton and Motherwell, the former with a covered shopping mall that is a real social asset, the latter with an unusually imaginative system of external concrete units; for now it is such small points that separate architecture from building, the individual from the nondescript. Both are by Ian Burke. Success has also been attained in co-operative ventures between local authority and commercial developer, and one of the best is the centre at Blackburn in West Lothian (1966). This is a canopied shopping street of very modest scale, straddled by a hotel. Under the bridge so formed, the blue brick walls are chalked with goal-posts in winter, cricket stumps in summer. There is a handy car park, which also serves the circular public library and other community buildings nearby. An interesting detail is the successful use of a difficult proprietary material that has swept Scotland since the early 'sixties, the reconstituted granite known as Fyffe-stone. It is often seen in a ghastly parody of snecked rubble walling on buildings where lip-service to tradition or amenity is required, with results that always recall ready-made rustic fireplaces. Here it is far more effective, being used in straightforward parallel lines both for pavements and (in alternate thick and thin courses) for the library walls.

This scheme by Wheeler and Sproson gives point to an existing and still expanding grey area of houses, and shows what can be done in a modest way by a partnership of commerce and local authority; it is only a lack of managerial expertise that prevents more authorities from raising the money (as any developer has to do) and following suit. But there are similar examples which have made a positive contribution to established town centres. At Galashiels the west side of the High Street has been rebuilt with a perfectly simple terrace of houses built out over a shopping arcade to form a continuous canopy; the south end, facing Lorimer's town hall, provides a well-used meeting place with seats, where people and even a piece of new sculpture seem quite at ease. Dumbarton has an outstandingly successful pair of developments on either side of its High Street, one with shops and low-rise offices, the other providing a car park and water-front meeting place, with detail of fine simplicity. The use of the same materials for both, and the way in which people's needs and pleasures have been foreseen, both contribute to the feeling that here for once the twentieth century has come to terms with a town.

The larger multiple shops, not speculative but purpose built, are the nearest equivalent to the Victorian and Edwardian department store. The chief difference is that daylight is no longer considered necessary on the sales floors and some levels may be used for storage only, so the modern shop tends to have a blank, impersonal look; none more so than the frightening bastille of the Co-operative building in George Street, Aberdeen. An elegant solution of this problem was found by Robert Matthew, Johnson-Marshall and Partners at the British Home Stores building in Princes Street, Edinburgh (1965). It begins with two storeys of almost continuous glass and then masks its storage levels with a curtain wall whose pale granite strips appear quite weightless. This was one of the first and is still the best of the redevelopments that follow the guidelines of the Princes Street Panel. Their rules set limits on plot ratio (the proportion of floor area to site area), heights and materials, and lay down certain formal elements for all new buildings; a blank vertical margin at the outer edges so that each single development projects forward from a common plane, and a provision for an elevated pavement on first floor level in something of the same manner of the Rows in Chester. It is the most interesting attempt at constructive planning constraint in twentieth-century Britain, but its weakness appears on the skyline where the new buildings (with the one exception mentioned) boast a motley crowd of tanks, lift houses and penthouses – some of them quite sizeable buildings – which look like cardboard boxes thrown up on top of the wardrobe after Christmas; unfortunately they are all too visible from the Mound to the south. If this sort of roofscape replaces the pointed towers of the old Palace Hotel on the corner of Princes Street and Castle Street it will be a poor exchange indeed.

As for the new shopfronts in which twentieth-century design has its main opportunity, the tendency to ignore the existing quality of a street is abetted by the plausible theory that the right to trade implies the right to attract trade in whatever way the shopfitter decrees. Of new shops inserted in old shells the most successful are those whose designers, sometimes under a planning officer's persuasion, have been content to work within the old frame; this is especially desirable where the facia and cornice form part of a continuous row, and most Victorian shops have plenty of height for a new facia, if necessary, to be inserted underneath. Within this frame convention can be abandoned. Some of the most effective new shops are those which break down the traditional barrier between displaying and selling, and try to draw their customers straight into a tempting sales area. These are privileged annexes to the outdoor townscape of a shopping street, and may be an escape from the noise and danger of traffic.

Conversely the errors of twentieth-century shopfitters are well known; not many architects have deigned to practise and still fewer to instruct themselves adequately in this branch of design. There are the long windows, big enough for a car show-room but frequently displaying nothing larger than a packet of cornflakes; the equally long facias with the accustomed names in house-style plastic lettering; and above them the sickly remains of whatever buildings happened to be there to have their legs amputated at the hip. Generally of course this maiming is not new; it has happened wherever a street of houses has become a street of shops. But today it is preventable by statutory means (at least for a listed building or in a Conservation Area) and there are even, with the current decline in the number of shops in most towns, opportunities of reversing the process, as has been started in Edinburgh's George Street. Two particular assumptions need to be corrected. The first is that offices with public counters cannot operate behind a house front without converting the ground floor into shop windows. The building societies who finance the buying of houses and the companies who insure them should surely not subscribe to this idea, but they are still doing so in Union Street, Aberdeen, where there may soon be no complete house fronts left. The other is that if the shopfront attracts enough attention on street level the old building on top can be left to rot. Even if the upper floors are used, as they frequently are, as makeshift stores, the owner of a street frontage has a civic duty to maintain it. With double glazing to keep the noise out, and even the noise itself reduced by pedestrianization, there are chances of reversing this kind of erosion too; the ghost town over many a shopping street could be lived in again.

THE ARCHITECTURE OF THE FILING CABINET

Another form of investment is in the speculative office block. Here the local authority is never directly a partner in the development but sometimes a tenant, as more commonly are the civil service and the fitly named statutory undertakers. Both are eager for space in the slightly cheaper but very much nastier range, and no effort in public relations can repair the second rate image they thus acquire.

Given the demand for office space, the new office block is the best machine ever devised for turning land into money. The owner of a less perfect machine like an obsolete theatre, or a financial dead loss like a redundant church, is naturally tempted to sell out having first made sure of permission for redevelopment; only a strong planning authority can resist this. The typical new block, probably unlike the building it has supplanted, is not part of the organic pattern of townscape – though a row of shops on the ground floor can help. Townscape stops at the door, and the inside is known only to those who work there. Outside, the serried windows betray nothing but the existence of a separate world into which they have gone. Thus disembodied, such a building relies for its effect on whatever abstract quality it may possess, both in itself and in relation to others, and the best are those whose architects are aware of this. Occasionally, where nothing else will be damaged in the process, there is room for blatant ambition, as in the astonishing complex designed in 1963 by Covell Matthews and Partners in George Street, Glasgow, including the David Livingstone Tower of Strathclyde University – a whole townscape in itself. But any visual connection with an established townscape imposes constraints. Granted that most office blocks are obtrusive or uniform or both, the important thing is that their bulk shall be well placed and their uniformity pleasing. The multi-storey Canning House at Edinburgh's west end (1963, tenanted by the Post Office) was one of the last to slip through the net of Lord Holford's high buildings policy. It is careless in detail, with no attempt to mask the usual collection of boxes on the roof, and is thus doubly intrusive as a terminal object seen along two Georgian vistas that are otherwise unchanged, Rutland Street and Walker Street. The First New Town of Edinburgh, in which Georgian houses have managed to co-exist fairly happily with business buildings for more than a century, has a number of exemplary new offices. Carron House by Morris and Steedman (1968) is a brilliant quotation of the Georgian pattern in terms that break away from what is now the dead convention of the window-pierced wall. At the other end of George Street, though set back from the main building line where it would have made too sharp a break with this same convention, is the pure curtain wall of Michael Laird's first extension to the Standard Life office (1964, pl. 29f); the second, round the corner in St Andrew Square, is content to join in the dialogue of basic Georgian geometry – vertically in masonry, horizontally in steel and glass (1968).

A CHANGING HIERARCHY

What of the old stars of the townscape scene? The banks have
merged, and so (for different reasons) have the churches, both
leaving a trail of redundant buildings. There are few new ones
of either kind in the older towns. Nor are there many new
schools on urban sites; Gillespie, Kidd and Coia's extension to
Our Lady and St Francis' School facing Glasgow Green is an
entirely happy exception (1964, pl. 30b), and here for a moment
the twentieth century speaks with the authority of its predecessors. It is an urbane statement but a rare one, for schools,
together with churches, town and county halls and post offices
(but happily not yet the public libraries) have all with their own
good excuses migrated from the centre, which runs the risk of
becoming a sham if the old shells are reused or a shambles if
they are redeveloped. Conservation, in the sense of preserving
the reality of urban life, presents an urgent challenge.

In this changing scene the greatest responsibility rests on the
designers of those public buildings that must by necessity be
members of the town centre. The Crown has unfortunately not
yet learned to wear its authority lightly, and telephone exchanges
in particular have an authoritiarian air that is too close – though
presumably not by intention – to the architecture of fascism.
Among local authority buildings Peter Womersley's Roxburgh
County office at Newton St Boswells is the most encouraging
(1970). Its authority is four-square but easy; isolated at present,
but inviting a townscape dialogue in the new, more loosely-knit
idiom of the twentieth century.

A PLACE TO LIVE

Housing has already been mentioned in connection with some
of the comprehensive schemes sponsored by enlightened local
authorities (p. 180). The private contribution has indeed been
minimal, for the market has only offered three options; the old
house modernized, the remote arcadia (from Wimpey's respectable suburbanity to the dreadful indulgence of Dalgety Bay in

188

Fife), or for a few altruists the determined rigours of a housing society scheme, tied to the hardships of both worlds – the discipline of public and the rising costs of private housing. Roland Wedgwood's Southfield estate to the west of Edinburgh earns some of the highest marks in this last class, being a valiant effort at identifiable urban quality over a large area, but without the uniting influence of a single shop or public building (1966).

Local authority housing of the mid century has mostly been conventional and 'low-rise', which means one to four storeys high, its small units and wandering layout conforming to the popular free-enterprise types of the 'thirties. The Scottish Special Housing Association, an official agency whose job is to supplement local authority efforts where required, have been more imaginative, particularly over layout; some would say *less* imaginative, but the straight two-storey terraces of many of their carefully maintained schemes are eminently civilized and sensible compared with what tended to happen elsewhere. Hundreds of maze-like layouts of semi-detached houses have been dumped by housing committees on the edges of their towns without a thought to social needs. Glasgow Corporation's vast estates at Castlemilk and Easterhouse and Edinburgh's at Pilton and Niddrie are among the most notorious. These and dozens of others cannot be called towns or even parts of towns. One of the best opportunities offered by the community council system under the new local government structure is a nation-wide local effort to improve them. Even the smaller towns and villages have generally failed to establish a good townscape relationship with their new housing areas, and fewer still have built houses at their centres. Dalkeith has been mentioned (p. 181), and so will a few other towns in the next chapter under the heading of conservation (p. 203). But even a modest central area scheme like that of Fife County Council at the village of Torryburn (1966) is a rarity [pl. 29d].

Low-rise housing having acquired a bad name, which most recent British efforts deserved but the type as a whole did not, the high-rise boom of the 'sixties came to leave its mark on the town. In Scotland its forerunner was Sam Bunton's early post-war scheme for the bombed town of Clydebank; its apotheosis

189

his thirty-four-storey towers at Red Road in Glasgow (1960) where on your way to the kitchen you have to duck under the diagonal braces of what proved to be the too flexible (though massive and expensive) steel frame. Multi-storey housing was embraced not only as a panacea but as a status symbol of progress. Its literal fall from grace with the Ronan Point disaster in the south (1969) has obscured its virtues and occasional successes. Sir Basil Spence's flats at Hutchesontown-Gorbals in Glasgow were perhaps over-romantic; the privilege he tried to confer on public authority housing turned out to have a patronizing air. Sir Robert Matthew's workmanlike rivals which adjoin them [pl. 29c] were in the event more successful. Both dating from the early 'sixties, the two schemes enjoy one of the finest urban building sites in Britain and the advantages of good grouping and site treatment (with low-rise buildings round about) which are essential to the success of this type in townscape terms.

Discounting, difficult as it is, their social implications, tall blocks have two obvious qualities. They speak, on their high level, to each other and to their lower neighbours. Their group relationship is of course crucial; a straight or staggered row implies an advance of giants, as in Aberdeen which is keeping to its ten-year-old multi-storey policy in view of chronic and recently increased land-hunger. Aberdeen also demonstrates, in its Hazelhead scheme, the capabilities of mixed high and low-rise. In the otherwise infinite landscape of suburban development the tall blocks demonstrate their second townscape potential, as landmarks and as senior buildings. Their most agreeable use, widely spaced on an undulating grassy landscape between established trees (as at Callendar Park on the outskirts of Falkirk) virtually removes them from the subject of townscape.

IX. CONSERVATION

'Preservation is about buildings and conservation is about places' declared the *Architectural Review* in November 1970; a perfectly workable distinction which will be observed in this chapter. But despite the *Review's* efforts, and Bernard Feilden's useful ideas towards further definitions in the same issue, the vocabulary of the subject is still confused. It is not surprising that this uncertainty is reflected in a general failure to define policies and objectives, either in discussion or in practice.

The main lines of the historic argument about terms may be summarized as follows. The Society for the Protection of Ancient Buildings, founded by William Morris in 1877, sought to protect them specifically against restoration; this meant the substitution of imitation work for the genuine article when the latter was missing or damaged or just historically inconsistent, and many architects at the time were overdoing it. To Morris, as to Ruskin, restoration implied deception. But the word is now used without this suggestion of disapproval, as a general term rather like preservation, only rather more positive. Preservation may mean no more than the arrest of further decay, as at one of the Ancient Monuments taken into official guardianship under the Act of 1913 and now in the care of the Department of the Environment, which significantly has had its own full share of renaming. Restoration is usually thought of as going a bit further, with the replacement of missing parts.

In the definitive vocabulary, *preservation* can only remain a general term; it is work done to prolong the life (not necessarily the useful life) of a building. *Restoration* however has a clear technical sense. In connection with pictures and other works of fine art, it is used to describe any justified element of new work to replace missing parts of the old. This meaning can

191

logically and satisfactorily be extended to buildings or indeed to the larger scene.

Conservation is another fine art term, meaning work done to consolidate and protect the original fabric. Other disciplines such as dentistry and the conservation of the natural environment have also attached their meanings to the word, and these of course are much nearer to its presently accepted use in relation to towns. As such it was first given widespread currency in 1966 by R. H. Crossman as Minister of Local Government in England. Conservation in this sense includes a preservation element (the keeping of buildings) but its main principle is the keeping alive of whole places. It involves everything and everybody in the urban scene.

The good results of this revolution in official thinking (for it had long been the doctrine of a vocal minority) will be described below. Unfortunately it also did some harm by confusing the issue in a new way. Both in words and in action, conservation was in, preservation was out. It was no bad thing for the preservation lobby to be reminded that most buildings have to justify themselves in terms of use and not just as monuments to piety. But it was now even suggested that preservation was out of date and irrelevant; that any conservation plan worth the name must have an element of demolition or at least change, and further, that individual buildings should not be preserved and restored but 'conserved', i.e. brought up to date. There is still a wide difference of opinion between this school of thought and the one which, while admitting that updating or even demolition of existing buildings may sometimes be desirable, still insists that the possibilities of preservation and restoration should always be properly explored. The *Review* was wise to suggest that conservation is about places.

Another useful but uncommon term is *intervention*. First used in this context in lecture notes by Professor James Marston Fitch of Columbia University (a pioneer in the terminology of the subject) it denotes any special action to achieve an objective in preservation or conservation. Both these ideas tend to be associated with intervention in the shape of restrictive laws, persuasion, campaigns, grants of money. So it is too often forgotten that the part which intervention plays in the survival of buildings and places is often small or non-existent. The chief agent in conservation and preservation is the property owner working without any outside prompting or subsidy. The ultimate aim of any sensible conservation programme is to eliminate intervention altogether.

NINETEENTH-CENTURY IMPROVEMENTS IN EDINBURGH

In many Scottish towns considerable areas built up in the 'golden age' of the sixteenth and seventeenth centuries survived well into the nineteenth. But their condition was parlous. The better-off residents having long ago moved into their urban terraces or suburban villas, these old quarters were left to provide the main stock of artisan housing, congested, derelict and disease-ridden. When redevelopment came, no conservationist intervention stood in the way of its headlong progress, though here and there a building might be spared and preserved on historical grounds. Thus Provand's Lordship still stands opposite the over-restored west front of Glasgow Cathedral, and in 1853 the house which is an important architectural and townscape feature of Edinburgh's High Street, narrowing it just before the entry into Canongate, was reprieved on account of its supposed connection with John Knox (p. 56).

Old Edinburgh in the early nineteenth century was something of a special case. It had not ceased to be the administrative centre of the capital. Its history had been brought to life by Sir Walter Scott and its picturesque (that is, townscape) qualities celebrated by commentators and illustrators alike. But anyone of consequence now lived in the New Town. Such redevelopment as took place in the old was not primarily intended to improve housing conditions but to make way for road improvements, notably under the Acts of 1785 (South Bridge) and 1827 (southern and western approaches). Both involved major engineering works to traverse the hilly terrain, and the ground had to be acquired and cleared and finally the roadside sites refeued. Professor Youngson in his *Making of Classical Edinburgh* has shown how in the latter case Thomas Hamilton, as architect to the Commissioners and designer of George IV and King's bridges, was found to have been over-optimistic in thinking that these schemes would pay their way; indeed Melbourne Place (George Smith, architect, on the site of the new Midlothian County offices) was still building in the 'fifties, and Nos. 45 to 55 further down George IV Bridge (Henry Hardy) were not started till 1860. It is surprising that one architect was expected to be the manager of this complicated project, as well as the designer of a large part of it.

The conservation policies attached to these and subsequent works in Edinburgh are of particular interest. Total redevelopment was generally accepted, as when the antiquarian John Britton says in *Modern Athens* in 1829:

> The over-hanging stories and lookern [dormer] windows of the buildings, by which the Lawnmarket and the West Bow are connected, as represented in the accompanying Engraving, have a picturesque appearance, when delineated on paper; but few persons will regret their removal, to make room for modern improvements.

In the event the splendid wood-framed building in the forefront of this view survived until 1892, long enough to be photographed [pl. 11c] and be the trademark of Nelson's publishing house. The more solid lands and houses at the foot of the West Bow [pl. 31b] escaped the demolisher and the restorer until they were given a new lease of life by the joint efforts of the city engineer (in placing a demolition order on them in 1969) and the architect Ian Begg, who turned the crisis to advantage and saw to their preservation. Hamilton's new line for the West Bow, which was to run up on to George IV Bridge under the name of Victoria Street, left nothing else standing. But before he resigned as architect to the Commissioners in 1834 he made a meticulous elevational drawing of the West Bow and Lawnmarket frontages, the best record of old Scottish burgh architecture we have.

The north side of Victoria Street is the work of Hamilton's successor George Smith (1840). As an example of conservationist redevelopment it is unequalled anywhere. It performs its new traffic function, making (as Professor Johnson-Marshall has said) an early clover leaf, if only half of one. With its near-regular arcade beautifully linked to the old fronts at the foot of the Bow, it is a straightforward work of its time. Its flat stone roof is the pavement of Victoria Terrace, a useful pedestrian link [pl. 31c] above which is the regulated diversity of church-fronts and house-backs, partly the work of other architects; an extraordinary skyline consummated in the view from the Grassmarket by the spire of Gillespie Graham's Tolbooth Church (p. 119).

Sir Robert Matthew's County Offices (1960, p. 231) lack the finesse of their predecessor, Smith's Melbourne Place. Stylistically the latter followed the brief suggested in connection with the 1827 Act, 'the old Flemish style of architecture, or whatever style appears most consonant with the character of this ancient part of the City of Edinburgh, which is so much identified with the history of former days.' The 'Flemish' style, which we would probably call Jacobean, represented the first stirring of a nationalist architectural revival.

The Edinburgh Railway Station Access Act of 1853 went further:

Provision for securing harmony in the new Buildings with those of the old Town.

And whereas in the buildings to be erected along the sides of or adjoining the said street, it is desirable to preserve as far as possible the architectural style and antique character of that part of the old Town . . . be it therefore enacted that Sir William Gibson Craig, of Riccarton, Baronet, the Honourable Henry Cockburn, one of the Senators of the College of Justice, and Sir William Johnston, of Kirkhill, Knight . . . are and shall be referees of the Company for securing and effecting the purposes above mentioned.

The new thoroughfare, duly named Cockburn Street, was designed by Peddie and Kinnear in 1860 in a varied baronial style (still somewhat Jacobean) which acknowledges its steep gradient and even recreates some of the intimacy of an old Edinburgh close. Its success is sufficient proof that this architectural policy was more than mere window dressing. By the late 'fifties the revived Scottish baronial style with its organic vigour (in contrast to Georgian regularity) and its obvious patriotic appeal, was synonymous with architectural progress. For the work done under the City Improvement Act of 1867 the brief was even more specific:

> These elevations shall be of plain but marked character, in harmony with those fine specimens of national architecture in many of the neglected and over-crowded areas.

Unity was assured by the Council, as Trustees under the Act, financing and instructing the work themselves, with powers to dispose of it after completion. Their architect David Cousin, Superintendent of Public Works since 1847 and thus responsible for the laborious task of drawing up the parliamentary plans for both Acts, became ill from overwork and handed the job over to John Lessels, who was thus the designer of Blackfriars Street and St Mary's Street. However their joint initials and the date 1869 appear on the gable at the latter's north end, the first section to be completed [pl. 31a]. This development does not strain after fragmentation or quaintness. It is a truly urban version of the baronial style.

These two Acts gave Edinburgh two adjoining areas of high architectural and townscape quality. What may seem to us a rather anachronistic design policy is vindicated not only by an important contribution to the famous view of the old town from Princes Street, but by the curious fact that this Victorian work is today (at least to the visitor) the largest consistently credible area of 'old Edinburgh'. Curiously too, its only failure in its own time was in its prime purpose as housing. Only a skilled worker could afford the rent of one of these tenement flats. Neither in cheapness nor in sheer quantity were they a substitute for the ruinous old dwellings they replaced.

Edinburgh's 1867 Act was put into effect under Lord Provost Sir William Chambers, Glasgow's of the previous year under John Blackie, another distinguished publisher and reforming Lord Provost. In Glasgow the Council were constituted as trustees for the acquisition and clearance of 90 acres (displacing some 30,000 people) and the provision of new houses on the land.

This enormous operation proceeded very slowly, throwing a greater strain than in Edinburgh upon the remaining old properties and boosting the demand for the new generation of purely speculative artisan tenements in the new suburbs. Similar redevelopment was even more ruthlessly pushed forward under the 1871 Improvement Act in Dundee, but no more account was taken of old buildings than in the formation of Reform Street thirty-eight years before. Neither city followed Edinburgh's characteristically self-conscious architectural policy for redevelopment.

Towards the end of the century Sir Patrick Geddes made an equally important but in some ways more intelligent contribution to the conservation of the old Edinburgh scene. Fired by the same sort of ambition to see the city as a European cultural capital that had inspired Provost Drummond's creation of the New Town, he set to work on the old. His name is most often associated with the Outlook Tower on Castlehill (1893), already in existence as an observatory when he bought the property. From the camera obscura he surveyed, as visitors still do today and as he himself in his other vocation would examine a biological specimen, the life and growth and decay of the city. But his interest was much more than academic, and he practised conservation at least as much as he preached it.

Geddes's 'conservative surgery', as he termed it, was an advance on the disruptive and expensive techniques of earlier clearances, and included a large element of preservation. Purchase, improvement and imaginative restoration, extension or rebuilding (according to circumstances) were the treatment he applied to some eight properties in the old town, handing over his personal responsibility in 1890 to the Town and Gown Association. At the head of the Royal Mile two former student residences may still be seen; Ramsay Garden (S. Henbest Capper and Sydney Mitchell, 1892–4, pl. 32a) and the three-gabled block at 451–63 Lawnmarket (Capper, 1893). In the backlands Lady Stair's House (G. S. Aitken, 1896) is an elaborate restoration on behalf of Geddes's friend Lord Roseberry. At the foot are Geddes's restorations at 11–15 Canongate (1893) and Whitehorse Close. The latter (J. Jerdan, 1889) was re-

restored in 1963 by Sir Frank Mears and Partners, whose late principal had been Geddes's son-in-law. The same firm do not seem to have considered the preservation of the Robertson's Close development on the important corner nearby, although it was another Geddes commission, but demolished it to make way for municipal housing to a new design (1970).

Geddes was a practical master of townscape. It would be too easy to condemn as unhistorical the architectural fancies he encouraged, and indeed it would not be entirely correct. A century in which the Scottish tradition has been identified with a puritanical love of masonry has brought us near to forgetting that wood and plaster, the erratic outline of 'overhanging stories and lookern windows' were just as much a part of it.

CONSERVATION IN THE TWENTIETH CENTURY: THE NATIONAL TRUST FOR SCOTLAND

The inheritor of the Geddes tradition was the fourth Marquess of Bute. In the Canongate he preserved and restored Acheson House (Robert Hurd, 1937). On the north side of Adam's Charlotte Square he acquired four houses, removed dormer windows and lettering, restored window sills lowered in 1872 and put back the astragals. The scheme was effective over almost the whole of this side, and in 1937 the entire Square came under the protection of the unprecedented *City of Edinburgh Order*. This was the year of the Adelphi destruction which prompted the founding of the Georgian Group based in London, but the comparison gives no further ground for satisfaction. William Adam senior's Dundee Town House had been even more scandalously demolished three years before.

Lord Bute was also a propagandist on behalf of the National Trust for Scotland, founded in 1932. After the Housing (Scotland) Act of 1935 had been roundly condemned in their annual report as having 'no doubt unwittingly, put a premium on destruction', he made a widely reported luncheon speech in the following year asserting the quality of Scots domestic building and saying in effect that the Scots people should be allowed to enjoy it. As a first step he financed through the Trust a national inventory of old houses in Scottish towns which was completed over the next four years by the architect-historian Ian Lindsay. Sequences and groups were particularly noted. The second world war, though it checked much further loss for a time, unfortunately prevented the delivery of the lists to town councils and other possible initiators of conservation effort.

In its first year the National Trust for Scotland became the owner of Crookston Castle, showing that it was in the preservation business as then understood (this ruin now belongs more appropriately to the Department of the Environment as an Ancient Monument). Two more modest acquisitions represented 'historic interest' (Bruce's Stone on the Field of Bannockburn) and 'natural beauty' (a farm on the isle of Mull).

Next came a more challenging subject. Dr James Richardson, HM Inspector of Ancient Monuments, was passing through the Burgh of Culross whose state of imminent collapse had been whimsically recorded by Jessie M. King thirty years before. He noticed the removal of timbers (prior to demolition) from Sir George Bruce's house (p. 60), and further observed that the timbers were decoratively painted. With commendable speed the Trust bought the building and Dr Richardson's own department undertook its maintenance.

Intervention to preserve a building still roofed and entire was at that time remarkable enough, though obviously justified by its merit as a 'museum piece'. It was clear however that not just one building but virtually the whole Burgh was now being abandoned. In the second year of its existence the Trust bought the half-derelict town centre, that is the 'study' and a total of nine sixteenth- and seventeenth-century houses round the Cross [pl. 8c] and started bargaining for two tenements next to Bruce's house (the 'palace').

Forty years later and more than a hundred thousand pounds of charitable money spent, it is now possible to take stock of this far-sighted enterprise. The obvious difficulty has been that inactivity, though it permits survival, is the very worst basis for conservation. Immensely important in the history of Scottish towns and till recently enjoying its historic autonomy as a Royal Burgh (a privilege that had become a burden), Culross was in all other ways very unimportant indeed. So there was a long period in which the preservation of houses (eventually more than thirty), with their even more costly internal improvement, had to be its own reward. The smallest new industry set up in the Burgh, the smallest support from the Town Council for the idea of a housing policy based on conservation – either would have made the task easier and more real in the first stages. Now that it is almost complete, tourists do a lot to fill the gap for a few months in the year and the services they need are attractively provided. Two early ideals were modified in the later stages. New houses were built near the centre by the Town Council, in the face of some opposition from the Trust (1966, pl. 8a). The 'stage set' of Back Causeway was thus impaired, but the marriage of old and new is successful in townscape terms and the town has lost its feeling of self-reproach that it was stuck in the past. Secondly the Trust itself was obliged to vary its altruistic low-rent policy and seek economic tenants and improving purchasers for some houses. Sure enough, private wealth eventually came in, and with it the personalities both human and architectural (the latter seen in small deviations from the safe norm) which bring life to the face of a town.

In Dunkeld after the war the Trust maintained its low-rent policy from start to finish, but in very different circumstances. The area of operations, Cathedral Street and the Cross [pl. 32d] adjoined the A9 to Inverness, an important tourist route. The county authorities not only shared in the preservation and improvement of forty houses, but co-operated with the Trust over details like road surfaces and street lighting, as did the Hydro-Electric Board and the Post Office on the undergrounding of cables. Ten years after the Trust's first acceptance of some crumbling rows of houses from Atholl Estates in 1954, the work was complete. One house on the north side of Cathedral Street was in fact past repair and a replica was put in its place, a straightforward infill procedure that earned a doctrinaire rebuke from the Saltire Society's Housing Panel in 1962 (p. 178). They gave the scheme an award, but went so far as to suggest that an opportunity for a modern contribution to the Dunkeld scene had here been missed.

200

Culross and Dunkeld represent the first phase of the Trust's campaign for the 'Little Houses', an attractive if not always very suitable term. The second, which grew out of it, was conducted on a wider front and with very much less expense of the Trust's funds. In 1958 a pair of houses at Rumford, Crail, were repaired and improved as a single dwelling and put on the market. It was two years in selling, but the Trust pressed on with similar projects not only in Crail but at the High Street and harbour of the neighbouring burgh of Pittenweem. The work was financed by a revolving fund to which the Pilgrim Trust contributed, and has been a turning point in the survival and revival of the historic townscape in virtually all the coastal burghs of the East Neuk of Fife. The devoted but careful management that any such scheme demands was supplied by the Trust's local agent, Hew Lorimer the sculptor, son of the architect Sir Robert Lorimer.

OFFICIAL POLICY: THE FIRST PHASE

Ian Lindsay was placed in charge of the listing of 'buildings of architectural or historic interest' in Scotland in the terms of section 28 of the 1947 Planning Act. In its differences from the equivalent procedure in England, the policy he laid down for his investigators was particularly auspicious for the conservation of the Scottish townscape; most of all in its specific allowance for group value and for the inclusion of Victorian and even more recent buildings, provided only that they were not the work of a still living architect. But progress in listing was lamentably slow, and even after the owner of a building had been told by the Secretary of State (in somewhat threatening terms) of its inclusion in the statutory list, all he had to do was 'give notice' of his intention to alter or demolish it. This put the ball back in the planning authorities' court, and the majority were not playing. Moreover, of the somewhat false set of teeth in the Act, only the Building Preservation Order was potentially effective. But in Scotland it was soon blunted in 1963 by Lord Clyde's judgement in the Court of Session awarding £35,000 compensation for loss of development rights to the firm which had bought Edinburgh's Tron Kirk in the full knowledge that there was already a preservation order on it. As a result of this surprising precedent the total number of orders served in Scotland is still in single figures.

Such mildly restrictive legislation was not much use in practice unless it was accompanied by a more positive initiative. When this came, it was generally from preservationist bodies who had little direct stake in the issue and naturally received small thanks from those who had more. In this unsatisfactory forum the object was always the same; to persuade the planning authority, or failing this the Secretary of State, first that there was an issue, second that it required a decision or a statement, and third to come down on the side of preservation, which was tantamount to standing in the way of progress. All these type-cast tragi-comedies had implications for townscape, and each was interesting in its own way. In Edinburgh the Secretary of State's advisers decided in 1959 that the sacrifice of George Square was permissible because it was of inferior quality to Charlotte Square. In the affair of the Venetian baroque Life Association building in Princes Street, the Scottish Secretary himself 'reluctantly' declared in 1967 that the advantage lay with redevelopment in conformity with the city's Princes Street scheme rather than preservation; he and the developer both overlooked the fact that an Edinburgh Architectural Association study had proved the two to be reconcilable. In 1962 Crimonmogate House next to the Music Hall in Aberdeen was not considered good enough to stand in the way of a supermarket and the latter received the batty benediction of a Civic Trust Award. David Dale's house in Charlotte Street, Glasgow, was distinguished in architecture and history, but its great townscape value had been irrecoverably lost. Its replacement is of high architectural quality [pl. 30b], which is more than can be said of the redevelopments on the sites of most of the casualties suffered by Glasgow in this bleak era. This is a partisan account, but at this time it was impossible to take anything but a partisan position. Told from any point of view the story would illustrate the uselessness of a weakly restrictive preservation policy.

A more positive official attitude originated with the Historic

Buildings Act of 1953. Although it never seized the opportunity of taking stock of the whole of its task and asking for proper funds to discharge it, the newly formed Historic Buildings Council for Scotland was quick to expand the scope of its grants from 'outstanding buildings' to outstanding groups as well. The early grant for the repair of the Harbour Cottages in Kirkcudbright (1955) perhaps stretched even this definition too far, but grants of this kind were a necessary and inexpensive gesture towards the one very real sort of conservation that had so far caught people's imagination in Scotland. The ultimate justification of this policy was the conservation of the eighteenth-century ducal town of Inveraray – an operation in a positively ducal and thus quite unusual scale made possible by the acquisition of virtually the whole place by the Department of the Environment (then the Ministry of Works) who thus succeeded the Duke as feudal superior, with supreme powers of action and control. Ian Lindsay and Partners were the architects and the scheme began in 1958, to be finished in three years. Sixty-four tenemented houses had been preserved and improved at the amazingly low average of £2049 each, the cost being shared between the housing authority and the Historic Buildings Council for Scotland.

Along less established lines far less was done. Bath's Town Scheme (a triple partnership of government, local authority and owners) began in 1955, but it was fifteen years before an equivalent arrangement could be successfully launched in Georgian Edinburgh. In 1967 a Scottish Minister, Lord Hughes, indignantly rejected the idea that Scotland should follow England's example in commissioning conservation studies of historic towns.

LOCAL ENTERPRISE

Nevertheless progress was being made on local fronts. Private agencies like the Killearn Village Trust (1932) and the St Andrews Preservation Trust (1937) had already begun to take a direct hand in conservation-minded preservation, and the National Trust's activities encouraged the formation of many more such bodies, especially in East Fife. A number of local authorities had acquired and preserved isolated buildings in the 'thirties, but the first sizeable group-preservation – or rather restoration – scheme was not begun until soon after the war, in the Broad Street area of Stirling. Most of the finest buildings were considered too far gone and virtually rebuilt, the rest being redeveloped 'in keeping', but to an uncharacteristically low density so that the result is rather a shadow of the bustling, congested town centre it must have been. In this operation Sir Frank Mears and partners collaborated with the Burgh architect.

A similar approach was adopted in Edinburgh's Canongate. In 1952, at the prompting of Robert Hurd, Lord Provost Sir James Miller (better known for his contribution to the city's residential fringes) launched a scheme which did much to restore the tattered credibility of the Royal Mile as a historic street. Shoemakers' Land, Bible Land and the splendid eighteenth-century tenement of Chessel's Court were preserved; most of the rest was redeveloped in an up-dated version of the original style in which the detail became more obviously modern in the later phases. Robert Hurd and his successors worked here in the tradition he had established before the war at Bakehouse Close, using a certain amount of wood cladding, and wood-float rendering (as opposed to harling) which accords well with the fine-cut masonry of the new arcades on the street. The walls are boldly coloured. In spite of its stylistic middle path this scheme is better than a compromise, and forms a valid continuation of the pioneer work of Geddes. Above all, it preserves a close and usable townscape character, and in all respects compares well with similar post-war reconstruction on the continent, at Munster for example, to which it has a striking resemblance.

Town centre housing redevelopment on traditional lines was also carried out at Dalkeith and Clackmannan, at Selkirk (Sir Frank Mears and Partners), old Stonehaven (the Burgh Architect) and Thurso, together with some restoration (Sinclair Macdonald, pl. 32b). Its pitfall is a certain substantial fussiness which belies the Scots tradition; an effect which is sometimes emphasized, though not in every instance, by quite alien features like low front-garden walls. This indeed is a fault in Basil Spence's housing scheme near the harbour at Dunbar (1953), which is otherwise a successful attempt to devise a modern equivalent for a traditional type. One vital point to be decided in this sort of exercise is the exact nature and purpose of the 'modernity'. Developments like Wheeler and Sproson's terraced housing at Milnathort (1967) have shown that a today's equivalent may be very near to the original, which had a basic and timeless style.

The same architects' policy at Somerville Street, Burntisland (finished 1955) was adventurous and significant. It was to combine the preservation of the south side with modern redevelopment on the north, the west end being closed by a long block of flats which runs through towards the High Street. Though obviously not applicable in all cases, the deliberate combination of new and old is here for the first time successfully attempted. The idea was developed in the same architects' larger scheme at Dysart, started in 1958 (pl. 32e). In this case selected old buildings (some would say too few) are used as the architectural and townscape key to an extensive new development of flats and houses. Contrasts and similarities in architectural idiom are nicely calculated, and the variety of old building types gives point to the even greater variety of the new. This municipal scheme provides an interesting contrast to the one down at the old harbour, where W. Schomberg Scott's Pan Haa' terraces adjoin a group of old houses in a revolving fund project jointly undertaken by the National Trust for Scotland and the Crown Estates Commissioners (1969). Disowning their sturdy neighbours, the new houses gaze with almost home-counties politeness at the North Sea.

The two greatest successes of local enterprise have been at Portsoy and Haddington; the first limited in scope, the second all-embracing. Portsoy however is remarkable because, here as nowhere else, preservation and housing have been treated as an identical job (p. 102). This is conservation in the fullest sense. Inspired and directed by the architect John Meldrum from Banff, work began at the harbour in 1963 and is moving steadily up into the town.

Haddington (p. 237) makes the same point on a bigger scale, again illustrating the importance of an inspiring personality. As early as 1955 Frank Tindall, the County Planning Officer, drew up a development plan on what would now be called advanced conservation lines, and in time convinced the burgh authorities that it was the right plan. It began in a small way; a single pilot scheme, the restoration of a condemned and derelict house for himself and his family, then a guide-book explaining what a fine place Haddington is. Mutual congratulation over the preservation of the Town House broke into an open row about cobbles in the streets. Most of them were eventually tarmacked over, but the Planning Officer lost the battle in such a way as to win the war; or rather the peace, because the rest has been achieved by agreement. This depopulated and by-passed county town now attracted light industry from the United States, and 250 'overspill' families moved in from Glasgow (some into restored houses) to swell the labour force. Good sites were earmarked for new development, and a positive policy for all listed buildings was backed up in 1962 by the first co-ordinated repainting scheme to be completed in Scotland (St John Street in Perth was similarly improved soon afterwards).

The cities of Edinburgh and Glasgow, from their very different points of view, paid some respect to conservation in their development plans; Edinburgh cautiously, with a policy of control in the New Town that was soon to be overtaken by its own success, and Glasgow desperately, in defence of a historic core beleagured by an industrial desert. Glasgow's problem is indeed a very different one. The owners of listed buildings in the Georgian-cum-Victorian central area are mainly commercial concerns which have, or imagine they have, a vested interest in the continuance of the city's tradition of change. A typical catastrophe was the redevelopment in 1970 of McGeoch's warehouse, where Sir John Burnet in 1905 perfected the townscape art of turning a corner in the grand manner; his building was perfectly stable and there was no gain in floor area. Despite such admirable gestures as the corporation's rescue of 'Greek' Thomson's masterpiece the St Vincent Street Church (1858) at a cost approaching a hundred thousand pounds (1964), Glasgow's composite richness has been and is still being disastrously eroded. Lord Esher's report on Conservation in Glasgow (1970) made a masterly diagnosis and put forward sound recommendations for treatment.

OFFICIAL POLICY: THE SECOND PHASE

The earlier stages of government policy had done little to relieve what amounted to an unproductive state of war between the supposedly opposite factions of preservation and development. For the former, it was especially hard to understand why the Secretary of State would not pronounce upon issues which did not seem to have been fairly assessed at a lower level by local authorities. Part of the reason was (and still is) the wide scope of his responsibility. A thumbs-up sign for one Scottish interest may mean thumbs-down for another, politically more important, one. Besides, he was reluctant to dictate to planning authorities or to prejudice his own judicial position should an issue become sufficiently hot for him to order a public inquiry in which he would himself have the final decision.

Decisive indeed were the few public inquiries to be held; not merely on the immediate issues involved, but in establishing the general principle that an apparently nebulous question ('surely it's just a matter of taste') can and should be discussed in real terms; that architecture and townscape are a part of planning. Inquiries also give a fair hearing to anyone who has anything coherent to say and the slightest pretext for saying it. The mammoth inquiry of 1966 into the Quinquennial Review of Edinburgh's Development Plan comes to mind, the existence of certain historic areas and buildings being one of the few tangible facts in the whole argument. Not unnaturally, the Scottish Secretary approved the reporter's recommendation that many points, including the proposed inner ring road, should be further considered. An important issue of high building was settled at the inquiry into the proposed seventeen-storey extension of the George Hotel in the middle of the First New Town (1958). The revised and now completed scheme by Harry Wylie, which received a Civic Trust commendation in 1973, shows how commercial interest can conform with the reasonable constraints of conservation.

But the first recognizable turning point was the Civic Amenities Act. It marked, in the words of the Scottish Development Department circular to local authorites, 'the change from negative control to positive planning for preservation'. Its main directive to planning committees was to designate areas whose character should be 'preserved and enhanced', and which would be known as Conservation Areas. The effect was to encourage those authorities or officials who already had a conservation policy by giving a respectable label to their activities; and to provide a conference table round which a planning officer could get together with his colleagues, the architects and engineers and administrators who had not previously recognized their own roles in conservation. But the overall response was disappointing. The initiative was firmly left with local authorities, with a minimum of central guidance from the Scottish Development Department's planning division, very little from the historic buildings division. The Department had not followed its own exhortation to 'get together'. For these and other reasons, including an unjustified fear of having to compensate the victims of special development controls within Conservation Areas, fewer than a quarter of the potential Areas in Scotland have been designated since the date of the Act.

Another important but little used provision of this Act was the power it gave to local authorites to make grants to historic buildings. As in England, where this had already been possible for the past five years, this applied to the buildings which for any reason were not eligible for Historic Buildings Council grants, and particularly churches. Despite the special townscape importance of many church buildings, they have so far been cut off from any other form of grant aid (though a pilot scheme has just been launched), and technically even from listing. For this there are historical reasons. In England the churches have never come to terms with preservation interests since the bitter conflicts of the nineteenth century. The Church of Scotland is a democratic organization traditionally opposed to central direction of any kind, and frankly uninterested in the architecture of their kirks except as accommodation for worship and the Word. Churches however, including those in use, are placed on the official lists and in practice many parishes have co-operated in conservation projects; just as well, for the 1928 reunion of the Church of Scotland and the Free Church gave the country a double quota of redundant churches.

A much greater transformation has been effected by new Planning Act of 1969. It is not yet clear how the new principle of Structure Plans will affect conservation questions, but the improved machinery for the protection of listed buildings laid down in part V is working remarkably well. Instead of merely having to give notice of his intention to alter or demolish a listed building, the owner or would-be owner now has to obtain formal Listed Building Consent for this as part of the required planning permission. All applications for Consent have to be advertised for three weeks, and comment is specifically expected from the Scottish Civic Trust, the Scottish Georgian Society and the appropriate local organization if there is one.

When this system was brought into force in 1971 the Societies – and for that matter the individualists who had kept out of them – suddenly found that they had been given the chance they had always asked for, but also a responsibility even greater than they had expected. Those applications that pass without comment amount to about a half of the national total. For the remainder, a simple objection is not considered enough; it has to be convincingly explained, and positive recommendations have to be made wherever possible. A very large element in many 'objections' is the furnishing of plain facts about history, architecture and townscape. Some planning authorities put applicants in direct touch with objectors to arrive at a solution, and consultation often continues throughout the work, which in many cases includes restoration as well as alteration.

The Secretary of State's role is even more limited than before, but much better defined; he is the final arbiter, but reluctant to interfere. The responsibility for the success or failure of this system rests heavily on the planning authority. Where their plans and policies favour conservation, as generally in Edinburgh, real co-operation is possible and it is not long before the results are seen in terms of social benefit. But where plans depart with more or less good reason from conservationist principles, and there is no agreement about objectives, the system comes unstuck. There is clearly a tendency, if not a need, for this to happen in towns whose economy is expanding. In Aberdeen for example, many alterations in character are contemplated or have already been committed within conservation areas (as with the demolition of the New Market), without any previous test of the benefits of a more rigorous conservation policy. The sort of communication which now exists over individual planning issues still has to be established for wider questions.

TOWNSCAPE CONSERVED

It is not the general practice in Britain to put up notices so that the approaching visitor knows that he is approaching a 'Ville Historique'. This designation might be applied to, say, St Andrews, old Stirling or Culross, towns which have kept their ancient shape and buildings, and where there is a sense of walking about in the past. Of younger towns, Inveraray and New Lanark might be included and so might the greater part of the New Town of Edinburgh.

The museum-piece town is the subject of a good deal of ridicule. But can anyone who has been to Colonial Williamsburg continue to accuse it of being dead or artificial? Interpretation, as it is called in the States, makes it a real homing-point for American and overseas visitors all the year round. Scholarship and workmanship together ensure that what they see is the genuine article – or as near to it as possible. Just as important as the restored buildings are the traditional activities in and around them. Visitors can watch the silversmith at work, buy his candlesticks, and eat the fresh gingerbread from the kitchen of the Raleigh Tavern. The full-time purpose of Williamsburg is to be visited and experienced.

There are few towns which do not share this purpose to some extent. But they tend to be a mixture, a continuous revision of activity and townscape up to the present time. Where in them should the line be drawn between preservation and restoration on one hand, and change on the other? The only universal standard is a very general one; that both old and new in their separate ways, and where necessary in concert with each other, should be credible.

This quality of credibility is shown in all sorts of ways. Use and usage are vital; it is best for a house to be used as a house, but we are now quite accustomed to seeing houses used as offices at town centres. How far is it then permissible to change the character of a house when it becomes an office? In such a case the function and credibility of the office are usually considered first, but it is important that they should come to satisfactory terms with the credibility of the house, or the whole thing will be a makeshift.

In two sorts of cases the argument becomes acute; when buildings are redesigned within an existing shell, or when they are moved to a new site.

Townscape value often gives so much credibility to buildings that their survival as shells may be thought worth while. John Nash's Regents Park terraces are an obviously justified example. St George's Church in Edinburgh's Charlotte Square, whose copper dome and gilt cross float over the trees at the end of the George Street vista, is another. It underwent complete internal rebuilding by the Crown and was reopened as the new West Register House in 1965, the credibility of the new use being successfully established on the outside by the bold glazing of the three great openings behind the portico. A similar internal transformation was carried out when the granite classical Trinity Church in King Street, Aberdeen (p. 130), was converted into an Art Centre in 1961. As part of Professor Robert Nichol's policy when he was Planning Officer in Glasgow, redevelopment of important Victorian buildings in Buchanan Street (p. 235) was only allowed if the frontages were retained; a realistic principle and at first glance an effective one. Yet now that the next step has been taken and the street has become a successful pedestrian precinct, there is more time to consider details. For a start, the frontages of the Western Club, the Royal Bank and the Stock Exchange have all been subjected to surface treatments that have devalued them, as is discussed below. But equally important, what survives of the exteriors is now belied by interiors that are obviously designed on different principles. The redevelopment by Celtic Securities of No. 23 Waterloo Place in Edinburgh, retaining the entrance hall and all the rooms on the street front, shows the gain in credibility from a more careful treatment (1972).

The moving of buildings is an exceptional operation totally condemned (even where total loss was the only alternative) by the Society for the Protection of Ancient Buildings ever since their foundation. However the loss of *genius loci* is no consideration in townscape, which takes a building and its site on their merits. A large section of Edinburgh's medieval Trinity College Church, demolished in 1848 to make way (perhaps unnecessarily) for the railway, was rebuilt by John Lessels in 1872 as part of a new church in the improvement area to the north; the newer work has now in turn been demolished. In Glasgow a condemned bank building in Queen Street was pressed into service by an enterprising Master of Works as a frontage for the Langside Public Hall in 1902. With the new end elevations he supplied, it occupies its very different open site with complete architectural and townscape authority. More recently in Aberdeen there was a controversy about the 'Wallace Tower', a charmingly turreted house which had been free-standing but became in time a key building in the close-knit townscape that grew up around it. The big store now covering the whole site is less of a credit to Marks and Spencer than the fact that they paid for the transplanting of the tower to a well-chosen site at Tillydrone Road, just north of Old Aberdeen (1972). These jobs were done stone by stone. At Gray's Close in Dundee High Street (just to the east of Reform Street) the whole frontage of Gardyne's House, complete with date stone of 1641, is about to be trundled bodily for a few metres in order to make room for a new Boots's store behind a curly-gabled eighteenth-century façade; altogether a real test of integrity, whose success will depend on the architect's attention to convincing details.

Techniques of the use and repair of stone are an interesting guide to changing fashions and attitudes. Earlier in this century stone was an exclusive object of reverence to lovers of old buildings. In hundreds of cases of well-meant restoration the rubble walling, with its special flavour of honest antiquity, was quite dishonestly stripped of its coat of harling; and often most unwisely, for the harling had been there for a reason. Sailors' Walk at Kirkcaldy, for example, had been built of soft stone, became eroded in places to a depth of six inches after twenty-five years of exposure, and had to be reharled in 1958. The seventeenth-century Tolbooth at Dunbar was 'restored' in the same way and with the same consequences, but the trouble there has still to be remedied.

If exposed rubble was somehow virtuous, painted stone was sinful. Regional practice in fact varies so much that it is impossible to generalize. Even the painting of ashlar, which is universally condemned, may occasionally be the best thing if deterioration of the stone is extensive and funds are not available for proper refacing. Marshall Place in Perth is a bad example because the necessary plastic (that is cement) repairs have been carelessly done and the Georgian unity lost through far too great a variety of colours. Carlton Place in Glasgow, where Geoffrey Jarvis successfully imposed a two-colour scheme on these much abused river frontages in a Civic Trust improvement project of 1959, is a good one. In Georgian Edinburgh, much of whose character depends on the continuity of its splendid stonework, the New Town Conservation Committee only sanctions natural stone repairs unless the area to be patched is very small or virtually invisible. It has also declared against the painting of masonry altogether, except on the standard Georgian shopfront.

The present fashion for cleaning masonry has obscured the important issues involved. No one would question that the removal of superficial dirt or soot is good for the maintenance and appearance of stonework. It can often rectify conditions which lead to the breakdown of walling or ornament. This breakdown, when it occurs, is one reason why many owners have sent for the 'stone cleaner', whose operations usually go far beyond cleaning. So much stone is actually removed that the whole shape of a building may be distorted or its lines impoverished. As a result of such treatment Irvine town hall is now little better than a skeleton. Examples in Buchanan Street, Glasgow, have already been mentioned and it is instructive to compare them with the nearby Library of the Royal Faculty of Procurators. This very florid building by the same architect as the Royal Bank office (Charles Wilson, 1854) has been much more successfully stabilized by the often despised method of painting. Another in Buchanan Street, David Hamilton's Western Club of 1840, has been quite needlessly *spoiled* by painting; or rather by the application of a textured surface which obscures the hard, clean lines of the masonry with a rough, dirt-attracting coat.

The other most frequent pretext for 'cleaning', quite apart from any breakdown of the stone, has been the desire to give a building a 'new' appearance. Like the stripping of harling from traditional buildings, this is often motivated by misguided stone-worship; equally often by the wish to make a frontage more conspicuous than its neighbours, a particularly unfortunate objective where a Georgian terrace is concerned. To produce the wished-for effect, very much more than the removal of superficial dirt is required, for the stone itself has probably changed colour with time. This weathered top layer is therefore either physically removed or (an increasing practice in recent years) chemically treated to restore something like its original appearance. The latter course is preferable insofar as it does not alter the precise shape given to each stone by the tools of the builder, though its long-term effects have still to be seen. Physical 'cleaning' by sand-blast, disc or bush hammer produces not only a different shape, but nondescript textures which may well encourage deterioration.

Stone is reputedly the most durable of materials. Its deterioration, often accelerated by remedial treatment or cosmetic surgery, raises the final question about preserving a building. How long will it last? The stabilized ruin, the meticulously restored museum-piece (not that there are many of these), the church piously restored from what it had become to what it never was, the seventeenth-century house with the modern conveniences of the mid twentieth century, or the Georgian house which has been gutted and made into an office – how will

214

they stand and what will they all mean in fifty or a hundred years' time? Will our historic architecture then be represented by a collection of unreal fragments, neither useful to their owners nor true to their original design?

With towns, the possibilities are both better and worse. Better because they consist of groups of buildings, each of which can make a case for its neighbour. Worse because towns are nothing if they are not functional; even more than the individual buildings of which they mainly consist, they stand or fall by their usefulness. If it is granted that we have towns which are useful and enjoyable, and that we want them to survive and prosper for as long as possible, what can we do about it?

One very tempting answer is that we should concentrate on the best towns and leave the rest to chance. Surely this would be wrong. Although any programme of intervention and aid must have its priorities, the idea of cosseting a minority of places as works of art, and treating the majority as merely useful, denies the possibility that all towns could be both of these at once. Moreover a selective programme would, as it were, tend to leave us with the cake and cheat us of the satisfying bread-and-butter of the ordinary townscape.

A more real objective would be to establish the conditions in which towns will be able to survive. We have already come quite near to this as far as negative controls are concerned, but the planners who administer these controls also hold the key to something more positive. Although it will always be the owner and the developer who make the individual decision, it is up to the planner to connect them with an effective strategy.

It will always be worth while to examine our motives in conserving and preserving – and our methods too. Our own use and pleasure is a perfectly legitimate aim. It will only be a selfish one if through neglect (or even by short-sighted restoration) we hand on buildings and towns that are less intelligible than we found them.

X. TEN TOWNSCAPES

ABERDEEN

UNION STREET AND CASTLE STREET TO KING STREET

As so often in this spacious county the sky predominates, often matching the pale grey of Rubislaw granite which was till recently the only permitted material. Laid out in 1800 to a length of three-quarters of a mile, and correspondingly wide, Union Street was a grand conception executed in low key, for most of the fronts were and still are those of two- and three-storey houses. Original doorpieces survive at Nos. 226 and 224, and arcaded Georgian shopfronts under flatted blocks can still be seen at Nos. 203, 124 and 17 (Finlay's tobacco shop) plus the similar treatment of the Athenaeum's ground floor at the far east end, where Union Street becomes Castle Street. The remainder are now converted with offices above, indifferent shopfronts below, and towards the west even these are shabby or unoccupied with the decline of their old-fashioned trade. The building societies are taking the better shop sites, through-traffic most of the road space.

As a westward exit UNION STREET [pls. 33a-c] is unceremonious, as if the main object were to get quickly out of town to Deeside and the mountains. The only terminal feature at this end, well down the right hand fork, is the square gothic tower of Christ's College (1850). So it is best to start here (in what is actually called Union Place) and walk towards the centre. Look eastward, and the initially daunting length of the Street is relieved in three ways. First by the gables and spires of two churches, Gilcomston South to the left and West St Andrew's to the right; then by the gradual descent towards the busy intersection with Market Street and St Nicholas Street; finally by the promise of larger buildings on the gently up-hill stretch

216

beyond, terminated by an extraordinary baronial apparition in the distance. But there are other incidents on the way. After the long blank supermarket front which conforms in nothing except building line and granite facing, the severe Ionic portico of Archibald Simpson's Assembly Rooms (1820) steps formally out on to the pavement. Just after it, Silver Street leads into Golden Square (1810) which is choked with parked cars, but the point block on the vista is far enough away to be decently effective. Then a dramatic break in the granite line; off to the north go Union Terrace, the sunk gardens with giant draught-board, the further-sunk railway tracks. The street sails on over Union Bridge, from which the northward panorama includes Simpson's Royal Infirmary(1833) as a distant focus and the tall red *brick* spire of his Disruption Churches (1844) as a middle-ground surprise.

On this side the building line resumes with a good Georgian block, on the other side with Trinity Hall (1846), or at least it would, if a line of flimsy-fronted shops had not been built along the whole south side of the bridge, blocking the view and partly obscuring the end of the perpendicular gothic Hall which is now abandoned, its former users (the Incorporated Trades of Aberdeen) having moved to a less highly rated site. To the left the buildings are again interrupted, but their line is maintained by the Ionic columned screen (1830) through which you can see the monuments and welcome trees of St Nicholas's churchyard.

And so to the cross-roads; four commercial corner-blocks, of which Montague Burton (*c.* 1937) best understands the granite idiom. To the left is St Nicholas Street, to which Union Street has long yielded its claim to be the principal shopping centre, its opening dominated by a thinly monumental Marks and Spencer (1962). To the right Market Street leads down to the harbour with more dignity if less fun; there was indeed a Market, a great covered basilica by Simpson (1839, destroyed in 1972).

The widening out into CASTLE STREET is supervised on two sides by Archibald Simpson's Athenaeum (1819) whose interior was burnt out in 1973. Opposite are the hugely Flemish Town Chambers (1860), almost swamping the old tolbooth spire of 1627. Straight ahead, the enormous building that has beckoned

you all the way down the street proves to be the Salvation
Army Citadel (1893) in a stretched baronial manner. But it is
little more than scenery, and much of its thunder is now stolen
by the ten and twenty-storey blocks of Virginia Court and
Marischal Court beyond (1969). The drum-based Mercat Cross
(1686) finds a modicum of sympathy in the ordinary domestic
buildings of the south side (including the old-style chimney
gable of 51–3) but is accesssible only to intrepid pedestrians.

Archibald Simpson has the last word, for his Clydesdale Bank
(1839) on the turn into KING STREET celebrates the last virtuoso phase of his granite classic manner. The corner itself
provides the entrance by way of a curved portico, the flanks
unite three storeys into tall units without overpowering the
domestic scale around. This side of King Street, however, has a
concentrated public splendour that you may have missed
hitherto, for next comes the Medico-Chirurgical Hall (1818)
from the beginning of Simpson's career; then after a shop-
arcaded interlude John Smith (the City Architect of the time)
has his say, with the columns of the Customs House portico
(1832) followed by the flat, pilastered flank of the North Church
(1829), the austere masterpiece of Aberdeen's granite neo-
classicism. On the other side uniform three-storey terraces defer
to all this and to Simpson's poker-fronted Episcopal Cathedral
(1816) in their midst. On goes King Street, straight as an arrow
to the north.

AYR

NEW BRIDGE STREET AND SANDGATE TO ALLOWAY PLACE

The drowsy Dungeon clock had number'd two,
And Wallace Tow'r had sworn the fact was true . . .
When lo! on either hand the list'nıng Bard,
The clanging saugh of whistling winds is heard . . .
Our warlock Rhymer instantly descry'd
The Sprites that owre the Brigs of Ayr preside . . .
Auld Brig appear'd o' ancient Pictish race,

The vera wrinkles Gothic in his face . . .
New Brig was buskit, in a braw new coat,
That he, at London, frae ane Adams got . . .

NEW BRIG
Will your poor, narrow foot-path of a street,
Where two wheel-barrows tremble when they meet,
Your ruin'd, formless bulk o' stane and lime,
Compare wi' bonie Brigs o' modern time?

AULD BRIG
Conceited gowk! puffed up wi' windy pride!
This mony a year I've stood the flood an' tide;
And tho' wi' crazy eild I'm sair forfairn,
I'll be a Brig, when ye're a shapeless cairn!

Robert Burns, *The Brigs of Ayr*

Auld Brig's prophecy came true in 1878 when New Brig was
half destroyed by flooding, and replaced by the present bridge
[pl. 34], carrying the traffic over the river Ayr from Newton and
joining up with Sandgate by way of NEW BRIDGE STREET.
This begins with 1–3 on the left, in Adam's own Culzean Castle
style; Adam certainly put in a design for the bridge, but it was
Alexander Stevens who finally got the job in 1786 – and also
designed Nos. 1–3 with twin bows overlooking the river and a
pretty shopfront on the street; its reeded pilasters introduce a
theme that keeps cropping up on this walk.

On the other side Harbour Street runs down to the quay, so
the block on the right does not rise from the water but sweeps
round the street corner in a suave Georgian bow. At its further
end No. 8 has another peculiar motif above its reeded shopfront –
curiously elaborate window sills with pom-pom brackets. It
finishes with a more tightly rounded corner balanced by that of
No. 10 on the other side of the narrow Boat Vennel, a cere-
monious entry justified by the fact that the early sixteenth-
century Loudoun Hall lurks down it, out of sight. Then alas,
on the key site facing down High Street, a double-width mosaic
fascia whose left hand half is surmounted by an artificial stone

front and steel windows; it is a nondescript way to be introduced
to the twentieth century, and what it looks at in High Street is
unhappily not much better.

It is impossible not to dwell on Georgian detail, for this is what
diversifies on a small scale the overall uniformity of the street.
SANDGATE, which follows, is a case in point; a well-mannered
rectangle with a few Georgian eccentricities followed by larger
Victorian ones, but the shape and contour (the latter a gradually
easing uphill slope) are still paramount. Leader of the architectural hierarchy that still prevails is Thomas Hamilton's dizzy
Town Steeple (1828) with gryphon-guarded clock. It has a
perfectly seemly Georgian shop at its base, and a remarkably
suitable extension along High Street. Then comes No. 3 (Little-
johns, superior grocers) with its pilastered shopfront, this time
Ionic, and beautifully painted upper floors which have more
pom-pom sills. Hereafter the Georgian frontages on this left
hand side are only interrupted by the intrusive long fascia of 15
(not bad in itself) and one red sandstone giant before they come
to Holmes and McDougall at 37, booksellers and stationers; they
have a good front finely lettered, with a Venetian window to
Sandgate and another to the tempting lane of Newmarket Street
round the corner. Soon after the opening the former Town and
Country Club makes Sandgate suddenly narrower – one would
say dramatically if it did not jut out in such a leisured manner
with its delicate cast iron veranda, mildly baronial above.
The former Royal Bank building by (Peddie and Kinnear,
1860) pushes out before it, its palace front taking more formal
advantage of the situation.

The right hand side has a good Georgian run (though only 26
still has its reeded shopfront) up to its own climax, the fine
neo-classic bank on the corner of Academy Street. The next
block, pleasantly varied, comes to Cathcart Street – columned
porches leading up to an off-centre glimpse of the pedimented
church front. The good vernacular block on the other side of the
opening is at the moment in a bad way; beyond it are three
strangely assorted bank buildings – baronial, Italian and modern
mannerist (1969), the last laboriously dissociating itself from
convention in all respects save its lovely stone; it belongs to the

Royal Bank of Scotland, formerly occupants of the palace across the street.

What follows is a free-for-all on both sides; shanty-shops, and a brash new post office looking blankly across at somebody's idea of a Romanesque Church while its charming red sandstone predecessor moulders. Hereabouts the Edwardian age wins a barren victory. Fort Street runs in from the right, the junction marked by the Kennedy statue.

Georgian order now resumes, and with the easy brilliance (three parts pragmatic in origin) which somehow eludes the modern planner. Alloway Place is straight on, but on its left hand side Barns Terrace (*c.* 1835) takes a side-step away from the road. And in the same sort of way the south side of Barns Street to the left (1800) is lined up with that of Wellington Square to the right (1806), the latter making room for the prospect of the domed County Buildings (1816). The Square has an endearing horticultural layout but the Fergusson and Neil statues are too fussed by 'Italian' flowerbeds to make much impression. Balustrades from the 'Adam' bridge are piously incorporated in the seaside pavilion whose strange silhouette looms beyond.

Ayr is a likeable and an infuriating place. It has inspired not only a certain amount of loyalty to its existing qualities but also, especially since it became a popular resort town, a strong urge to renewal and fragmentation. Today it can bring out the worst in the nostalgic visitor; a longing for the past which is visibly disappearing, a reactionary loathing of all innovation. Unfortunately the latter is justified on the present showing.

BANFF

Although this may not please all of its people all the time, Banff is the completest old town in Scotland. Little is left, apart from the street plan, of the medieval Royal Burgh confirmed by William the Lion. But the town still has a foothold in the seventeenth century and an uncommon wealth of straightforward building from the eighteenth, sparsely but all the more tellingly adorned with the marks of status and architectural fashion.

The nineteenth century respected this character and subtly added to it – a sign not merely of good manners but of remarkable stability, and a vigorous tradition. The present age, in which Banff is still very much alive, has contributed a general policy of conservation; there are surprisingly few gaps.

The best approach is on the A947 which has come all the way from Aberdeen. To the east is the fishertown of Macduff, christened in 1783 by the second Earl of Fife. Duff was the Earls' family name, and is also that of their tremendous baroque mansion designed by William Adam in 1725. To the west is Banff, and between the two towns the Deveron flows into the sea, crossed by Smeaton's bridge of 1770. The road was re-aligned in 1960, and although this has not quite spoiled the noble panorama it unfortunately wiped out the lodge and gates with which the house, standing back in the trees, made itself known to the town.

HIGH STREET AND LOW STREET

Like many harbour towns, Banff is ranged along a slope. The ancient High Street runs along the top of the ridge with Low Street parallel to it, further downhill. The prelude, where you can make your choice between the two, is an open slope super-intended by the late Georgian Academy building and the houses of Institution Row climbing up to it. At the point of decision stands Collie Lodge (solemn Greek Doric of the same period) now appropriately used as an information office for visitors.

First then the HIGH STREET, whose entry is marked by the quietly playful Georgian steeple of the parish church – only in fact it is Victorian, of 1842. On the left a nice row of two-storey houses finishes with a gable-endie, followed by the tall chimney-gabled tenement built by the Banff Shoemakers in 1787. On its further end gable is the shadow of another which belonged to an even finer specimen; the supermarket that replaced it in 1963 is one of the few signs of conflict between the town and its heritage. Across the street are the town houses of important men (No. 5 belonged to Lord Banff) but their fashion of building

is just the same; the only difference is that they stand a little
way back from the pavement and have a tactful minimum of
classical trim, like the doorpiece of No. 1 which was built in
1764. Also set back, but resembling nothing else in the street
except its own rectory, is the Tudor Gothic Episcopal Church of
1830 by Archibald Simpson of Aberdeen. Moray House on the
same side, with its intricate fanlight, was built in the eighteenth
century and belonged to Robinsons, threadmakers in Banff. So
did the chimney-gabled house around the corner in Boyndie
Street. George Robinson and his son were provosts of Banff for
for most of the period from 1784 to 1831. Boyndie House itself
(the Forbes of Boyndie lodging) is dated 1740 and goes one
better with a full-width gable of lovely curved profile. High
Street then continues northwards as Castle Street. This was
opened up in 1750 when John Adam replaced the medieval
castle with a Georgian mansion for Lord Deskford, and eventually reaches Battery Green on the point, by way of the Georgian
seatown, passing a porticoed church and the handsome Italian
town hall *en route*.

LOW STREET [pl. 35a] starts off Victorian, but with due
attention to Banff's established classical idiom. The old County
Buildings are rather volubly Italian, but are set back from the
street. The Fife Arms Hotel whose porch pushes into it on the
other side is in the timeless Georgian idiom of the eighteenth
century which lived on well into the Victorian age; it was in
fact built by the Earl of Fife in 1843, and its two-storey northward extension with pend ('Stabling & Horses for Hire') accords
beautifully with the smaller scale of the rest. From here there
is a clear view up to Boots the Chemists at the north end; its
commanding position is helped by the slight dip in the middle,
but over its straight ridge appears the hipped roof of Lord
Deskford's house on the historically dominant site of the old
castle. Past Bridge Street, which slips down on the right to the
old market place and harbour, Low Street rather unexpectedly
widens and assumes a grander scale. One of the Adam brothers
came here in the 1760s to design the wonderfully austere Town-
house spire, with fluted obelisk steeple, Archibald Simpson in
1836 to contribute the characteristic Clydesdale Bank. Both are

quite at home here amid the prevailing vernacular of the eighteenth century, and the one wild Victorian extravagance is strait-jacketed in granite, and thus forgiven. The medieval Mercat Cross stands on the Plainstones in front of the Town-house, and to one side of it Admiral Gordon's mid-Georgian mansion hangs back, slightly aloof but lending dignity to the scene. A handy traffic obstruction is provided by the pretty crown-topped fountain in front of Boots, whose building is the first of a Georgian row climbing westward up the steep passage of Strait Path to the High Street.

From Low Street – for this is nothing like the sum of what Banff has to offer – you can walk down to the turreted corner house at High Shore [pl. 9c] and on to the churchyard which has lost its church but still has plenty of tough and grisly headstones from the seventeenth century. The waterfront is lined with old buildings doing good service, including the houses of Deveron-side where the Banff Preservation Society first took a direct hand in the job of rehabilitation, beginning with the one at the north end in 1965. Unfortunately they look out over a long, bald concrete sea wall. The masonry of the old one had certainly been breached in places, but was such a drastic cure really necessary?

CUPAR

A Royal Burgh since 1237, Cupar has long lost its sheriff's castle but is still the county town of Fife. Standing at the Cross you can look west along Bonnygate towards Kinross, or south down Crossgate and its successor Millgate which takes the road over the Eden to Kirkcaldy; road junction and river crossing explain its location.

BONNYGATE AND ST CATHERINE STREET

The two old streets form an inverted L, with Kirkgate threading its way between the two limbs. In Regency times it became a T, St Catherine Street making the other arm of the cross-bar and leading indirectly to St Andrews at the eastern tip of the county.

Anyone who remembers the outstanding collection of shopfronts that Cupar boasted twenty years ago will be disappointed today. But it still has its most basic assets; a compact centre intensively used, distinctive skyline and layout, and beautiful yellow sandstone.

Coming in from Kinross, West Port begins raggedly with three petrol stations and finished with two early Victorian church fronts facing each other in some embarrassment, one now a school hall and the other a cinema. But the former provides, with its spike-topped belfry, the first of a procession of spires. The next two of these belong to BONNYGATE; the Baptist Church (1866) with a cautious line of conifers, and St John's with its tall needle spire (1877) standing back behind limes as symmetrical as itself. But a domestic scale has already been established by good late Georgian terraces on each side; 132–6 nicely kept and lived in, their opposite numbers painfully stretched to accommodate a shop fascia 50 m. long, a small-town record even for the Co-op. After this lapse the more durable seventeenth-century modernism of Preston Lodge (1623, pl. 10e) makes some amends.

The churches and their trees are followed by the genial Georgian of a shopping street whose owners seem too busy and independent to change anything but the shopfronts. At 29 Reid and Son, Italian Warehousemen and Wine Merchants, still have three iron balconies, fine lettering and the original domestic window arrangement. On the south side the same sort of mixture; the thinly grand Masonic Hall (1811) is just important enough to restore the building line after a gap made for car parking. No. 40 is a real Scots oddity. It projects a little into the street but doesn't extend quite far enough sideways to support the skew of its own gable; this job is obligingly done by a corbel built out from 42, but 40 takes further advantage of the arrangement by putting a little fillet across the gap, with a squint window looking down the street; all this in aid of a stair which has to get up in between them. A further diversion is provided by the miniature battlemented tower of 32 (1912) with red sandstone dressings and a splendid shopfront of the same date; James Montador, complete with hanging fish sign. But alas for the other fronts; 28 retains only the shadow of what was one of the finest in Scotland – and the good draper's sign of a sheep. By now Bonnygate, which swelled to its greatest width in front of St John's, has narrowed again before opening out at the Cross [pl. 35b]. Here, in front of a Bank of Scotland which does its best to conform, you have a choice.

To the right is CROSSGATE, a spacious market area with granite setts along its more formal side in front of the Town Hall. Opposite is a conscientious redevelopment by Woolworths (1970) and then the Duncan Institute (1870, 'for the working classes of Cupar') with an amazing twisted spire; this is the pivot at which Crossgate begins to turn and narrow, eventually (as Millgate) curving round out of sight with green hills above the far rooftops.

Straight ahead is ST CATHERINE STREET [pl. 35c] starting with the former Town Hall (1815) at the corner of Crossgate, to which it presents a big bow-front. Having conceded that the business of the ground floor must be shopping, it asserts a much larger scale than its neighbour for the upper floors and finally goes full circle with a dome, lantern and clock. It also sets the cornice line for the County Buildings (1820) in St Catherine Street itself; they were tactfully extended by the County Architect in 1960. On the other side the slated and lucarned spire of the Corn Exchange (1862) is higher than the Town Hall dome but stands well back and complements its outline – square and craggy as against rotund. The same sort of contrast is effected by the gable of St James's Episcopal Church (1870) jammed between the high-class Georgian housefronts and the Royal Hotel; the former uneasily shared by the big three Scottish banks, the latter poorly extended with a single-storey bar. But the Street ends well with an excellent war memorial against the green background of the park; this is where the Georgian master-plan would have put a jail building to close the vista. Traffic signs, not too conspicuous, are the only indication that this is somehow the way to St Andrews; a victory for townscape and the principle of town-containment.

DUMFRIES

BUCCLEUCH STREET, HIGH STREET AND ENGLISH STREET

The A76 enters the town along Glasgow Street, whose left hand side is at present weakened by wholesale clearance right down to the river. Will the space be filled – and if so, how? Luckily Galloway Street cuts across the far end with a small-scale Georgian row, culminating in the gable and painted sign of the Spread Eagle at the townward end. It also offers, through the gap beyond, a glimpse of a mysterious, distant tower. Turn left, and the street takes you between two more Georgian blocks and on to the bridge, after which it becomes Buccleuch Street, with the red needle of Greyfriars Church at the far end.

From the bridge the view downstream is of White Sands, a broad riverside space architecturally nondescript but performing every possible function for people and vehicles. This is where Dumfries's famous cattle and pig markets were held. Above it rise the roofs of the town centre, and the 'Devorgilla' bridge [pl. 5a], built about a hundred years after Dumfries became a Royal Burgh, still links it (for pedestrians at least) to Maxwelltown and its loftier heights on the right bank. Above the villas, and above the riverside housing which strikes a nice balance between urban and suburban, our tower now stands supreme. It is a windmill, Grecianized into the Town Museum in 1836.

Much of the Georgian BUCCLEUCH STREET has been redeveloped with beefy giants in the universal red sandstone of the region, like the Victorian Court House and the Edwardian Post Office – the latter now in need of a new job. Most of the fourteen surviving houses are painted so that their fine red masonry looks like stucco, but half are still relatively intact despite change to business use. Into this friendly dialogue between the early and late nineteenth centuries, the twentieth makes an obscure interruption with the single-storey extension to the Town Hall. Ahead, the grander late-Georgian fronts of Castle Street move out from behind the painted portico of the

Baptist Church to confront you. But the Victorian has the last word, with the soaring gothic of Greyfriars Church (1866) finally closing the vista.

CASTLE STREET runs across the T-junction at the end. To the left, painting has brought out the crispness of the facing Georgian terraces, and their arched tabernacle doorways. The excellent ironwork includes a fantastic curly light over the steps to No. 4. But at the far end the effect falls to pieces, no Georgian developer having feued the corner sites at the intersection with George Street. To the right a long supermarket shopfront holds up a re-erected Georgian façade which still bears traces of the operation – a number painted on each stone. But its five Palladian windows are unhappily blanked off for storage. The best shop is Victorian (Tosh, Fish and Game) at No. 14. The other side of the street expands into a sort of square in front of Greyfriars Church. It is in fact a traffic junction, but the views in all directions are enticing and an unlikely mixture of architectural personalities (including late Victorian fireworks and modern gentility) manage to achieve its enclosure. The obligatory Burns statue stands in the middle.

On the left, this space squeezes you gently into the narrower HIGH STREET. On the right the building line pushes in more decisively (George Young and Son, Bags and Umbrellas), suggesting a walk down Friars' Vennel to the river. On into High Street, and the first narrow section is effective in shape, ghastly in its butchered or thinly imitated Georgian detail. Then to the left it breaks suddenly into Queensberry Square, where an early and thus interesting pre-war supermarket (1932) with blankly monumental top-hamper confronts the Trades Hall of 1804, altogether a more sociable building despite the filling in of the ground floor with unsympathetic shops; one of them, the Bradford and Bingley Building Society, was momentarily up-to-date when built in 1971 but will have to wait some time for its period charm to be felt. But this is still a splendid space, and the extraordinary gem of the Mid Steeple [pl. 36a], set coolly in the middle so as to preside from either direction, here gives you a choice: right, through a narrow pedestrian squeeze, or left so that you pass another and equally repellent

Building Society frontage. Montague Burton did a more reticent job about 1936, but thought better of it and slapped on an irrelevant post-war facia. For the rest, this side has a fine array of three-storey Georgian fronts, one with a wall-head chimney gable, before English Street comes in and sees, on the other side, the festive fronts of the King's Arms and County Hotels. The centre of the junction is marked by a luxuriant iron fountain. Steeper now, and once again narrowed, the High Street goes on past what must have been, before they lost their glazing, the lovely shopfronts of 24 and 28. The chaotic building line on the right is called to order by the fruity Carlton Hotel. Then it is Nith Place that curves on down to the river, looking back up the hill with the eighteenth-century pedimented front of No. 24.

ENGLISH STREET is narrow, with a hump and a bend in the middle; predominantly three-storey Georgian, with masonry painted above, and shopfronts introduced or altered below. Its angle with High Street has an invaluable corner splay, and then 19 has its original pedimented door and a splendid pub front, the Barrel. The three storeys twice duck down to a smaller two-storey scale but culminate in a pedimented chimney gable atop the rise – important when seen from either direction. The right hand side begins with a Graeco-renaissance bank and the former Music Hall whose upper frontage is a pantheon of the busts of great composers; both in ripe red sandstone, un-painted but over-cleaned. Crisp Georgian corners lead into Queen Street and then there are some bad gaps, but on the back of No. 50 is the information that it was 'built in 1579, rebuilt 1806', which is roughly the date of most of the Street. The left side provides another vital chimney gable before the Dumfries Motor Company breaks up the scale. The street widens, and before it forks off (split by a church) to Lockerbie and Carlisle, accommodates a great show of red sandstone, finely grouped although St Mary's Church on the left (1837) has a surprised look – a firescreen-gothic frontage stranded on a hillock. Despite the big-scale competition, the honours for quality must go to Adam's Queensberry monument (1779) that used to stand in Queensberry Square, and the weeping elm in front of the Cairn-dale Hotel.

EDINBURGH

CASTLEHILL TO HOLYROODHOUSE

Royal Mile! The name has the sanction of four hundred years of history, for Alexander Alesius called it the *Via Regia* as long ago as 1529, but what is the present reality? First, and unalterably, it is an event in geology, the long path down the tail of a volcano; secondly an event in space, the now continuous sequence of two burgh high streets. What it lacks, and may never regain, is the confined activity that made it in the first place; a mile of intensive development in which every little opening of pend into close was grudged (dozens of closes survive in name, a few in fact). Today's movements cut across it and leak out of it, a townscape change which is at least excusable on grounds of function. It is the purposeless holes, exposing wide views and blank gables like amputated stumps, that really do the damage. Pedestrianization, if the whole street cannot become more purposeful, could make it worse.

CASTLEHILL is a small set piece, as perfect and as odd as the art nouveau Witches' Fountain (1894) set in the wall at the top; and narrow, so that it makes a surreptitious exit from the broad Esplanade, stealing down behind the convincing gothicry of St John's Tolbooth Kirk (1841) to make a sneaking entry into the head of the Lawnmarket. On the way are rubbly restoration, a reservoir with dummy windows, a Scottish Baronial observatory with Geddes' Outlook Tower perched on top (nature's television, says the notice), a good shopfront at 539, a solid Victorian board school of 1886 and a meagre stone screen that fails to dignify the back entrance to the Church of Scotland Assembly Hall. All this in a tight curve, so that there is no clear view downhill.

You emerge to see Mylne's Court with its regular frontage addressing itself to the Upper Bow (this is a good way on to the raised footway of Victoria Terrace [pl. 31c], and the Tolbooth Kirk spire to the LAWNMARKET, a splendid space lined with the street scenery of three centuries and ending with the breach

230

made in 1840 by the new thoroughfare of George IV Bridge.
This is not a particularly good junction; for one thing it lays a
carpet of asphalt across the Royal Mile's granite setts. It opens
effectively northward (David Bryce's 1870 Bank of Scotland
boldly blocking the view down to the New Town) but feebly
southward after a weak start, the semi-transparent corner of
the new Midlothian County Buildings (1960) offering an example
of anti-townscape. It is however a good place to stop and look
back at the Lawnmarket. The convergence and contrast of the
two sides is dramatic; gables dominate to the left, straight
Georgian eaves to the right, though the latter are relieved by
the craggy skyline of Gladstone's Land and the fanciful gables
of Geddes' Royal Mile Improvement Scheme at 451–63.

This is also a vantage point for the HIGH STREET which
follows [pl. 36b]. To the left the Sheriff Court holds its position
well, and after a turreted corner comes a long cliff of tenements
dignified at the centre by the City Chambers (1753); an arcade
sustains the building-line across its open courtyard. On the
other side you can as yet see only three buildings; in the distance
the Tron Kirk (1637), in the middle the big projection of St
Giles, and in the foreground – well, here there is some doubt.
In fact it is not the older Midlothian County Buildings of 1900
that lead the sequence, but the well-head in the street alongside.
As a formal climax St Giles is more than adequate despite its
boxy Georgian refacing (1829), but unhappily the operation
left it cold and isolated, its three dependent squares cleared not
only of their odd accretions of buildings but of the city life that
teemed around the Kirk. The fifth Duke of Buccleuch (1887)
now surveys the roofs of touring coaches, one of which may be
standing on the heart pattern of pink setts that now marks the
site of the old tolbooth. John Knox and Charles II (1685) share
the job of parking warden in Parliament Square, which since
the great tidy-up has been a place of pomp with very little
circumstance. The space to the east of St Giles is better, with
comings and goings of councillors and officials round the
mercat cross, and a head-on view into the courtyard of the
City Chambers on the other side. Further on, another cliff of
largely Georgian tenements has now emerged from behind the

231

cover of St Giles, and it includes at 166 the prettiest of all the two-storey shopfronts which are a distinctive feature of this length of street. Just before the Tron Kirk it breaks into Hunter Square, a civilized Georgian space (from 1786) which is the nearest thing to a commercial centre in the whole of the Old Town, business interests having taken themselves off to the New. With the revived (though now secular) Tron Kirk in the middle, pedestrianization could do wonders here.

In the 1790s South Bridge cut across the High Street, and a century later its northern angles were reconstructed as a festive exit to the New Town, one of them beautifully linked to the baronial redevelopments of Cockburn Street (1860) and Flesh-market Close. The further part of the High Street is a fine and now quite distinct space – or will be, if the present appalling gaps can be continuously filled with tall and preferably narrow buildings. For more than ten years now it has been a scene of desolation, strangely dominated by the vastly upstanding colonnade of the Carrubber's Close Mission. What is really satisfying about this space is the way it ends. John Knox's House (pl. 10a, one of a good group of three, with a well-head to keep them company) juts out from the left, just as if nothing had changed in three hundred years. History comes neatly into focus with the tourist image – and what does it matter if that history happens to be based on a mistaken tradition?

The narrowing of the street left room for the Netherbow Port, whose plan is marked out in brass studs on the road. Here begins the CANONGATE, and here unfortunately ends the causeway of granite setts, the tide of asphalt having reached this far up-hill before it was stopped by general protest. In other respects it starts well. To the right stands the bluffly chamfered baronial corner of St Mary's Street [pl. 31a] which you may have seen (and the distant glint of the Firth of Forth beyond it) through the Netherbow gap from a long way up. To the left another gap, but a well managed one, where Jeffrey Street (a second Victorian redevelopment) branches off to reveal the stone cylinder of David Hume's monument (Robert Adam, 1777) and the needle of the Martyrs' obelisk (1844) across the valley on the Calton Hill. One thing draws you down the

Canongate's stone corridor (new and restored buildings that look flat despite their self-conscious rubblework), and that is the exotic frontage of Moray House with its spiked gate piers and luxuriantly bracketed balcony. The contrast with Robert Hurd's Bible Land and Morocco Land reconstructions (1952) is almost as telling; their nice mixture of ashlar and colourwash together with the rubble seems positively joyous. Curiously, the same firm's later work on the right returns to a stiff mannerism, with brittle, flattened arcades. But again there is an effective contrast, for through them you glimpse the beautifully restored solidity of Chessel's Court (1748).

With the confrontation of Huntly House (1570) and the Canongate Kirk (1688), overlooked by the fortified Tolbooth of 1591, you are at last surrounded by the substance – not merely the shadow – of a Scottish town before the Union. But alas, although the corner turrets of Holyroodhouse are already coming into view, the Canongate will steadily peter out from here onwards. Milton House (1886) is an honest Victorian Board School whose central gable and bell-cote contribute to the picture, but the marriage of old and new style that has been arranged on the other side is too clever by half. Much worse are the gaps, the exposed gables bringing both sides of the street to a halt with one ugly jolt after another; two great gashes on the left disclose the appointments, suburban in character, of the ex-servicemen's home at Whitefoord House, with garden seats in front. What they look at is worst of all – the long blank wall that leads down to the Scottish and Newcastle Brewers' building (1971); a monument of non-participation in townscape, with statutory stone frontage towards the Palace. The left hand side makes a last despairing lunge into the street (behind this is the twice-restored Disneyland of Whitehorse Close) before bending northward into Abbeyhill. There, straight ahead, are the Palace and Chapel of Holyroodhouse. But they lie beyond the roundabout. You may still want to visit them, but the townscape has lost its hold on the situation. The excitement has leaked away.

GLASGOW

BETWEEN STATIONS: QUEEN STREET TO CENTRAL

This is a piece for Georgian symphony orchestra, partly re-arranged for Victorian and Edwardian brass.

From the glass vault of Queen Street Station's sheltered townscape (1878, the most graceful of its kind anywhere) straight out into GEORGE SQUARE. This was formed by leaving two blocks out of the Georgian grid so that there are two entries at each corner, but the one from the station has been built over by British Rail (We are a commercial concern) without even a token set-back in the building line. The big oblong space is better used than organized. In what should be a powerful Victorian confrontation, the north-of-England-looking City Chambers at one end (1883) are masked by the war memorial; at the other, three remarkably consenting office blocks (built from south to north, 1869–74) are stifled by a wooden information bureau which has neither a temporary nor, compared with them, a permanent appearance. The youthful equestrians Victoria and Albert deserve something better to come between them. Of other statues the free-standing ones are more at home in the crowd, but the municipal planting round the others is pretty enough, and you can sit on the granite edging; the little trees seem in awe of the buildings. Scott presides in the centre, his classical column a concession to Glasgow's character, and looks down Hanover Street which narrows dramatically before changing its name to Miller Street, prestigiously warehoused. There are fine views out of the corners of the Square. West George Street is nearest the station and has a terrific curtain-raiser in the top hamper of the Merchants' House (1907); building on buildings is a Glasgow habit. St George's Tron Church (1807) stiffly and authoritatively shuts the vista which is unsatisfactorily lined with the aggressively nondescript station front obstructing the glass arch, and a monster red sandstone office of the let-us-now-praise-famous-men Flemish school. Diagonally opposite, Cochrane Street

234

ends with a warehouse that reminds New Yorkers of their Soho. Then St Vincent Street, straight as a Roman road but built up with commercial architecture that becomes higher and mightier as it ascends the hill towards the wonderful silhouette of 'Greek' Thomson's church in the distance (1859).

But for the moment turn down QUEEN STREET; a superbly dignified frontage on the right, with big pilasters all the way along over the shops, built about 1834 as an office for the great art collector Archibald McLellan. Then on the same scale the two columned blocks flanking ROYAL EXCHANGE SQUARE (1830, pl. 37a), with Wellington's horse marking the centre between them; for more equestrian geometry look back to Victoria and Albert. Behind him the portico of Stirling's Library, formerly the Royal Exchange [pl. 5b]. All round the Square the same grand scale continues above the shops etc. of the ground floor, the best of them Alexr Hunter with shotgun sign, the worst the blocked-in windows of the migrated Western Club, genteelly netted – to stop them seeing us, or us them? Into the Square the Stirling Library is tightly packed so that cars are almost kept out, walkers not at all. The portico of the Royal Bank (1827) is so close that it seems to be forming a queue, but columned arches on each side acknowledge the friendly pedestrian scale of these spaces. The left hand one goes past one lovely shopfront (Porteous, bookseller) having framed for us the view of another (Barton, Men's Wear) across the street.

This is BUCHANAN STREET [pl. 37c], now part-pedestrianized, which incidentally makes our earlier paths feel a bit less privileged. Three things make this the finest of shopping streets. First the shops with their comings and goings which can now also be sittings and standings. Second its simple form, 550 m. of close-built corridor sloping very gently south, to end not in a great monument but a pretty little gauge-00 Jacobean tube station (1896); not that it needs more, for the third thing is the entertaining diversity (but consistent quality) of practically every building in the street. On the skyline the senior landmarks are a green dome at the south end, another half-way up, and the skeleton dome and spire of St George's Tron Church at the

top. Between them the flat-tops like the former Western Club
(1840) on the corner of St Vincent Street, and the saw-edged
ones like its gothic neighbour the Stock Exchange (1875) and
the big gable of Miss Cranston's Franco-Flemish tea-room, a
layer-cake in stone (1896). Walls are just as varied; framed
window, tall column and bulging bay in every responsible
combination plus one or two wild ones. Even the twentieth
century rises to the occasion with the British Airways office
(1970). Most of the shop fronts are good old fashioned or fully-
glazed modern, the latter coming into their own in a pedestrian
street. Worst is the Halifax Building Society with deep, opulent
slate facia, not only for itself but what it does to the charming
Glasgow Herald Building overhead. There are only two other
reservations. For Club, Stock Exchange, tea room, now read
office block, office block, bank. It's better than losing them
altogether, but how much unreality can even the best of streets
bear? Second, most of the stone-cleaning has removed ornament along with the dirt. Some say that painting devalues a
stone building, but it can leave it in much better shape; not
so the applied masonry textures like that which seems to have
covered the crisp outline of the Western Club with dirty
porridge.

In GORDON STREET the palace front of the Royal Bank
(built for the Commercial Bank in 1885) is the finest thing even
in Glasgow's streetscape, even if a little aloof from the walker
on the pavement; the lucky ones here are those behind the deep-
set columned windows of the first floor. To the left down Mitchell
Street is the runner-up; Mackintosh's red stone corner tower for
the Glasgow Herald (1893) shooting up seven storeys at the end
of a nondescript passage before it breaks into a roof-top cele-
bration. Then this bar of the gridiron bends a little, giving a
raking view of Thomson's Grosvenor Building (1859) the most
exciting produce of his (and Glasgow's) obsession with the
problem of the commercial street frontage. Opposite it, past the
amazing Ca d'Oro (1872), is the Central Station of 1884 with
welcoming canopy also in iron. Ahead, the completest possible
visual block, so you are not for the moment tempted to see
more. This is not quite the quickest way of changing trains

(all that some people say they want to do in Glasgow) but can be done without hurry in twenty minutes.

HADDINGTON

This is a handsome town whose general shape [pl. 38a] is still that of David I's Royal Burgh, but whose prosperous face is mainly Georgian, kept alive by sound twentieth-century planning. There is no yawning gap here between past and present.

COURT STREET, MARKET STREET AND HIGH STREET

The A1 has by-passed Haddington since 1950, and coming from Edinburgh you turn off towards its town-mark, the town-house spire (1830). The entry is lined with Victorian and the Georgian villas standing back in their own gardens; new housing, instead of ribboning along it, leads out of it on each side. The real beginning is signalled by the statue of Robert Fergusson of Raith, MP looking into town from his column (1843). The first few houses of Knox Place (leading to the amazing gothic Knox Academy, 1878) are angled to watch your approach. Past the red stone gables and baronial topped tower of the West Church (1890) you come to the point of the long triangle of the medieval market space; once open, it has since been split into three main streets, each of which is terminated by an inn – or inns – that jut across the end but allow you to squeeze past and explore further.

The first space is COURT STREET. The Tudor style County Buildings on the right (William Burn, 1832) are supposed to occupy the site of a medieval royal palace, and beyond them is the pompous pedimented frontage of the Corn Exchange (1854). These and the little Georgian villa that is now the Police Station (it has fine tendrilled ironwork supporting its blue lamp) lie back behind a long row of limes which cut off a quiet sliver of street from the traffic. On the other side more early-nineteenth-century Georgian villas have come right into town and are now urbanized by conversion to offices and banks; the showiest is 44 (possibly by Haddington's local master James Burn, 1802), now the Bank of Scotland. The Victoria Inn having planted itself in the middle, Court Street then narrows and takes on a more conventional town aspect to form something like a square in front of the gable and Venetian window of the Court Room which was added to the town-house in 1788; its ground floor was once open, accommodating the market for barley and oats. A nineteenth-century grain warehouse is part of the street architecture on the right.

Keep left past the town-house and MARKET STREET begins, gradually widening until it is almost blocked by the Pheasant and the Compasses, with many good things on the way; the Courier office nudging in from the left, and a single crowstepped gable on the right, past which is a stolen view, down a narrow passage, of the Mercat Cross in the High Street. Indeed the two streets here come very close together, and it is a pity the backlands of High Street have had to be cleared, giving Market Street only a wooden fence and some north facing seats. The tall Crown Dairy and 60–2 are prestigious town buildings of about 1750. After it narrows, Market Street has three surprises. The first is the majestic palace front of 7–8, built about 1760 [pl. 38b]; Palladio's home town of Vicenza offers just this sort of foreshortened view. Second, an unnamed close in which the cart tracks, set in whin chippings, take you past the burgher manse to the former burgher kirk, a homely pantiled hall of 1806 with flashy Georgian glazing. Last, Mitchell's Close, a brilliant feat of conservation in which the taller side is restored as housing and the other, too small and overshadowed for this, forms a row of craft workshops (1964–7, pl. 9b). At the far end is an openly modern clinic by the same architects, Campbell and Arnott.

Alternatively you could have taken the opening to the right of the Victoria Inn. This is LODGE STREET [pl. 38c], where the old masonic lodge with its early arched pend has been given the eighteenth-century status symbol of a Venetian window, and the mini-palace front of 'Carlyle House' (Jane Welsh was actually born in the house behind) sees you out into High Street; a long rectangle effectively blocked at the far end by the George Hotel, toy-fortified in the early nineteenth century and absurdly coated with artificial rubble in the twentieth. Colour is the street's most obvious attraction; the repainting scheme of 1962 has now been fully assimilated. But there is still a telling proportion of grey stone, particularly at the Bank of Scotland and its neighbour, and at 35–6 whose plain pilasters are the architectural signature of James Burn; here even Boots have managed to keep a good Victorian shopfront. On the opposite side a still better and earlier pair of shops at 82–4 have Ionic columns. Late Georgian is the keynote of the street and signs of earlier character have been camouflaged, like the seventeenth-century stair turret of 43–5 which used to be the Blue Bell Inn, and the double gables of the Commercial Hotel which have been built up from chimney to chimney. The main Victorian contribution is the fanciful reconstruction of the mercat cross (1880), its finial formed by the grape-eating goat of Haddington's arms; a pity it is not in a defined space where it could be a pedestrian rallying-point. Cars are of course the main twentieth-century contribution, but just before the exit into Hardgate, behind 34 (one of the few fronts that retain early Georgian astragals), is Campbell and Arnott's brave effort to have the best of both old and new worlds in new housing at Ross's Close, more successful in its layout than its attempt to bring up to date a Scots vernacular manner of which Haddington has very little anyway.

INVERNESS

THE RIVER, BRIDGE STREET AND CHURCH STREET

To call this the Florence of the north would be absurd. To compare the Ness and the Arno is not. Moreover in each place the silhouette of the further bank owes its character to a succession of churches – a fact that emphasizes, of course, the difference between the two towns in quality of architecture. But this is about townscape.

On the flat west bank of the Ness the biggest building is the Victorian gothic cathedral (Alexander Ross, 1866) in its contemporary baronial close. This is something apart – a dignified upstream suburb. Downstream of the bridge Huntly Street runs along the river. Here a modest urbanity is established by a string of Georgian fronts effectively punctuated by four churches and – as if to press home the point that architecture is not all – a symmetrical art-deco cinema converted into Palace Bingo.

The eastward, town-centre side of the river [pl. 39a] has another four churches, and builds up towards the site of the medieval (now 1834) Castle. On this bank a large chunk of the river frontage has been sacrificed to make a car-park for the Caledonian Hotel, whose back elevation looks over it with the blank, vicarious stare of 56 standard bedroom windows. Next to the gap a single eighteenth-century house (now the Inverness Courier Office) asserts the old building line at the corner of Bank Lane; then come the concrete giants, spilling along the riverside from Bridge Street.

Despite the seasonal constipation of cars, this finest man-made riverscape in Scotland can still be enjoyed on foot, with the aid of the twin suspension bridges conveniently sited at the north and south ends of the town. But alas for the centre. You penetrate BRIDGE STREET (from the Great Glen or the north) between two developers' complexes; two wrongs which in townscape terms at least could make a right, if they did not totally ignore the toy-fort Castle (actually the County Buildings, by William Burn) whose turrets are barely visible over the top. The earlier, to the right, has three slabs striding up from the river on top of a pedestrian terrace that makes a useful canopy over the shops; an intelligible idea, made obscure and irrelevant by clumsy detailing. The block on the left makes no such effort to conceal the fact that it is too big for the site, but it is far better in detail – especially if you look at the sunk-level entrances along the river front and not the egregious tankscape on top. Up Bridge Street is a beautifully finished Georgian range of three storeys complete with hardly spoiled shopfronts, nicely matching the slightly earlier town steeple (1791) which has lost its town-house. Its Victorian successor of 1878, in lean baronial gothic, stands back on the other side of Bridge Street on a pavement whose Caithness slabs are of awe-inspiring size. As to the rest of the street you can take your pick, from the relaxation of late Georgian to the mannerism of the 1930s. Most characteristic of Inverness are the innocently florid Victorian of the

a

b

c

33 Aberdeen. Union Street, moving east; **(a)** with the Assembly Rooms to left;
(b) crossing Union Bridge, with new shops obstructing Trinity Hall to right; **(c)** with
the churchyard screen, Town Chambers and Salvation Army Citadel (p.216).

34 Ayr. The entry to New Bridge Street and Sandgate from the bridge, with the Town Steeple behind the twin bowed 18th century house (p.218).

a

b

c

35 (a) **Banff**. Low Street; the Fife Arms to right, with the tip of the Town-house spire beyond, and the hipped roof of Banff Castle in the far distance (p.221). **(b) Cupar.** The Mercat Cross, looking back to the west along Bonnygate, and **(c)** looking east along St Catherine Street past the dome of the former Town Hall (p.224).

a

b

36 (a) Dumfries. The High Street, with the Mid Steeple and Greyfriars Church spire (p.227). **(b) Edinburgh**. The High Street from Lawnmarket; from the right, Midlothian Country Buildings new and old, and the Kirks of St Giles and the Tron (p.230).

a

b

c

37 Glasgow. (a) Royal Exchange Square with one of the two arches that show the way past the Royal Bank into Buchanan Street. **(b)** Stirling's Library (former Royal Exchange) along Ingram Street. **(c)** Buchanan Street, with former Western Club, Stock Exchange and St George's Tron Church (p.234).

a

b

c

38 Haddington. (a) from the air, with Court Street, to left, forking into Market and High Streets past the Town-house; **(b)** looking back along Market Street, with 7-8 to right, to the Town-house; **(c)** Lodge Street, past the former Masonic Lodge to Carlyle House (p.237).

a

b

39 Inverness. (a) the east bank of the Ness, with three churches, Town Steeple and Castle; (b) the end of Church Street, looking past Bow Court and Dunbar's Hospital to the telephone exchange; 111-3 to left (p.239).

40 Montrose. High Street and the Parish Church spire; Sir Robert Peel to right (p.242).

festive Bank of Scotland, (former Caledonian Bank, 1880) and the Royal Arms Warehouse, stupendously gothic with Peterhead granite shafts.

In CHURCH STREET, fragments of disappearing character include (but for how long?) the Edwardian shoe-shop at No. 9. Panel-faced offices over plastic-faced shops have nearly won on both sides, and have so little sense of place that the shops and restaurants sensibly sited along the base of the Caledonian Hotel seem positively urbane. The hotel's upper frontage manages to raise a minimal distinguishing (if not distinguished) feature – a pile of balconies and a tank-box lined up over the entrance – to look down Union Street which was started in 1865. This, despite the unhappy gap in the centre of one side, is an unforgettable vista of fin-de-siècle confidence terminated by an informal view of the Station Hotel (1875). Church Street continues with a mixed interlude in which Alex Macdonald's wine shop at 49–51 is still worth praying for and a shoddy new Co-op already looks the worse for wear, before Alexander Ross (Inverness's architectural supremo in late Victorian and Edwardian times) fires with his second barrel, which is Queensgate. It is the best thing in all his central redevelopment, and some of his confidence rubbed off on the Crown architects who with incredible presumption (almost its own licence) replaced one whole central feature with a new Post Office in quite a different idiom (1965). It is a pity the architectural broadside of Queensgate aims at no better target than the untidy supermarket at the far end.

After Fraser Street, with its narrow glimpse of the river, comes an odd surprise; a yawning gap created by demolition to reveal Abertarff House, at 350 years the oldest inhabitant of the street, with round stair turret and brilliant white harling. This is sacred-cow preservation with a vengeance, for even allowing that it is a very attractive and worthwhile building, there has not been the slightest effort to relate building lines, or levels, or functions, to those of Church Street. Preservation, we are to conclude, is a separate activity from that of real life. The aggressive new frontage of harl and mosaic goes to the other extreme in claiming a decisive relationship with the street, whose domestic scale is now only broken by two good Victorian hotels and the awful up-dating of the Hotel Clansman at 103. It signals furiously 'We are sorry this is an old building which we can't quite afford to pull down, but here are some modern bits and pieces so that you won't be put off'. After which, provided you can manage not to look straight ahead, all is well [pl. 39b]. The exemplary recreation of Bow Court (1970) has a ground-floor arcade leading nicely up to Dunbar's Hospital (1668), and on the other side, after a lane past the churchyard to the river, is a lovely build-up of old houses at 111–13. You can thread between them through iron gates to the Old High Church (1796). Finally the plain Georgian bulk of Greyfriars Free Church turns its back on its older neighbours; its bigger scale does something to mitigate the authoritarian mass of the telephone exchange which has been threatening you most of the way down the street, and which you may well have noticed from the other side of the river. This is Crownscape at its worst.

MONTROSE

BRIDGE STREET AND HIGH STREET
THE RIVER, BRIDGE STREET AND CHURCH STREET

One of David I's Royal Burghs, Montrose occupies a peninsula bounded on the west by a tidal basin, on the east by the North Sea, and on the south by the river South Esk which connects the two; a stage set by nature for a Dutch town, and indeed there were windmills here in the early eighteenth century. To reach it from Dundee you have to cross the river in two jumps; first on to the island of Inchbraoch, from which there is a view of the solid houses of the harbour front and the needle of the church spire sticking up behind them, and then over a petrified suspension bridge in reinforced concrete (1928). At its far end the medieval castle used to stand, and you would have gone on into town by way of Seagate and Castle Street. But the newer way is along BRIDGE STREET; after a calm prelude of Georgian terrace it curves round to the right, giving a closer preview of the spire over the backlands built out behind the west side of the High

Street. There is still a quiet Georgian ante-room. Castle Place, before the beautifully scaled and detailed Public Library (1903) whose red sandstone is in contrast to the local pinky-brown. Here you finally turn the corner into one of the finest town spaces in Scotland – and from it, if you like, into some of the most charming backlands; the private way through to the Retreat behind 188 for example, or the public path past the church and over a little bridge into Panmure Place [pl. 25b].

The HIGH STREET is the same big rectangle that Johnson and Boswell saw in 1773, the latter remarking that 'many of the houses are built with their ends to the street, which looks awkward'. It was the narrowness of its burgess plots, presumably because of a heavy demand for them, that early gave Montrose the image of a town of gable-endies, traditionally comic but always memorable. It became all the more distinctive after 1748 when a central row of buildings was cleared away and the narrow gables looked out, Netherlands fashion, over the broad market area which is now interrupted only by the bold projection of the town-house. Built in 1763, this was given its present aspect in 1819; it divides the street visually into two parts, while allowing the life of the town to flow through and shelter under its arcaded loggia or *piazza*.

The southern compartment [pl. 40] is dominated not by the town-house, which actually turns a blank gable this way, but by the lesser projection and far greater height of the Parish Church tower and its lovely flying-buttressed spire (James Gillespie Graham, 1832) which is Montrose's town-mark. Over this space Sir Robert Peel presides (1852), looking northwards up the Street from his pedestal in the middle; his back turned on the battlemented bungalow of Castlested House behind its screen of trees and, more understandably, on Alex Smith's stores with its incongruous picture-glazing. To his right is a long, substantial terrace of his own time with many original shopfronts, 141 and 143 the best. Victorian Scotland often follows Georgian tradition in this way, and here provides a perfect complement to the soaring spire. To his left an assortment of frontages representative of 250 years of disciplined prosperity runs right up to the west side past the constriction caused by the town-house (just here they tend to be lower); gable-endie and Georgian flat-top, Victorian commercial display and modern indiscretion, together they achieve a rough and ready balance. Along this side, which retains a single gable-endie, the pavement is sunk as a result of road-levelling. The stepped kerb has a sympathetic line that helps to unite the whole diverse collection and enables you to enjoy the best of the shop-fronts, notably the Royal Arch bar at 32 and the tobacconist at 102.

In the northern section Joseph Hume, MP is in charge (1859); like Peel he faces the centre, which in his case means southwards. On the east side are two more gable-endies at 85 and 91, mal-treated with tile and vitrolite fronts respectively. Here also is the parade of banks, the baronial Royal (1864), the palace front of the Bank of Scotland (1839) and another of 1863 which has been successfully transformed into a supermarket [pl. 32c]. The vital job of bringing the street to an end is done by the plain eighteenth-century block at No. 2. Cutting across from the west side, it is one of the key buildings of the whole scene. As a bonus, so unpractically effective that it has been considered beyond the power of official listing to protect it, a domestic group of minute scale and complex outline, stone slated, stands today just beyond the High Street in Murray Place, framed in the narrow exit. It will be a miracle if you find it still there when you read this.

In Montrose as elsewhere, the crisis of conservation is more than anything a crisis of communication. Central control is not the answer. What does Edinburgh really know about Montrose? Not enough to make decisions, but plenty that could help Montrose to make them. For the most part, the present state of the town is a credit to its ability to decide well. But the exceptions are numerous and can be laid not only at the door of the town, like the botching of the mouldings at the town-house in cement, but of the planning authority, like the whole-sale sacrifice of old shopfronts. Haddington, where conservation has been made a routine subject along with housing, roads and employment, has done well out of it in every sense. Montrose, an equally valuable place though less accessible and not of county town status, has only recently got a conservation area.

FURTHER READING
AND REFERENCE BOOKS

This selective list is mainly of books published in the present century and, if not actually in print, at least available at the larger public libraries in Scotland. When a book or its author is mentioned in the present volume the main page reference is given before the bibliographical details. PB means the existence of a paperback edition.

TOWNSCAPE AND TOWN GROWTH (GENERAL)

Gordon Cullen's *Townscape* (p. 11 Architectural Press 1961 PB) is the classic on the visual side of the subject. Kevin Lynch's *The Image of the City* (p. 16 MIT 1960 PB) concentrates on the idea of visual distinctiveness in (American) cities, and *The Historian and the City* by Oscar Handlin and John Burchard (MIT 1963 PB) is a perceptive treatment of the relationship between past and present in general terms. There is more British but no Scottish material in the papers from an important Symposium *The Study of Urban History* (Edward Arnold 1968) edited by H. J. Dyos.

Internationally, there is E. A. Gutkind's heavyweight series *The International History of City Development* (Macmillan 1971) which also includes towns and is copiously illustrated. Of its eight completed volumes No. VI deals with *The Netherlands and Great Britain*, but pays little attention to Scotland except in a short description of its burgh system. Lewis Mumford's *The City in History* is a more manageable and subjective introduction to its subject on a world scale. Patrick Geddes (p. 197) wrote his *Cities in Evolution* (reprinted by Ernest Benn 1968 with an introduction by Percy Johnson-Marshall) in 1915, with emphasis on solving problems in particular places, notably Edinburgh.

For Britain, a valuable series has begun with Vol. 1 of *Historic Towns* (Lovell Johns 1969, edited by M. D. Lobel) which includes Glasgow. It is intended that future volumes should cover Aberdeen, Ayr, Edinburgh, St Andrews and Stirling, with the same excellent format of large maps and commentaries. In much less detail Colin and Rose Bell's *City Fathers* (Pelican 1969 PB) is a good general introduction to town and even village development, taking special notice of some of Scotland's Georgian new towns. Photographs have their limitations, and two books are noteworthy because they are illustrated with their authors' drawings. They are the pleasant but rather randomly selected *British Townscapes* (Edward Arnold 1965) by Ewart Johns, and Roy Worskett's *The Character of Towns* (Architectural Press 1969) which is usefully slanted towards conservation.

SCOTTISH HISTORY AND SOCIAL HISTORY

W. Croft Dickinson's *Scotland from the Earliest Times to 1603* and G. S. Pryde's *Scotland from 1603 to the Present Day* (Nelson 1962) are standard works, and the first writer is mainly responsible for the *Source Book of Scottish History* (Nelson 1952) with its quotations from contemporary documents of the earlier period. These are among the least evasive of histories, but the same also applies to Rosalind Mitchison's *History of Scotland* (Methuen 1970 PB) which is a much shorter introduction to the subject, concise but always real. The shortest, recommended to the visitor with only minutes for reading, is Basil Skinner's *Scottish History in Perspective* (Scottish National Portrait Gallery, HMSO PB). T. C. Smout's *History of the Scottish People 1560 to 1830* (Collins 1969 PB) is unlikely to be bettered as a general work on social history with a wealth of particular information. The Victorian period has only recently received much attention; there is no standard book but W. H. Marwick's *Economic Developments in Victorian Scotland* (George Allen and Unwin 1936) was the pioneer work. Of the general books which attempt to cover the whole field, easily the most useful is *Scotland* (Ernest Benn 1934) in the *Nations of the Modern World* series. It is by Sir Robert Rait and G. S. Pryde.

Two books of early photographs are especially worth mentioning; *Victorian and Edwardian Scotland from Old Photographs* by C. S. Minto (Batsford 1970) and the volume *Scotland* (David and Charles 1968) in the *Industrial Archaeology in Pictures* series, with captions by John Butt, Ian Donnachie and John Hume. Hume's *The Industrial Archaeology of Glasgow* (Blackie 1974) is less copiously illustrated but extremely useful.

For burgh history the key reference book is G. S. Pryde's *The Burghs of Scotland; a Critical List* (Oxford University Press 1965) which indexes them and gives their important constitutional dates.

Of two volumes on *Local Government in Scotland* (Dunfermline, no
date) No. 1 by J. D. Mackie goes up to the 1832 Reform Act and No. 2
by G. S. Pryde follows on from it. Pryde also had a hand in a useful
booklet of the same title (HMSO 1958 PB) whose object was to
explain the Scottish local government set-up of that time; it now
needs to be brought up to date.

TOPOGRAPHY AND TOURISM

The Early Maps of Scotland (Royal Scottish Geographical Society
1936) is a useful key, and *The Mapping of Scotland* (Bartholomew
1971) is a copiously illustrated booklet covering the whole history
of the subject. The two volumes of *A Contribution to the Bibliography
of Scottish Topography* by Sir Arthur Mitchell and C. G. Cash (Scottish
History Society 1917) give references to maps, charters and other
material.

Notable tours, like memoirs, cannot be listed individually but once
again there is a good key, with numerous extracts; Sir Arthur
Mitchell's List of *Travels and Tours . . . relating to Scotland* (Pro-
ceedings of the Society of Antiquaries 1901 and 1905). Much of this
sort of material is also included in P. Hume Brown's *Scotland before
1700 from Contemporary Documents* (Edinburgh 1893). Maurice
Lindsay's compilation *The Eye is Delighted; some Romantic Travellers
in Scotland* (Muller 1971) is recommended as a prospectus of longer
memoirs, all of which take notice of towns.

The *Statistical Account of Scotland* (p. 65) is an invaluable guide to
Scotland for the 1790s when it was written and put together, but
Sir John Sinclair's own *Analysis* (p. 88 Edinburgh 1826) is more
suitable for general reading. The *New Statistical Account* (p. 86) does
the same service for the 1830s and is more use for touring because it is
assembled county by county. The *Third Statistical Account* by C. P.
Snodgrass (Oliver & Boyd) has begun to tackle the more diffuse
situation of the mid twentieth century with some success. But of all
comprehensive reference books Francis H. Groome's *Ordnance
Gazetteer of Scotland* (William Mackenzie, various editions from
about 1885) is still unrivalled.

For today's tourist the best single volume is the *Shell Guide to
Scotland* by Moray McLaren and others (Ebury Press 1960) though
its scholarship is unfortunately flawed by occasional lapses, as when
Haddington is credited with much work by Adam; this hardly
detracts from its value, especially for remote places unnoticed in
other books.

Scottish Townscape

This deserves a special heading because of the recent cross-disciplinary works which have revolutionized the study of towns and architecture in Scotland. T. C. Smout's more general work has already been mentioned, but his long essay *The Landowner and the Planned Village in Scotland 1730–1830* (p. 96) is very relevant in this context. It is one of a number in *Scotland in the Age of Improvement* edited by N. T. Philipson and R. Mitchison (Edinburgh University Press 1970). A. J. Youngson's *The Making of Classical Edinburgh* (p. 77 EUP 1966) is the first real study of the reasons and decisions behind this Georgian master-work, and has a bearing on the whole story of eighteenth-century Scotland. He followed it with *After the Forty-five* (EUP 1973) which deals with economics and town and village growth in the Highlands during that period. *Inveraray and the Dukes of Argyll* by Ian G. Lindsay and Mary Cosh (EUP 1972) is a sumptuous book about the town as well as the castle. It is written this time from the architectural point of view, but gives an equally satisfactory account of people and conditions at the time.

TOWNS AND ARCHITECTURE

The giants are still MacGibbon and Ross (p. 55) though their *Castellated and Domestic Architecture of Scotland* (Douglas 1887–92) and *Ecclesiastical Architecture* (do. 1896–7) are not of course restricted to town buildings and include very little after 1700. G. Scott-Moncrieff's *The Stones of Scotland* (Batsford 1938) is a good general introduction in spite of his censorious attitude to Victorian buildings, but it was superseded by John Dunbar's *Historic Architecture of Scotland* (Batsford 1966) which is completely dependable and remarkably comprehensive, especially on burgh architecture. George Hay's *Architecture of Scottish Post-Reformation Churches* (Oxford University Press 1957) is an important source for this significant building type. Ian Lindsay's *The Scottish Parish Kirk* (St Andrew Press 1960) is more general and embraces a much wider period. There is no general work on town development and buildings, but individual places have been variously treated. The Royal Commission *Inventories* of the Ancient and Historical Monuments of Scotland, for example, have become increasingly concerned with town growth, as in *Edinburgh* (HMSO 1951), *Stirlingshire* (1963) and part of *Argyll* (1973). On particular buildings and developments the best source of information may be the official *List of Buildings of Architectural and Historic Interest*, which are not available for purchase but may be

248

seen at planning offices and public libraries.

Edinburgh has been luckiest. *Modern Athens!* (p. 118) has been reprinted in facsimile under the rather misleading title *Edinburgh in the Nineteenth Century* (Frank Graham; the original by Jones 1829). Grant's *Old and New Edinburgh* (Cassell about 1876) is a real panorama of buildings, people and developments. A. J. Youngson's remarkable *Making of Classical Edinburgh* has already been mentioned. Ian Lindsay's deceptively slim booklet *Old Edinburgh* (Cockburn Assn. 1939) was followed by his *Georgian Edinburgh* (do. 1948) with good photographs and brief, unequivocal notes on developments, buildings and architects; hardly a word had to be qualified in the new expanded edition by David Walker (Scottish Academic Press 1973). But adequate treatment of Victorian developments must await the publication of the latter's volume in the *Buildings of Scotland* series (Penguin). Buildings of all periods are included in *Edinburgh; an Architectural Guide* (Edinburgh Architectural Association 1969) but not comprehensively, and not all are illustrated.

Glasgow at a Glance (Collins 1965 and 1971 PB) is more complete; it is one of the best books of its kind for any town. Most of the notes on some 250 buildings were written by David Walker who was also Andor Gomme's collaborator in *The Architecture of Glasgow* (Lund Humphries 1968) which has outstanding photographs and excellent tabulated information and bibliography. Most of the larger towns have their chroniclers. Fenton Wyness, for example, has written the useful *City by the Grey North Sea – Aberdeen* (Impulse Books 1972) and *Aberdeen – Century of Change* (do. 1971). But others, notably Inverness and Dumfries, are already suffering from the lack of scholarly investigation into their townscape and architecture.

Smaller places are unevenly documented, but among the best architectural guides the series published by the St Andrews Preservation Trust are outstanding; their main author and contributor, R. G. Cant, also wrote the booklet on the burghs of the *East Neuk of Fife* (East Neuk Preservation Society). These, with *Old Glasgow, Old Stirling* and *Old Elgin*, all follow the excellent original format of Ian Lindsay's *Old Edinburgh*. More recently *Royal and Ancient Banff* (Banff Preservation Society 1966) has introduced the 'walk-round' format. Others, like Thurso and Cramond, have produced collections of specialized essays which shed much light on their foundation and subsequent development. Almost always the initiative has come from the local preservation society, convinced of the need to study and make known the heritage it seeks to preserve.

INDEX

of places and counties (old style), buildings (selectively), events and subjects

ABERDEEN, 29, 35, 36, 47, 149, pl. 4
  Townscape walk, 216, pls. 33a-c
  Castlehill, 38
  church, 43
  early 19th century, 129-31
  Footdee, 103
  Gallowgate, Schoolhill, 70
  Gordon's College, 70
  tolbooth, 62
  town chambers, 145
  Union Street, 98, 129-30, 139, 186, 216-17
Old Aberdeen, 33, 212, pl. 4
  cathedral, 40
  King's College, 42
  town-house, 74
Aberfeldy, Perthshire, 173
Alloa, Clackmannanshire, church, 61
Alness, Ross & Cromarty, church, 54
Ancient Monuments Act, 1913, 191
Annan, Dumfriesshire, 53
Anstruther, Fife, 47; church, 63
Archiestown, Moray, 97
Ardrossan, Ayrshire, 94, pl. 19e
Astragals (glazing bars), 115, 116, 161
Athelstaneford, E. Lothian, 99
Auchtermuchty, Fife, 48, 52, 73
AYR, 28
  Townscape walk, 218, pl. 34
  church, 63
  early 19th century, 133-5
  growth, 34-5
  town-house, 17, 134

Balnagard, Perthshire, 100
BANFF
  Townscape walk, 221, pl. 35a
  Boyndie House, 72
  High Shore, 59, pl. 9c
  mercat cross, 34
  Shoemakers' Land, 69
Banks, 138, 140, pls. 27c, 32a

Bath, England, 80, 83, 116, 119, 203
Beith, Ayrshire, 67
Bells, 47
Berwick-on-Tweed, England, 28, 29
  church, 63
  guild laws, 30
Birnam, Perthshire, 173
Blackburn, W. Lothian, 183
Blantyre, Lanarkshire, 105-6, pl. 19b
Board of Trustees for Fisheries and Manufactures, 67, 74
Board schools, 148, 175
Bo'ness, W. Lothian, 49
Bothwell, Lanarkshire, 42
Braemar, Aberdeenshire, 100
Brechin, Angus
  cathedral, 39
  Maison Dieu, 41
Brewing, 30, 76
Building Preservation Orders, 201-2
Burgh kirks, 40-4
Burgh laws, 29-31, 36, 48, 50-1
Burgh Reform Act, 1833, 142-3
Burghs of barony, 32
Burgus (burgh), 28
Burntisland, Fife
  church, 62
  Rossend Castle, 39
  Somerville Street, 205

Callander, Perthshire, 99-100
Cambuslang, Lanarkshire, 183
Canals, 109
Canongate, 32 (see Edinburgh)
Castle Douglas, Kircudbrightshire, 145
Castles, 37
Catrine, Ayrshire, 105-6
Cellardyke, Fife, 47
Cemeteries, 52
Charlestown, Fife, 98
Cholera, 149
Churches, 39-44, 62-4, 208-9

Civic Amenities Act, 1967, 13, 208
Civic Trust, 124
CLACKMANNAN, 72, 204
    tolbooth, 61
Closes, 49-50
Coatbridge, Lanarkshire, 126
Commissioners of Forfeited Estates, 67, 99
Commissioners of Supply, 87, 145
Corn Exchanges, 147
County Councils, 145
Coupar Angus, Perthshire, 73
Crail, Fife, 35, 36, 47, pl. 9a
    church, 42
    tolbooth, 61, 62
Crieff, Perthshire, 67, 87
Cromarty, Ross & Cromarty, 104
Crovie, Banffshire, 103
Cullen, Banffshire, 103
Culross, Fife, 18, 32, 47, 54, 199-200, pl. 8
    Ark, 71
    Parleyhill house, 72
    Sir George Bruce's house, 60
    'Study', 35, 59
    tolbooth, 61
Cupar, Fife
    Townscape walk, 224, pls. 35b, c
    church, 63
    mercat cross, 34, pl. 35b
    Preston ludging, 225, pl. 10e
    St Catherine Street, 136, pl. 35c

Dalkeith, Midlothian, 72, 181, 204, pl. 10d
    church, 41
    board school, 175
Dalmally, Argyll, 87
Dalmeny, W. Lothian, church, 40
Dalnacardoch, Perthshire, 87
Dean of Guild, 35-6, 121, 180
Deanston, Perthshire, 105, pl. 19a
Department of the Environment, 191
Dornoch, Sutherland, 39, 53
    castle and cathedral, 38, pl. 5b
DUMBARTON, 160, 184
    castle and Rock, 17, 38
    Glencairn ludging, 57
DUMFRIES, 53
    Townscape walk, 227
    bridge, pl. 5a
    Mid steeple, 62, pl. 36a

Nith Place, 70, pl. 12e
Doune, Perthshire, pls. 2d, e
Dunbar, E. Lothian, 53, 69, 87
    High Street, 50, 79
    tolbooth, 62, 213
    wall, 37
Dunblane, Perthshire
    cathedral, 39, pl. 6a
    hydro, 169
Dundee, Angus, 18, 19, 47, 57, 105, 149
    church, 43
    early 19th century, 131-3
    Improvement Acts, 132, 197
    jute palaces, 159
    libraries, 175, 177
    Morgan tower, 69
    Reform Street, 132, pl. 22a
    Stobswell school, 175
    Strathmartine lodging, 70
    'Wishart' arch, 37
Dunkeld, Perthshire, 87, 200, pl. 32d
    cathedral, 39
    industrial school, 148
Dunmore, Stirlingshire, 101
Dunninald, Angus, 99
Dunning, Perthshire, church, 40
Dysart, Fife, 36, 47, 205, pl. 32e

Eaglesham, Renfrewshire, 94
Earlsferry, Fife, 47
Ecclefechan, Dumfriesshire
    arched house, 69
Edinburgh; see below
Education Act, 1872, 148
Edzell, Angus, 53, 147
Elgin, Moray, 29, 32, 48
    arcades, 57, pl. 10b
    Castle Hill, 38
    cathedral, 17
    church, 44, pl. 6c
    friary, 41
    'Tower', 59
Entry to towns, 19, pls. 2c, 3a, 21b
Eskbank, Midlothian, 160
EDINBURGH, 13, 29, 36, 53, 56, 142, 149, 202-3, 206-7
    Townscape walk, 230, pl. 36b
    Ann Street, 113-14
    Bowhead tenement, 55, pl. 11c
    Calton development, 116, 121
    Candlemaker Row, 48
    Canongate church, 64

EDINBURGH, (continued)
Canongate tolbooth, 61
Canongate restorations, 204
Castle, 17, 37
Castle Street, 81-2, pl. 15c
Charlotte Square, 21-2, 82-3, 106, 198, pl. 15a
City chambers, 75, pl. 13a
City Improvement Act, 1867, 196
Cockburn Street, 195
'Conservative Surgery' by Geddes, 197-8
Co-op store, Bread Street, 180
Cumberland Street, 150
Dean Bridge, 142
Dean of Guild, 35-6, 121
early 19th century, 111-23
Elm Row, 121
First New Town, 78-83, 98, 120, pl. 14a
Forth Street, 115
Gayfield Place, 83
George Square, 77, 115, 202
George Street, 23, 79-80, 174, 186, pl. 14b
Gladstone's land, 57
Greyfriars, 41, 62
Heriot's hospital, 60, 147
Holyroodhouse, 45, 62, pl. 2a
Huntly House, 56-7, 60
'John Knox's' house, 56, pl. 10a
Magdalen Chapel, 48
Mary of Guise's house, 56, pl. 11c
Moray estate development, 113, pl. 23a
Moray house, 60
Mylne's court, 50, pl. 11c
Observatory, 85
Princes Street, 12, 81, 164, 179, 184-5, pl. 24a
pubs, 167-8
Queensberry House, 70
Queen Street, 81, 111
Quinquennial Review, 1966, 207
Railway Station Access Act, 1853, 195
Ramsay Garden, 15, pl. 32a
Regent Morton's house, 46
Register house, 84, 182
Royal Circus, 112, 116
Royal High School, 118
Royal Scottish Academy, 114, pl. 24a

St Bernard's Crescent, 114, pl. 23b
St George's church, 80, 83, 122, 211
St Giles' church, 42, pl. 36b
St James's Square, 82, 182
St John's Church, 119
St Mary's Street, 196, pl. 31a
St Stephen's church, 135, pl. 25a
St Stephen's Street, 150
Scott monument, 12, 118, pl. 24a
Second New Town, 111, pl. 25a
shops, 119-22, 164-6, 179-80
South Bridge, 84
Stockbridge board school, 148
Tolbooth church, 119, 195
Tron church, 63, 202, pl. 36b
University (old college), 15, 84
Victoria Street & Terrace, 194-5, pls. 31b, c
Victorian housing, 151-5
Victorian villa developments, 159
walls, 37
Waterloo Place, 117, pl. 24b
York Place, 119, 121

Falkirk, Stirlingshire, town hall, 126
Falkland, Fife, 18, 45, pl. 11a
Fettercairn, Angus, arch, 147
Feu system, 27, 29
Fife, 46-7, 201
Fires, 30
Fochabers, Moray, 92
Forfar, Angus, 38, 48
Forres, Moray, 29, 32
  castle, 38
  town hall, 145
Fortingall, Perthshire, 101
Fortrose, 39
'Four Burghs', 29-31
Fraserburgh, Aberdeenshire, 72, 101
  customs house, 110
  town hall, 144

Gables, 54, 58
Gaits (streets), 26, 33, 35
Galashiels, Selkirkshire, 47
  burgh chambers, 176
  High Street, 184
Gardenstown, Banffshire, 103
Garlieston, Wigtownshire, 99
Gas supply, 149
Gatehouse of Fleet, Kircudbrightshire, 145

Gifford, E. Lothian, 94-5, pl. 18a
  church, 63
Girvan, Ayrshire, 53
Glamis, Angus, 52, pl. 10c
Glasgow; see below
Glass, 160-1
Granite, 53, 130
Grantown-on-Spey, Moray, 97
Greenock, Renfrewshire
  customs house, 110
  town hall, 144
GLASGOW, 32, 39, 49, 58, 75, 77, 105, 141-2, 206
  Townscape walk, 234, pls. 37a-c
  Abbotsford Place, 124, 150
  Adelaide Place, 124
  Argyle Arcade, 165
  Assembly Rooms, 76
  Blythswood Square, 124
  Buchanan Street, 211, 235
  Buck's Head Building, 162-3
  Carlton Place, 123, 174, 213, pl. 22b
  Central Station Hotel, 169
  Charing Cross Mansions, 163
  Charlotte Street, 76, 202
  city chambers, 142, 144, 177
  City Improvement Act, 1866, 196-7
  Cosmo cinema, 179
  courthouse, 125
  customs house, 133
  Daily Express building, Albion Street, 179
  Egyptian Halls, Union Street, 162
  Fish market, 161
  Gorbals, 124, 190, pls. 27b, 29c
  Great Western Terrace, 157
  Great Western Road, 139
  Grosvenor buildings, Gordon Street, 162
  Grosvenor Terrace, 158
  'Hatrack', St Vincent Street, 164, pl. 26c
  High Street, 76, pl. 15b
  Hutcheson's Hospital, Ingram Street, 125
  Iron Building, Jamaica Street, 162
  Kibble palace, botanic gardens, 161
  Merchants' steeple, Bridgegate, 49
  Miller Street, 76
  Moray Place, 157
  Our Lady & St Francis' school, Charlotte Street, 188

Provand's Lordship, Castle Street, 40, 193
Queen's Crescent, 158
Queen's Park Terrace, Eglinton Street, 157
Queen Street station, 161
Royal Exchange, 125, pl. 37b
St Andrew's church, 73
St Andrew by the Green church, 76
St George's Tron church, 125, pl. 37c
Sauchiehall Street, 124, 164, 175
School of Art, Renfrew Street, 164, 175
Scotland Street school, 175
Shawfield house, 70, 75
Stock Exchange, 163, pl. 37c
tolbooth, 61, 144, pl. 13b
Trongate, 48, pl. 13b
Tron kirk, 62-3, pl. 13b
Victorian tenements and terraces, 156-9
Walmer Crescent, 157
Walworth Terrace, Kent Road, 156
Westbourne Terrace, 157
Wilson Street, 76
Woodlands Hill, 125, 158, pl. 28

Haddington, E. Lothian, 29, 68, 72
  Townscape walk, 237, pls. 38a-c
  church, 43
  conservation, 206
  county buildings, 146
  Mitchell's close, 50, pl. 9b
  town-house, 17, 68
Hamilton, Lanarkshire, church, 64
  shopping centre, 183
Harling, 52, 69, 213
Hawick, Roxburghshire, mills, pl. 23e
  town hall, 145
Helmsdale, Sutherland, 104
Highland & Agricultural Society, 96
Historic Buildings Act, 1953, 202-3
Holland, 47, 49, 58-9, 62-3, 72, 75
Hotels, 100, 128, 169-70, 173, 207, 240
Housing Act, 1924, 156
Housing, Victorian, 150-6
Housing, twentieth-century, 188-90
Huntly, Aberdeenshire, 97-8
  High Street, 72

Ideal town plans, 98
Inveraray, Argyll, 91-2, 98, 203, pl. 18c

Inverkeithing, Fife, 36
  Fordell *ludging*, 59
  town-house, 75, pl. 12a
INVERNESS, 29, 36, 87, 173
  Townscape walk, 239, pls. 39a, b
  Abertarff house, 59
  castle, 38
  market arcade, 165, pl. 27f
Inverurie, Aberdeenshire, Bass, 38
Iron, 47, 128, 160-2, 163, 166
Irvine, Ayrshire, 72
  Seagate castle, 60
  skyline, 17
  town hall, 144

Jedburgh, Roxburghshire, 38
  Canongate, 71

Keith, Banffshire, 96-7, 105
Kelso, Roxburghshire, 32, 47, 100, 149
Kenmore, Perthshire, 100, pl. 20b
Kilbarchan, Renfrewshire, 17
Killearn, Perthshire, 203, pl. 2c
Kilwinning, Ayrshire, 41
Kinghorn, Fife, 36
Kinloch Rannoch, Perthshire, 99
KINROSS, 91
  steeple and county buildings, 73, pl. 12d
Kintore, Aberdeenshire
  town-house, 74
Kirkcaldy, Fife, 46-7, 213
KIRCUDBRIGHT, 32, 72, pl. 12c
  'Maclellan's castle', 59
Kirkintilloch, Dunbartonshire
  church, 63
  High Street, 71, pl. 23f
Kirkwall, Orkney
  cathedral, 39
  Tankerness house, 60
Kirriemuir, Angus, 53, 105

Lamington, Lanarkshire, 100
LANARK, 53
Langholm, Dumfriesshire, 93, 100
Lauder, Berwickshire, church, 64, pl. 10f
Laurencekirk, Kincardineshire, 94
Leadhills, Dumfriesshire, 108
Leith (Edinburgh), 36, 47
  Bernard Street, 110, pl. 3b
  Assembly rooms, 126

customs house, 110
Dr Bell's school, 148
Lamb's house, 45, 58-9
Lerwick, Shetland, 38
Leuchars, Fife, church, 40
Linlithgow, W. Lothian, 29, 37-8
  church, 42-3
  tolbooth, 62
  redevelopment, 181
Listing of buildings, 198-9, 201
Locharbriggs, Dumfriesshire, 54
Ludgings (town houses), 50, 54-5
Lugar, Ayrshire, 107

Mauchline, Ayrshire, 53
Maybole, Ayrshire, castle, 38
Mercat Crosses, 34, 94-5, pls. 2d, 8b, 12a, 18a, b, 35b
Milnathort, Kinross-shire, 205
Montrose, Angus, 29, 34, 50, 139-40, 143
  Townscape walk, 242, pl. 40
  bank into supermarket, 244, pl. 32c
  church, 17, 140
Motherwell, Lanarkshire, shopping centre, 183
Moving of buildings, 212

NAIRN, 32
National Trust for Scotland, 198-201
Navigation Laws, 1660, 49, 67
Newcastle, England, burgh laws, 29
Newcastleton, Roxburghshire, 98, pl. 19d
New Lanark, Lanarkshire, 106-7, pl. 20a
New Scone, Perthshire, 92
New Winton, E. Lothian, 100
Newton St Boswells, Roxburghshire, county offices, 188
North Berwick, E. Lothian, 169, 172
  N. Berwick Law, 17, pl. 2b

Office buildings, 186-7
Orbiston, Lanarkshire, 106
Ormiston, E. Lothian, 54, 95-6, pl. 18b
Orkney, 53

Paisley, Renfrewshire, 33, 67, 105
  county buildings, 145
  town hall, 144
Panoramas, 18

PEEBLES, 29, 37
Penicuik, Midlothian, 107
PERTH, 29, 35
  bridge, 127
  church, 43, pl. 6b
  early 19th century, 127-9
  entry over bridge, 19, pl. 21b
  infirmary, South Street, 137
  James VI hospital, 70
  Kinnoull lodging, 55
  St John Street, 206
  St Leonard's church, 137
  St Leonard's in the Fields church, 129
Piazzas (arcades), 57, 74-5, 243, pl. 10b
Pitlochry, Perthshire, Atholl Palace hotel, 169
Pittenweem, Fife, 47, 57
  tolbooth, 61
Planning Acts, 1947, 36, 180, 201; 1969, 209
'police' Acts, 149
Poor Laws, 1845, 146
Portknockie, Banffshire, 101, 103
Ports (gates), 34
Portsoy, Banffshire, 72, 102, 205
Post offices, 120, 175, 241
Preston, E. Lothian, 93
Public Health Act, 1857, 150
pubs, 167-8, 229, 238
Pultneytown, Caithness-shire, 104

Railways, 20, 134, 169
Reform Act, 1832, 142-3
RENFREW, 29
Rigs (gardens), 49
Roads, 86-8, 145, 172
Rosebank, Lanarkshire, 101
Rothesay, Bute, castle, 38
ROXBURGH, 28, 29
Royal Burghs, 29-32, 49, 143
Royal Commission on Scottish Housing, 155-6
Royal Fine Art Commission for Scotland, 82
Royal Society for the Encouragement of Arts & Manufactures, 161
Rutherglen, Lanarkshire, 29
  town hall, 145, pl. 26a

St Andrews, Fife, 32, 35, 47, 203
  castle, 38

  cathedral, 17, 40
  church, 43
  friary church, 41
  lang rigs and closes, 49-50
  priory wall, 37
  Queen Mary's house, 45
  St Salvator's college, 42
  Southgait port, 37, pl. 7a
  South Street, pl. 7b
St Monance, Fife, 47, 72
  church, 41
Saltire Society, 177-8, 200
Saltoun, E. Lothian, 94
Sanitation, 112, 149-50
Sanquhar, Dumfriesshire
  post office, 120
  town-house, 74
Scale, 21-2
Scalloway, Shetland, castle, 38
Schools, 147, 188
Scottish Civic Trust, 209
Scottish Georgian Society, 209
Scottish Local Government Act, 1929, 143
Scottish Special Housing Association, 189
SELKIRK, 204
Sheriffdoms, 28, 29
Shieldaig, Ross & Cromarty, 104
Shops, 119-22, 164-7, pls. 19e, 27e
Shopping arcades, 165, pl. 27f
Sinclairs Hill, Berwickshire, 101
Slaughterhouses, 146-7
South Queensferry, W. Lothian, priory church, 41
Spittalfield, Perthshire, 104
Spittal of Glenshee, 87
Stanley, Perthshire, 105
Statues, 22-3
STIRLING, 29, 37
  arcade, 165
  Athenaeum, 135
  Broad Street, 204
  castle, 17, 45
  church, 43
  eastern entry, 19, pl. 3a
  Leckie ludging, 50
  Mar's Wark and Argyll ludging, 60
  tolbooth, 62
  Wallace monument, 135
Stobo, Peebles-shire, 101

Stone, 53-4, 95, 114, 122, 130, 157, 176, 179, 183, 213-14
Stonehaven, Kincardineshire, 93, 204
  county buildings, 145-6
Stornoway, Lewis, 101-2
Strathpeffer, Ross & Cromarty, 173
Street names, 48
Stromness, Orkney, 38

Tain, Ross & Cromarty, 173
  tolbooth, 61
Tarbert, Argyll, castle, 38
Telephone exchanges, 188, 242
Textile industries, 66-8, 71, 99, 104-7, 123, 133, 141
Thornhill, Dumfriesshire, 93
Thurso, Caithness-shire, 98, 204, pls. 19c, 32b
Timber, 47, 54-7, 194, 198, 199
Tobacco trade, 49, 123

Tolbooths, 34, 61-2
Tomintoul, Banffshire, 97
Torryburn, Fife, 189, pl. 29d
Townscape, definitions, 11
Transplanted towns, 91
Turnpike Act, 1751, 87
Turriff, Aberdeenshire, 53, 146

Union of Crowns, 1603, 46-7; of parliaments, 65-6
Ullapool, Ross & Cromarty, 104

Villa (feudal village), 28, 96
villa developments, 159-60

water supply, 149
Whithorn, Wigtownshire, 29, 32
Window tax, 161
Wynds (lanes), 26, 35